-REPORTING ON HITLER-

REPORTING ON HITLER

Rothay Reynolds
and the British Press
in Nazi Germany

———

WILL WAINEWRIGHT

Biteback Publishing

First published in Great Britain in 2017 by
Biteback Publishing Ltd
Westminster Tower
3 Albert Embankment
London SE1 7SP

ISBN 978-1-78590-133-1

10 9 8 7 6 5 4 3 2 1

A CIP catalogue record for this book is available from the British Library.

Set in Arno Pro by Adrian McLaughlin

Printed and bound in Great Britain by
CPI Group (UK) Ltd, Croydon CR0 4YY

MIX
Paper from
responsible sources
FSC
www.fsc.org
FSC® C020471

For BDH

CONTENTS

PHOTOGRAPH PERMISSIONS

I am grateful to the Hewson family for allowing me to reproduce the photographs of Rothay Reynolds, his parents and siblings. Also included are three photographs taken by Anthony Hewson in 1938 during his visit to Reynolds in Berlin. All photos appear by permission of the Hewson family unless the source is otherwise mentioned.

A NOTE ON NEWSPAPERS

"For providing information about events, none were better placed than newspaper correspondents. Wherever was excitement, there were they. They raced about the world in search of what was most urgent, most timely; interviewed the great, and witnessed the stuff of headlines. Inside information was at their disposal, and on their typewriters they played each day's tumult. Like bloodhounds following a scent, they carried news, a ravening pack. Trains, aeroplanes, motor-cars, carried them to the scene of all disasters; war and rumours of wars set them in motion."[1]

THE THIRTIES, MALCOLM MUGGERIDGE

The 1930s has been described as the golden age of newspapers in Great Britain. In a world before television, with radio in its infancy, newspapers were the predominant means by which everyday men and women could learn news of the outside world. Newspapers were more trusted than they are now (whether or not that trust was justified is a separate question). There were scores of them – in 1938 fifty-two morning, eighty-five evening and eighteen Sunday newspapers were printed in the United Kingdom. In deciding which newspapers to focus on, this book follows the lead of Frank Gannon, whose 1971 study *The British Press and Germany, 1936–1939* prioritises what he calls the 'major' newspapers. These comprised seven national dailies, two important Sunday papers and the *Manchester Guardian*, which had an influence and reach far beyond its status as a regional paper. A short guide to the ten titles, which are listed below, follows at the end of the book.

Daily Express
Daily Herald
Daily Mail
Daily Telegraph
Manchester Guardian
Morning Post
News Chronicle
The Observer
Sunday Times
The Times

CAST OF CORRESPONDENTS

A mass of *dramatis personae* feature in the narrative that follows. But at the heart of this story are the unique band of men and women who, like Rothay Reynolds, were working for British newspapers in Europe. What these correspondents experienced in Berlin and other continental cities, and the resulting dispatches they sent back to London, are of prime importance. This is a short guide to their roles.

Vernon Bartlett: *News Chronicle* correspondent, roving role.

Paul Bretherton: *Daily Mail* correspondent, roving role.

Harold Cardozo: *Daily Mail* correspondent in Paris.

Ian Colvin: *Morning Post* and later *News Chronicle* correspondent.

Sefton 'Tom' Delmer: *Daily Express* chief foreign correspondent.

Norman Ebbutt: *The Times* correspondent in Berlin.

Eric Gedye: *Daily Telegraph* correspondent in Vienna, later *New York Times*.

Shiela Grant Duff: *Observer* correspondent during Saar plebiscite.

Hugh Carleton Greene: *Daily Telegraph* assistant and later correspondent in Berlin.

H. D. Harrison: *News Chronicle* correspondent in Belgrade, later Berlin.

James Holburn: *Times* assistant and then correspondent in Berlin.

Ralph Izzard: *Daily Mail* assistant in Berlin, later Germany bureau chief.

Wallace King: *Daily Herald* correspondent in Berlin.

Charles Lambert: *Manchester Guardian* correspondent in Berlin.

Iverach McDonald: *Times* reporter in Berlin and elsewhere.

Noel Monks: *Daily Express* journalist in Berlin and elsewhere.

H. H. Munro (Saki): *Morning Post* foreign correspondent.

Noel Panter: *Daily Telegraph* Munich correspondent.

Selkirk Panton: *Daily Express* reporter in Vienna and Berlin.

G. Ward Price: *Daily Mail*'s chief foreign correspondent.

Douglas Reed: *Times* correspondent in Vienna, later joined *News Chronicle*.

Rothay Reynolds: *Daily News* correspondent in St Petersburg, *Daily Mail* Berlin bureau chief, *Daily Telegraph* Rome correspondent.

Karl Robson: *Morning Post* correspondent in Berlin.

John Segrue: *News Chronicle* correspondent in Berlin.

Philip Pembroke Stephens: *Daily Express* correspondent in Berlin.

Frederick Voigt: *Manchester Guardian* correspondent in Berlin, then Paris, then diplomatic correspondent.

Eustace Wareing: *Daily Telegraph* correspondent in Berlin.

- PROLOGUE -
DEATH OF A CORRESPONDENT

Photo portrait of Rothay Reynolds, late 1930s.

I t was high summer in Jerusalem and growing uncomfortably hot for the small congregation gathered at the church. Many in attendance were English and unused to such heat, even after living in the city for several years. It was August 1940 and Britain's League of Nations mandate to govern Palestine had been in force for two decades. Almost a year into a new war with Germany, minds drifted increasingly to friends and relatives at home. Palestine's future remained a headache for leaders in London, who regarded it as a distraction during a tumultuous period. But the British mandate remained, forcing them to stay.

The metal cross at the altar was too hot to touch; even the ancient stone walls had warmth. A dress code of formal wear made matters worse in the heat and the handful present shifted uneasily in their pews. Oddly, they were at the church for the funeral of a man they had met just weeks before. Among them was the chief surgeon at the government hospital, who had not been able to save him. A group of British nurses had sent a wreath of flowers.

It was the funeral of a 67-year-old Englishman named Rothay Reynolds. He would not have come to Jerusalem had it not been for the war – one of the many individuals displaced amid the chaos. For reasons few of them knew, Reynolds had made the long and hard journey from Italy, an exhausting month-long trip that took its toll on his health. He was in a weak state when he arrived in the ancient city, and it worsened when he contracted malaria. A few days later he caught pneumonia and finally succumbed.[2]

A door creaked slowly open and Reynolds's coffin came forward, draped in the Union flag. British military police acted as pall-bearers and bore him to the front of the church for a service officiated by a Franciscan friar in a flowing brown tunic. It was a fittingly sacred end for Reynolds who, in his younger years, had been ordained an Anglican priest before converting to Catholicism. 'He is the sort of person who would be glad to die in Jerusalem,' wrote a friend back in Britain. After the service he was laid to rest in the Roman Catholic cemetery on the side of Mount Zion. 'In fact, one can't feel sorry for him in any way; his life was so full and so good,' the friend said. 'One can only feel sorry that one will never see him again.'[3]

But who was he? The congregation in Jerusalem had dutifully given Reynolds a fine send-off, despite not knowing much about him. It was a typically English act in honour of a man who had ventured into their quasi-outpost of the British Empire and met his end. The people who knew him, relatives and friends at home, were forced to mourn his passing from afar. The congregation guessed Reynolds was an interesting man – to travel as far as Jerusalem in the middle of a new world war was no easy feat – but they had little inkling of his startling background.

Obituaries published in Britain gave some idea. They revealed that Reynolds was one of the best-travelled foreign correspondents of the era. As chief of the *Daily Mail* newspaper's Berlin office between the wars he had known Adolf Hitler personally, and had chronicled his rise to power. He first met the Nazi leader in 1923 and interviewed him several times in the years that followed. Reynolds, who in his final days had struck the small band of mourners as an ageing, nomadic and slightly peculiar individual, was more significant than they knew.

Old friends in the press ensured readers in Britain were made aware of his significance. The day after the funeral, six journalists, including correspondents for the *Manchester Guardian* and *United Press of America*, sent the following joint letter to the editor of the *Daily Telegraph*, the last paper to have employed him.

> A number of colleagues who worked abroad with the late Rothay
> Reynolds of your staff would like to add their tribute to the memory
> of a man who was for many years the doyen of the British newspa-
> pers in Berlin. We would like to lay stress upon his utter fearlessness.
> He never feared to stand up to Nazi officials, however much they
> blustered, and he always retained a suavity and dignity which almost
> invariably won the day. He refused to be muzzled and his direct,

accurate descriptions of events in Germany must have caused the Nazis great displeasure.

Reynolds was a man of great personal charm, widely read and deeply cultured. He was famous throughout a continent for his elegant hospitality and his kindliness. He began life abroad as a chaplain to the embassy church in St Petersburg, and although he left Holy Orders on his conversion to Roman Catholicism, he always retained something of the priestly attitude to life. Hundreds of victims of Nazi persecution and terror received from him material and moral support in an uneven fight with an evil system.[4]

Other public tributes followed. 'He was one of the few British journalists who had the foresight to interest themselves in the Nazi movement at a time when it seemed quite off the map,' was the verdict of an obituary in *The Times*. 'He never had any doubt of what Nazism meant for Europe.'[5] Some saluted him in private. Frank Foley, an MI6 spy who had used his cover as the Berlin Passport Control Officer to help thousands of Jews flee Germany, wrote in sorrow to Kathleen, a sister of Reynolds. 'I am very sorry indeed to hear of your brother's death in Jerusalem and I know that every member of the British colony in Berlin and everyone who knew him will share in your grief.'[6]

Time passed and minds shifted elsewhere. The death of a foreign correspondent was worthy of some attention, but other matters pressed; a war was on and the fate of Britain hung in the balance. Reynolds had no children to ensure the details of his remarkable life were safeguarded. In the years after his death, his three surviving siblings – Ronald, Kathleen and Marjorie – passed away. None had married or left children. The story of their brother and his role in the interwar years remained untold.

———

It all began with a letter. During research into our family history, my mother had found a yellowing, type-written letter sent by Rothay Reynolds to his second-cousin, Cuthbert Reynolds. The two men had been of similar age and Rothay was godfather to Cuthbert's eldest son, Lionel. It had been written just before Christmas in 1939, shortly ahead of his final departure from Britain.

The letter provides a fascinating insight into Reynolds's state of mind. He recounts how he had returned from Berlin at the start of 1939 to live in Cambridge and write a book about his time in Germany. The result was *When Freedom Shrieked*, which was published in November 1939 and revealed the truth about life under the Nazis. 'It was the best contribution I could make to our cause,' Reynolds said in the letter. He reveals his anger at the Munich Agreement of 1938, when Prime Minister Neville Chamberlain's British government struck a deal with Germany that fatally undermined Czechoslovakia. He left Berlin a few months afterwards. 'It was good to get away, for after Munich I hardly cared to look a German in the face. It was the first time that I was not proud of being an Englishman,' Reynolds wrote.

The letter has always fascinated me. It is a thrilling document of history and reveals in stark terms the thoughts of a man who had witnessed momentous events. Cuthbert was my great-grandfather, but he died years before I was born. My mother and I were captivated by the story of our relation, Rothay Reynolds. Why was more not known about this intriguing man, who appears to have witnessed so much and yet been forgotten?

Again, time passed. We remained fascinated by Reynolds, but other distractions took priority. I completed my degree and began my own career in journalism. He remained at the back of my mind. Then, after a few years of reporting in London and New York, my interest in him suddenly revived. Perhaps it was the dry nature of what I was writing about – the ups and downs of the global hedge fund industry – that made me appreciate how interesting Rothay Reynolds's career had been. He had met Hitler many times and interviewed Nazi leaders. He had fled Rome and travelled to Jerusalem during a world war. And these were just the things we knew about. What other incredible stories had he reported on? What events had he witnessed?

My mind was set. After returning to London from New York in February 2014, I decided to pursue a story very different from my usual articles about the world of banks and high finance. I began collecting all the information I could find about Reynolds's life. I visited Berlin, St Petersburg, Vilnius and Warsaw to retrace his footsteps in the cities in which he had worked as a foreign correspondent. I spent days in the British Library's 'Newsroom' archive to read the reports he had written for the *Daily Mail*. I tracked down two men, both in their mid-nineties, who had known Reynolds personally. It became an obsession.

The more I learned about Reynolds the more hooked I became on the idea of telling his story. From an early career in the church to working all over Europe as a foreign correspondent, the many adventures of Reynolds's life became more and more clear. One part stood out from the rest. His time in Berlin, living first in the Weimar Republic and then under Nazi rule, put him at the epicentre of a unique moment in history. As one of the first foreign correspondents to interview Hitler, he had a place in history all of his own.

The story that emerged was not a straightforward one. He had worked in Berlin for the populist *Daily Mail*, which had been a vocal supporter of Hitler in the 1930s. The newspaper's owner Lord Rothermere had been a fervent admirer of the dictator, which made it almost impossible for its correspondents to report accurately on the horrors of life in Germany. Reynolds 'struggled hard to fulfil the difficult task of being Berlin correspondent of Lord Rothermere's *Daily Mail*,' according to Douglas Reed, one of his friends in the European press pack.[7] But some correspondents at the *Mail*, including its star foreign correspondent G. Ward Price, appeared to share the proprietor's support for Hitler. Many British newspaper owners and journalists, as well as politicians and aristocrats, supported Hitler during the 1930s. They agreed with him that Germany had been wronged by the Treaty of Versailles and supported his economic reforms. Where did Reynolds's sympathies lie?

The idea behind this book originated as the tale of one man, but the story soon broadened in scope. Reynolds was seen as the 'doyen' of British newspaper reporters in Nazi Berlin, but many other talented foreign correspondents from the UK worked in similarly difficult conditions. The story of Reynolds, caught between Hitler and a press baron eager to maintain good relations with Germany, was their story too. What had started as a biography of Reynolds expanded to incorporate some of their tales and describe the conditions faced by journalists reporting on Hitler. Rivals and friends, such as Norman Ebbutt of *The Times*, had to contend not only with the controlling propaganda machine of Joseph Goebbels, but also the fact that many newspaper proprietors in Britain supported Hitler and happily shut their eyes to the increasingly awful truth of life in Germany. Reynolds did his best, but not until he left the *Daily Mail* and published *When Freedom Shrieked* could he reveal his true feelings about the regime.

After Reynolds died, he left his prized collection of books to Prinknash Abbey in Gloucestershire, which houses an order of Benedictine monks with whom he felt a strong spiritual bond. He is still thought of fondly at Prinknash. The archivist there, Aelred Baker, was one of many men and women who have helped me tell this story. They are thanked in the acknowledgements section at the end of the book, though any mistakes in what follows are my responsibility. 'He is worthy of remembrance,' Baker wrote about Reynolds in a 2004 article. The more I read and learned about him the plainer this fact became. This book is an attempt to tell his untold story, as well as recognise the efforts of a band of journalists working in unimaginably difficult circumstances.

-CHAPTER I-

THE RESTIVE CURATE

The fate of Sydenham, like many other areas of the UK, was changed forever in the nineteenth century by the arrival of a railway station. This revolutionary development came just a few years into Queen Victoria's reign and transformed the peaceful area, which is now one of south London's many bustling and interconnected urban centres. A full six miles south of the River Thames, two centuries ago it felt veritably remote.

The emerging rail network was just one of the changes sweeping London as the UK became the world's first industrial society. Not everyone was happy about the transformation. 'Before Sydenham became so much built over this was a very lovely spot,' wrote Joseph Edwards, a resident of the area in 1866. 'In those days no gas lamps lit the place at night, nor any drainage made the little stream offensive.'[8]

Edwards was irritated that sleepy Sydenham was not protected from change as huge population growth transformed London. His problems were far from over – a new neighbour soon arrived whose career choice irked him further. Frederick Reynolds, the son of a Gloucester ironmonger, was one of those incomers helping to reshape the city. A young businessman on the make, he viewed the industrial revolution as a path to riches, and modern advances as a source of wealth rather than irritation. Reynolds made his money as director of the London Electric Lighting Company, which expanded coverage of street lighting throughout the capital.

Reynolds arrived in Sydenham near the start of his career. Though it took several years for his new neighbour to make his money, Edwards no doubt fumed at his efforts. Firmly built with a thick, dark beard and a hair-line already receding from the front, the budding entrepreneur made his home at Rothay House, a large, detached abode backing onto the London to Brighton train line. In 1871 he married Dora, a south Londoner from the nearby area of Gipsy Hill. She was two years his senior with mid-length dark hair and a slightly severe-looking face.

Rothay's father, Frederick Reynolds, was the son of a Gloucester ironmonger and made a fortune installing London's first electric streetlights. Frederick's wife, Dora Reynolds, gave birth to their first child in the family home of Rothay House in 1872. Rothay preferred to use his middle name rather than his first name, Alfred.

A year later the pair, both in their twenties, had their first child. Alfred Rothay Reynolds was born in the family home on 17 September 1872. He was named Alfred after his maternal grandfather while his middle name stems from the name of the house. The story of how the house acquired this unusual name is lost, but it was taken up with enthusiasm by their firstborn. Alfred was used for formal occasions but most of the time the boy was called Rothay – or Roy, to members of his family.

He was born at a time of change for the country as well as London. In the 1870s the British Empire was approaching its zenith, with the pink ink of empire colouring large swathes of the world map. India had been part of the empire for fourteen years in 1872 and Queen Victoria still had almost three decades remaining on the throne.[9] The great liberal politician William Gladstone had begun the first of his four spells as Prime Minister, while Benjamin Disraeli dominated for the Conservatives. Victorian Britain was the pre-eminent global power and the London of Reynolds's birth was its beating heart.

Home life was comfortable throughout his childhood. Rothay House, which no longer stands, was in the affluent Peak Hill area of Sydenham. There was a lot of green space and it was peaceful by the standards of today's traffic-filled world, even if residents such as Edwards were uncomfortable with the changes. By the time Reynolds was nine he had been joined by a sister and brother, Kathleen and Leslie, and two more would follow, Ronald and Marjorie. Four of the five siblings lived to old age, testament to the healthy upbringing Dora and Frederick could provide in an era when many childhoods were spent in employment rather than education. The home was staffed by three servants – a cook, housemaid and nurse – to help Dora with domestic matters.

The family was deeply religious. The children were brought up as devout Anglo-Catholics and Rothay felt the draw of faith keenly. Anglo-Catholicism is a branch of Christianity that grew in popularity in the nineteenth century and found followers such as the author T. S. Eliot in the twentieth. Its believers are Anglicans but, as the name indicates, their faith is closely based on traditions and practices that pre-date the Reformation. While a religious upbringing was far from uncommon at the time, Reynolds's branch of faith was slightly unusual.

Rothay House may have provided a name for their firstborn, but the Reynolds parents deemed it insufficient to cope with the demands of their growing family. In 1883, the year Rothay turned eleven, the Reynolds moved to Blomfield House in Bromley, a district of south London to the southeast of Sydenham. Unlike Reynolds's birthplace, the house in Bromley still stands.[10] Long since converted into separate flats, it is a grand, though in some ways ramshackle, Victorian mansion and would have been a fitting home for a large family and its household staff. It had an important additional benefit: from the top floor of Blomfield House, Frederick observed neighbouring parts of London and assessed whether the streetlights he had helped install were working. On some nights his children would hear exasperated shouts from upstairs, quickly followed by a slamming door as their father left to address technical problems in other parts of the city.[11]

By 1892 Frederick's business had installed 360 public street lamps and was providing current to many more, as well as about 16,000 lamps for private customers. A fundraising advert in the *Pall Mall Gazette* said additional shareholder investment would help the London Electric Lighting Company provide current to 150,000 more private lamps.[12] It was a business on the up and proved the making of Frederick Reynolds. Later in life it led to political access and civic prestige. A photo exists of him standing outside Downing Street next to Herbert Asquith, Britain's Prime Minister between 1908 and 1916. Frederick Reynolds was also appointed Justice of the Peace, a mark of his position as a respected elder citizen.

Frederick took a close interest in how his children were brought up. Rothay was a small, mild-mannered child with light brown hair. His education started with a governess who made a lasting impression – years later he recalled awkwardly learning to play the piano as a child while a patient governess named Miss Fuller counted time.[13] Private tutors were employed when Reynolds was a little older, at the age of about eleven, to school him at home in the sciences and arts.[14] At the age of fifteen Reynolds was briefly enrolled at Dulwich College, an illustrious all-male public school in south London with a history dating back to 1619. His attendance demonstrates the wealth his family had acquired by that point, which allowed Reynolds to be educated with children of the elite, some of whom would become leading figures of the age. The Antarctic explorer Ernest Shackleton and the creator of Jeeves the Butler, P. G. Wodehouse, who edited the school magazine, were both in attendance there at a similar time.[15] Another writer, Raymond Chandler, the author of thrillers and detective books, was educated at Dulwich a few years later. Reynolds studied an engineering curriculum focused on the sciences and learned thermodynamics from the working steam engine operated in the school's basement.[16]

A flair for languages quickly emerged. Class lists reveal Reynolds was middling in all subjects except French, where he was ranked top of a class

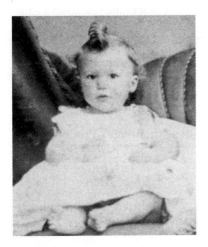

Rothay pictured as a baby in the 1870s. Rothay as a boy in the late 1870s.

of twenty-three. He would remain a deft linguist throughout his life, speaking Russian, French, German, Polish and some Italian. His education in the classics also stayed with him – in a letter written years later he used an idiom from Greek mythology to describe how an awkward predicament had left him between Scylla and Charybdis.

Wodehouse remembered his time at Dulwich as 'six years of unbroken bliss', but for Reynolds it was not to last. He studied in the summer and Christmas terms of 1888 before leaving unexpectedly. No evidence survives to explain the sudden departure. Whatever caused it, Frederick does not seem to have maintained a grudge against England's public school system. Ronald, a decade younger than Rothay, was sent to Malvern College, a public school in Worcestershire, for four years at the end of the 1890s.[17]

Reynolds continued his education with tutor friends of his father. He was a studious child and the spell at Dulwich, though short, helped with his learning. The family was tightly knit and the siblings remained close throughout their lives; later in life the four surviving brothers and sisters lived together in a house in Cambridge. Reynolds's great affection for his parents is evident from the poem he dedicated to them at the beginning of his first book, published years later. 'To my Father and Mother,' he wrote, followed by a sonnet which begins:

My gondola adventures to the sea.
I stand and hear the plash of falling spray
Grow fainter, as the high prow glides away
Upon the summer waves' uncertainty

The romantic verse, which evoked a sense of seaborne adventure, is the sole surviving example of his own poetry. In it, Reynolds may have been harking back to an earlier voyage taken with his parents. Frederick and Dora took

Rothay, Leslie and Kathleen on holiday to Dublin in 1894, travelling on a Royal Mail passenger steamship.[18] Ronald and Marjorie were judged too young to make the trip. The Reynolds children were often taken on trips around Britain and to nearer parts of Europe, instilling a love of travel that led several of them to live abroad in later life.

Religion would prove central to the first important decisions Reynolds made in life. His interest in religious ideas from an early age led him to pursue theological studies and at the age of twenty he won a place to study divinity at Cambridge. He moved there in the autumn of 1892, beginning a connection with the university city that remained with him throughout his life. Reynolds studied at Pembroke, founded in 1347 and one of the university's oldest colleges. Pembroke is home to the first college chapel built in Cambridge, which seems fitting given Reynolds's choice of course.

Reynolds adjusted quickly to life in Cambridge and was inspired by its famed libraries and ancient lanes. The peaceful and relaxed environment of Pembroke College and its grounds was a perfect place in which to study and think about his future. His surroundings were striking: from the Sir Christopher Wren-designed chapel to the grand and imposing library, Reynolds got a taste for fine architecture that remained with him. Whether living among the onion domes of Tsarist Russia or the wide, Swastika-lined boulevards of Nazi Berlin, the tranquil squares of Cambridge were never far from his mind.

Among his teachers were two leading theological scholars, Henry Swete and Herbert Ryle. Swete was appointed Regius Professor of Divinity at Cambridge in 1890 and was popular with students, delivering the best-attended lectures in the faculty. Despite internal opposition to his appointment initially, he served in the role for twenty-five years.[19] Ryle was Hulsean Professor of Divinity at Cambridge before later becoming Dean of Westminster. He took on the latter position in 1911 when preparations were underway for the coronation of George V at Westminster Abbey. Serving in the role during the war, he was responsible for many special services to mark particular battles and events overseas.[20]

Both Ryle and Swete recommended Reynolds for his next move after Cambridge: a career in the church. His three years of religious study confirmed in his mind the decision. In light of his strong childhood faith, it was unlikely to have surprised his family. He turned twenty-three in 1895, the year he graduated, and wasted no time in pursuing his calling. In August he enrolled at the Clergy School in Leeds for nine months of 'instruction in pastoral theology' and 'practical training in parochial work'.

During the process, fellows from his old college, Pembroke, wrote a letter to the Lord Bishop of Durham to testify to Reynolds's learning and suitability for a life in the church. They said he lived 'piously, soberly and honestly' while at Cambridge and had never held beliefs 'contrary to the doctrine and discipline of the Church of England'. Their support was absolute. 'We believe him to be a person worthy to be admitted to the sacred office of deacon.'[21]

Notions of unity and support for the weak lay at the heart of Reynolds's belief. A letter he wrote later in life provides a clue to this. He used a passage on religion written by one of his ancestors in the eighteenth century to explain his faith to others. 'My children,' the excerpt begins:

> I entreat you to live in unity and love with one another and help one another if it is needed. If any of you should be poor in this world and God should give any of you riches, you that are strong, help those that are weak. Stick close as a family and the God of Heaven will bless you.[22]

His training for the deaconship in Leeds culminated in his ordination at a special service at Durham Cathedral held in May 1896.[23] As Reynolds listened to a sermon in the grand surroundings of the cathedral, his religious path was mapped out. He would spend the next year as curate of St Hilda's, a parish in the northern city of Darlington, the last stage before he could be ordained a priest. He lived a humble existence, surviving on a stipend of one hundred pounds for the year, no more than £7,000 in today's money. He was ordained as a priest in another service at Durham in 1897 at the age of just twenty-four. Reynolds was young, but appears to have had no doubts about his future.

On the last day of August in 1897 Reynolds was sitting at his desk in Darlington. The young curate was struggling over a letter he was writing to a clergyman in another part of the country. He had never met Reverend John Green but had heard about his plans to form a community of monks who would go into the world to help the poor and lost souls of society find meaning in a religious life. Green, a Cistercian monk in Gloucestershire, was searching for young men who might be interested in helping him with this work, and had contacted Reynolds via a mutual friend.

Reynolds's letter to Green survives today deep inside a battered chest of documents held in the archives at Douai Abbey in Berkshire. The letter provides some insights into his views at the time. After brief pleasantries, he addresses the subject at hand. 'I hardly think that the work you write of will suit me,' he writes sharply. 'To begin with I could not leave my work here easily until next spring or summer, of course you want someone earlier.'[24] But timing was the least of Reynolds's obstacles to the plan. He agreed that the Christian faith could help to cure social ills, but did not think Green was being radical enough. 'I feel very strongly that the religious life is absolutely necessary to restore England to Christ, but I feel that what is wanted at the present time is not an adaptation of monastic life, but the old life as we have it set out in the rule of St Benedict and nothing short of that. At least that is what I should like for myself.'

Reynolds was a purist. 'My own belief is that men must become religious, that is the first and greatest part of their life, and then work will grow out of their life,' he wrote. 'They must come together to lead a particular life and not to do a particular work.' Having so forcefully expressed his opinions, he remembers he is writing to a man he has not met before. 'Will you forgive an entire stranger for writing to you in such a fashion as I have done?' concludes the missive, written by hand over three small pages. 'Kindly treat this letter in confidence.'

Still a month shy of his twenty-fifth birthday, Reynolds was confident enough to write such letters to far more experienced figures in the Christian community. Green's plan was not for him, but his reference to wanting to live the 'old life' shows how he was already looking beyond his work as a curate at St Hilda's.

He remained at Darlington another year until moving in 1898 to the parish of St Alban's in Sneinton, Nottingham, again as a curate. During this period both churches were involved in controversies over 'high' Anglicanism.[25] Reynolds, brought up an Anglo-Catholic, was used to religious practices with which some Church of England congregations were not comfortable. The young curate may not have played a leading role in the controversy, but he was unable to cure the tension. It was the clearest harbinger yet of his future conversion to Catholicism.

The controversies echoed a similar situation that occurred around the same time in the family home in Bromley, which Reynolds had left behind. In 1896, Dorothy Mousley, the orphaned daughter of Frederick Reynolds's sister, Polly, went to live with the Reynolds family. During her studies she became greatly attracted by Roman Catholicism and wrote to a Franciscan friar to seek advice. At this point Frederick, afraid his daughters would be swayed by such views, sent Dorothy to a family in Wales to cure her of her 'popish leanings'.[26] Though Frederick brought his children up as Anglo-Catholics, indicating some sympathy with the church of Rome, he firmly wished them to remain within the Anglican church. But the damage, as Frederick saw it, was done. All five of his children later converted to Catholicism. Leslie and Ronald, both of whom were active in Catholic social work in London, took the step in 1904, while Rothay and his sisters followed at intervals in subsequent years.[27]

Reynolds grew increasingly restive during his time as a curate with the two northern churches. His slim build and Cambridge-bred aura of intelligence belied a restless nature and a constant search for new opportunities. He was a young man utterly committed to his faith, which he viewed as the 'first and greatest part' of his life, and his correspondence with Green demonstrates how he was not afraid to speak out. But he found the narrow, procedural debate over Church of England practices incredibly stifling. It was just a distraction getting in the way of the real purpose of religion as he saw it: the transformation of society from the ground up. His idea to achieve this was a rebirth of monasticism, with men coming together to live the simple life as set out by Benedict, an Italian saint born in the fifth century. The debates within Christianity before and after the reformation would disappear, Reynolds thought, if the religion reverted to its early roots.

This led, as the letter to Reverend Green suggests, to Reynolds almost becoming a monk himself. In this period he travelled throughout Britain forging close and lasting links with monastic orders, in particular the Benedictines. Records remain of his visit to monks at Milton Abbas in Dorset in the summer of 1899 and Caldey Island, off the coast of Wales, in 1901. Reynolds stayed on the island for a week, saying Mass each day in

Latin. He was moving closer, month-by-month, to taking up the monk's life for good.

There was one order of monks to which he was especially close. Seventy miles south of Darlington, in Painsthorpe, Yorkshire, dwelt a group of Anglo-Catholic monks led by Abbot Aelred Carlyle. This band of Benedictine monks had been a leading Anglo-Catholic community and emphasised the Catholic heritage of the Anglican Church.[28] They had been the first Benedictine monastic order accepted into the Church of England. But times were difficult. The monks were under pressure over the question of how smoothly their Anglo-Catholicism fitted within Anglicanism. In 1913 the dam broke and they were received into the Roman Catholic faith.

The order's struggle over the question mirrors the internal conflict faced by Reynolds, who was closely connected to the group. One contribution he made to the Painsthorpe monks stands out. In 1904 he played an instrumental role in founding *Pax*, a new quarterly magazine for their community that is still produced today. Reynolds was thirty-two at the time and it was the first time he had been published.

Some years later, Carlyle's monks – who were to settle permanently at Prinknash Abbey in Gloucestershire in 1928, where they remain today – discovered the anonymous editorial in the first issue of *Pax* was authored by Reynolds. The article demonstrates the affection Reynolds felt for the order and his closeness to it. 'The community, now living at Painsthorpe, has been in existence for more than ten years, and its circle of friends is continually increasing,' he wrote. 'The difficulty of keeping in touch with so many is great, and we have come to the point reached by so many communities, when a magazine becomes a necessity.'

Reynolds then turned to Benedict, the patron saint of Europe who inspired the founding of the order, and explained why the magazine had been named after the Latin word for peace. 'St Benedict is, above all, the

Saint who proclaimed Christ's message of peace in an age of unrest and social upheaval,' he wrote. 'The title given to the present publication is not, then, due to fancy or caprice, but has been adopted because it represents the spirit which those fighting under the rule of St Benedict desire to cultivate in themselves and to propagate among others.'

Reynolds was a campaigning Christian – which would prove important during his time in Nazi Germany. He believed religion could cure social ills. To him, monks of the order were not living but 'fighting' under the rule of St Benedict. 'We have spoken of fighting, and with reason, for the Christian paradox must never be forgotten, that peace comes through war,' he wrote. 'It was after the din of battle that the St Benedict emerged the Saint of the Placid Countenance.'

'Alfred Rothay Reynolds was a great friend of the Prinknash Community in the early years of the twentieth century', according to Aelred Baker, who serves as archivist for the order. In the decades that followed, Reynolds found time to write several articles for *Pax* on subjects ranging from Russia's 'Festival of Summer' in 1916 to 'Poles at Prayer' in 1939. Such was his closeness to Carlyle's order of monks that he seriously considered joining them and pursuing a monastic life. But he never followed through on promises to do so, retreating for the third and final time in July 1902. A monk's life of seclusion and contemplation was not for Reynolds. Faith was central to his life but the outside world was just too interesting. Reynolds was not forgotten by Carlyle's order, which regards him highly over a century later. He remembered them in his will, leaving his collection of books to the order.

The years after university were busy for Reynolds. Even in the midst of his time serving English churches and communing with monks he found the time to return to Cambridge and obtain a Master's degree in 1901. He lasted longer in Nottingham than Darlington but the two churches and his monastic diversions could not sate his yearning for new experiences. He visited Carlyle's order again in August 1904 before leaving quietly. Planning was well-advanced for his next religious appointment, one that few people could have anticipated. He left his position with the church in Nottingham and agreed to relocate to the Russia of Tsar Nicholas II. He moved to St Petersburg in 1904 as an assistant chaplain to the Anglican church attached to the British Embassy. Still feeling unready to serve as a priest, moving to such an exotic location offered him the new opportunities in languages and culture that he craved. It was a decision that would change his life forever. His years in Russia would prove decisive to the restive curate's future course.

-CHAPTER II-
LAND OF THE TSARS

S tanding as dusk falls in the centre of St Petersburg's *Dvortsovaya Ploshchad* – Palace Square – is a strangely paradoxical experience. It is remarkable because of the awe-inspiring scale and impressive grandeur of the Winter Palace, which dominates the open space before it. Yet it is also unsettling – mainly because the people are missing. As a landmark it is comparable to Trafalgar Square in London or St Peter's Square in Rome, yet those places would be filled with tourists. St Petersburg has the attractions to compete with those tourist hubs, but recent events had led to a sharp fall in visitors when I travelled to the city in October 2014.

I landed almost 110 years to the day after Reynolds's first arrival in Russia. My trip was easier than his. While Reynolds faced a long journey over land and sea, the ease of modern air travel meant I could fly from London to St Petersburg in under four hours. There were similarities, though, in the political situation. Vladimir Putin's decision to annex the Crimean region and covertly spread unrest in Ukraine had sent relations plunging to Cold War levels a few months before my arrival.

It meant the atmosphere of uneasy relations between Russia and the West was comparable to when Reynolds arrived. At the start of the twentieth century, Russia and Britain were far from the best of international friends. Russia was seen as a mysterious land peopled by strange and rather untrustworthy souls. This situation improved with the Anglo-Russian entente of 1907, and again when the two countries were allies in the First World War. But when Reynolds arrived in 1904, such comradeship would have felt an extremely distant notion.

St Petersburg was founded early in the eighteenth century by Peter the Great, one of the most important leaders in Russia's history. He was a close follower of the West's traditions and fashions and St Petersburg is known as Russia's 'window on the west' for being its city most open to non-Russian influences. But with its onion domes and Cyrillic symbols, St Petersburg felt an alien place to English travellers at the beginning of the twentieth century – and it felt that way even in the twenty-first.

The Winter Palace in St Petersburg, home to Russia's royal family
until the 1917 revolution. (Photograph by the author)

Reynolds would have disapproved of the timing of my trip. He thought the country was 'detestable in Autumn' because of the cold and grey weather, which was suitably drab on my visit. St Petersburg boasts some amazing sights, none more so than the Winter Palace, but is a disorienting place for a non-Russian speaker. On one occasion I stood outside Kazan Cathedral as worshippers streamed out after a service. Steady rain fell as a saxophonist busked in the shadow of the formidable ninety-six-column colonnade. A remote-controlled drone flew high above. It felt an immensely strange atmosphere – the modern-day equivalent of the disorientation Reynolds may have experienced as he settled into Russian life.

The Church of the Savior on Spilled Blood was built on the site of Emperor Alexander II's assassination in 1881. It was completed while Reynolds was living in Russia. (Photograph by the author)

His decision to move there in 1904, at the age of thirty-two, was a move of extraordinary bravery, driven by his desire for new experiences and challenges (and learning the language was certainly that, even for a linguist like him). He grew to love the city and developed an affinity for Russia and its people that led him later to write two books about the country.

Reynolds's religious ardour was also an important factor in his decision to move. His posting as assistant chaplain to the British Embassy church was the perfect way for him to experience Russian culture. Religion exerted a heavy influence on life in the country he now called home. As soon as he arrived he was struck by how religion 'forces itself on the attention' in Russia.[29] 'God and His Mother, saints and angels, seem near; men rejoice or stand ashamed beneath their gaze,' he admiringly wrote. 'The people of the land have made it a vast sanctuary, perfumed with prayer and filled with the memories of heroes of the faith. Saints and sinners, believers and infidels, are affected by its atmosphere.'[30]

If religion was the first thing Reynolds observed in St Petersburg, the city's scale and distinctive character was a close second. He was mesmerised and said it was 'a magnificent city, magical in the grip of winter, detestable in autumn, alluring in the spring-time. Its streets are broad, its squares and open places large, the size of its palaces and public buildings makes them imposing even when their architecture is poor.' His imagination was particularly fired by the cathedral spire within the Fortress of St Peter and St Paul: a 'tapering pillar of gold, rising high above the tower'. At sunset it becomes a 'shaft of flame', he wrote.[31]

Reynolds did not enjoy his living quarters, a city centre flat in a barracks surrounding two large courtyards. 'Nobody ever loved a flat,' he remarked dismissively.[32] But he enthusiastically involved himself in Russian culture and life. He learned to speak the language fluently and was impressed by the mother tongue of his new home country. 'Russian is soft and melodious, and hard and nasal sounds, which remain in Polish, a language bearing a close resemblance to it, have been almost entirely eliminated.'[33]

He arrived in Russia during the early stages of a tumultuous revolutionary period, which culminated in the Bolshevik Revolution and execution of the Tsar and his family in 1918. Few would have predicted such momentous events when Reynolds arrived in 1904, but signs of turbulence were growing. Chief among the country's problems was the countryside, where years of poor agricultural policy had fuelled discontent among the peasantry. Politically, Tsar Nicholas II – the cousin of George V, to whom he bore a strong physical resemblance – ruled autocratically without a Parliament. He showed little appetite for change or reform despite his 'Father of the Nation' epithet. Minorities including Catholics and Jews were subjugated, while harsh 'Russification' policies incensed the Finns, who revolted at the forced imposition of the Russian language and disbandment of Finland's army. Overseas, increasingly tense relations with Japan ignited in February 1904 when Russia's Pacific fleet was targeted by a surprise attack in Port Arthur, which eventually fell to the Japanese the following January.[34]

These pressures combined to trigger the revolution of 1905, a bout of unrest that put Nicholas II's rule under unprecedented pressure. The fall of Port Arthur sparked demonstrations in the capital, and a petition signed by 135,000 people seeking better working conditions and wages was delivered to the Winter Palace. But the peaceful protestors were met not by concessions but rifle fire. On the 'Bloody Sunday' of 22 January 1905 more than a hundred were killed, causing outrage throughout the Russian Empire and beyond. Intermittent strikes and unrest in the cities and countryside grew in the ensuing months, leading to Nicholas II's 'October Manifesto', which promised a new State Parliament or *Duma*. Its arrival appeared to usher in a constitutional monarchy, but within months many of the concessions had been reversed.

The year 1905 was significant for Reynolds personally, as well as for Russia. It was the year of his conversion to Catholicism, which, though years in the making, remained an important personal event. Diving into his new life in Russia had been an exciting and energising experience, but it had caused him to question deeply his Anglicanism. He loved the rich tone of religious life in Russia, which was 'perfumed with prayer' in a way the staid Church of England was most certainly not. Russians were devoted to the Eastern Orthodox faith, which regards Constantinople (Istanbul) and not Rome as its spiritual home. The experiences nonetheless elevated the Catholicism that had lain dormant within him.

Russia was not a uniformly welcoming place for followers of the Catholic faith when Reynolds arrived. Nicholas II, having inherited the throne from his father Alexander in 1894, continued the old policy of hostility towards the Catholic church. Symptomatic of this were his 'Russification policies' towards Catholic Poland and other countries within the Russian sphere of influence, which he tried to make 'Orthodox minions'.[35] However, the first Russian revolution in 1905 led to his decision to issue a decree of religious toleration that allowed Catholics more freedom to practise their faith. It was in this environment that Reynolds, after years of painful internal contemplation, finally decided to follow his brothers and convert to the Catholic church. For the remaining years of his life in Russia he worshipped happily at the Catholic Church of St Catherine in the heart of St Petersburg.

More everyday matters pressed. Reynolds's departure from the English church left him in need of a new source of income. He was inspired by his new life in Russia and had no desire to return to Britain so soon. Realising how interesting the events of 1905, and the accompanying political and social changes afoot in Russia, were to people back in Britain, he sought work as a writer and won his first job in journalism as St Petersburg correspondent for the *Daily News*. The newspaper, which is no longer printed, launched in Britain in 1846 under the editorship of Charles Dickens. It was positioned as a liberal alternative to *The Times* and enjoyed a successful period of increasing sales and influence in the early twentieth century under the editorship of the young and dynamic Alfred George Gardiner.[36]

During those fevered months of violent upheaval in 1905, when an incendiary public mood led to industrial and political upheaval, Reynolds's reporting instincts were stirred as never before. He had the journalistic luck to be living in a city undergoing great change and was never far from a potential story or situation of interest. He was well aware he was living through historic times, in which the lower orders were politicised by events as never before. 'The echoes of heated political debate used to float to me from the kitchen,' he wrote, 'especially on those days when the washerwoman took tea there and added the weight of her influence to the arguments of the cook.'[37]

In short, St Petersburg at that time was an ideal place to be a foreign correspondent. Reynolds took to it quickly. Within a couple of years in Russia he was able to gain access to events at which more seasoned foreign correspondents were expected, including the first meeting of the new *Duma* in April 1906. Reynolds described the fevered atmosphere of the revolutionary era in dramatic terms. 'What a chance for a revolutionist to blow up the whole lot of them!' he recalled a friend saying during a party attended by Prime Minister Pyotr Stolypin and other leading politicians.[38] The febrile environment in St Petersburg meant newsworthy events seemed to come his way with regularity. He rarely had to look for them. 'A bomb has just gone off in the street,' Reynolds wrote on one occasion, as if such an event outside his flat was an everyday occurrence.[39] One evening Reynolds was present during an incident in a restaurant when a student was murdered after an argument sparked by his refusal to stand during the national anthem.[40]

Reynolds's pieces for the *Daily News* provided vivid portraits of life in revolutionary Russia. In 1906, for one of his first articles, he interviewed a nineteen-year-old woman, Nadejda, about her participation in the revolution. 'It is going very badly,' she told Reynolds, 'and numbers of revolutionists are in prison. I see in the paper today that a great friend of mine has been arrested. She had thrown a bomb at one of the enemies of the people, and had not time to shoot herself when her work was done.'[41]

The revolution was a time of personal as well as professional opportunity for Reynolds – in its fires he forged the closest friendship of his life. In September 1904, the English writer Hector Hugh Munro, better known by the pen-name of 'Saki', arrived in St Petersburg as a correspondent for the right-wing *Morning Post* newspaper. The two men were of similar age and enjoyed similar pursuits; like Reynolds, Munro was a keen swimmer and tennis player. As two members of a limited pool of foreign correspondents working in St Petersburg, who arrived at a similar time, their friendship is not surprising.

Munro differed from Reynolds in one key respect. He was no fledgling journalist but an emerging author, whose short stories parodied the upper classes of Edwardian England. While in Russia he split his time between reporting on the country and developing his own fictional works. His writing style was informed by figures such as Oscar Wilde and Lewis Carroll, and Munro in turn was an influence on comic writers of the next generation, such as A. A. Milne, Noël Coward and P. G. Wodehouse.[42] Munro had yet to achieve that level of fame while working as a foreign correspondent, his foremost years of prominence beginning on his return to Britain in 1909.

During the revolution of 1905, Munro's sister Ethel was visiting him in St Petersburg and she was present for the drama and carnage of Bloody Sunday. The protest was led by Father Georgy Gapon, a Ukrainian priest in the Russian Orthodox church, who had discovered socialism after the death of his wife. His speeches persuaded masses of Russia's industrial workforce to strike and on Sunday 9 January (the twenty-second by Western calendars) he delivered a petition to the gates of the Winter Palace setting out their demands. Hector and Ethel Munro took up a position in the Hotel de France, located in the heart of the city, to observe proceedings.[43]

It was not long before Hector had left his sister and ventured outside for a closer look; and not long again before he was chased back, having become part of a Russian crowd beaten away from the Winter Palace by cavalry forces. Having then sought a different vantage point, the Munros narrowly avoided death as they came under rifle fire. The assault had started. The next day Munro hired a sleigh to witness the aftermath and saw the many corpses that remained strewn on the icy streets. It was macabre work, but necessary to inform his dispatches.

Compared to the events of the seismic Bolshevik Revolution that followed twelve years later, the 'revolution' of 1905 seems relatively insignificant in impact. But it was not a minor event for Russians living through it. An urban uprising in the country's capital had led to soldiers firing on their countrymen, a tragic indictment of the rule of Tsar Nicholas II. He may not have shot any bullets that day, but he was the military's leader and the events contradicted his 'Father of the People' image. Changes to the country's political, religious and agrarian spheres followed.

What did Reynolds make of it all? Though he stayed at the National Liberal Club while in London, he had a diverse mix of political views. He was a monarchist, supporting Nicholas II and the reforms undertaken during his time in Russia. Reynolds did not condemn the violence of Bloody Sunday. 'The Russian Government cannot be condemned for using severe measures to restore order in the country,' he wrote.[44] He observed Tsar Nicholas II's rule in a traditional sense. 'In Russian theory the emperor has a double part to play. He is autocrat and he is also father of his people.'[45] Reynolds's favourable view of the Tsar endured, as this admiring passage near the end of his time in Russia shows: 'When [Nicholas II] went to Poltava in 1909 to celebrate the two hundredth anniversary of Peter the Great's victory over the Swedes, [he] refused to listen to the advice of the police, and strolled about chatting with peasants. His homes at Peterhof and Tsarskoe Selo are small country houses, and the splendid palaces in both places stand empty.'[46] It is admiring fluff rather than critical journalism.

The reforms started in 1905 partly explain Reynolds's support for a monarch whose appeal to liberals was damaged by the violence of that year. He approved of the Tsar's manifesto in April 1905 in which he apparently renounced his authority over the religious lives of his subjects. The new policy of increased tolerance towards faiths other than the Orthodox church was a liberal move, chiming with Reynolds's political sentiment. The personal implications for him as a Catholic convert were of great importance too. And it paid off for the Tsar, or so Reynolds thought. 'When Nicholas II, on his own initiative, adopted a policy of toleration, a conservative newspaper of Moscow declared that his manifesto had destroyed the Orthodox Church,' he wrote. 'These fears have proved to be groundless. The manifesto has given new life to the church.'[47]

In politics the progress was more limited. While Reynolds supported the inauguration of the new Russian Parliament, he was well aware of how Nicholas II had ensured the *Duma* would pose no threat to his power. It did not take long for the Tsar's old habits to reappear. In the summer of 1908 Reynolds visited a prison in Moscow to speak to Sergey Muromtsev, the president of the first *Duma*, and eleven other members of Parliament who had been incarcerated. After his visit he reflected on how legal rights in Russia differed from Britain. 'The elementary safeguards of liberty are wanting.'[48]

Though political liberty was in short supply, Reynolds found Russian society to be less fusty and rule-bound than his homeland. 'I did not understand what liberty is until I left England and lived in Russia,' he wrote. A man 'is not considered dirty because he has been too lazy to shave, nor ill-mannered if he be unpunctual, nor eccentric if he goes into the stalls of a theatre in a check suit.'[49]

It seems unlikely Reynolds partook of those particular freedoms. He was clean-shaven and – crucially, for a journalist – had no reputation for missing deadlines. Furthermore, he took his tailoring extremely seriously. His brother Ronald once described him as 'Europe's best dressed correspondent'.[50] Despite apparently admiring Russia's social freedoms and its people, Reynolds was a man of standards, and in several ways the country disappointed him. Russian cuisine fell short of acceptable in his judgement. 'I have been to dinner-parties in Petrograd at which the food was dull and the conversation enthralling,' he wrote. 'The reverse is so often the case in London.'[51] Reynolds, who was able to combine a strong interest in gastronomy with a slim figure, was also accustomed to certain levels of service. 'It is a matter of uncertainty whether it will occur to anybody to bring one shaving water in the morning,' he wrote during an account of life at a country house, seemingly without irony.[52]

Reynolds spent most of his thirties in Russia, leaving in 1910 at the age of thirty-eight. Entering middle-age, he was established in a second career and had acquired specialist knowledge of Russia that would prove of great benefit on his return to London. He remained a bachelor, a status his time abroad does not seem to have come close to changing. But Reynolds was no loner. His ability to make friends from all walks of life was frequently commented on and his time in Russia had added a new set, most notably Munro. His spell abroad had also established him as a traveller, which would remain the case until his death. Did he regret the nomadic path on which he had embarked? There is a hint of melancholy in the following passage about Reynolds's visit to a countryside acquaintance in Eastern Europe: 'When I left Ivan's home there was a tinge of envy in my heart. Its simplicity was imposing. I was a wanderer; Ivan had his castle, standing in the midst of fields which were his own and would pass to his children.'[53]

-CHAPTER III-

WAR AND MI7

C atholic in faith and a journalist by trade, a very different Reynolds returned to Britain after six years abroad. He arrived in a country at the peak of its power thanks to industrialisation and the global networks of empire. George V succeeded his father Edward in 1910 but the Edwardian era lived on for four years after Reynolds returned to his home country: an age of innocence, with little indication of the devastation war would soon inflict on the nation and its families.

Reynolds had changed more than Britain during the Edwardian years. When he first left for Russia he had been close to ascetic in his personal life. Now in his late thirties, Reynolds had transformed into something approaching an Edwardian dandy. He drank coffee, preferred to converse in French, wore braces and used *Brillantine* in his hair. His first book, *The Gondola*, was a novel published in 1913 that featured a lead character named Richard Venning. A travelling convert Catholic journalist from Britain who has recently worked in Russia, it is clear who Reynolds had based Venning on. The character provides numerous insights into his own life.

'Journalism was demoralising,' Venning declared at one point.

If he had never been the correspondent of a London paper in St Petersburg, he would never have formed expensive tastes. He had sacrificed his love of simplicity for the benefit of the paper. Could he ever have got the scoops, which had made his reputation, without the help of little dinners in restaurants and boxes at the opera? Of course not.[54]

Journalism had clearly elevated the standards to which Reynolds was accustomed – especially compared with his time in the church, when he lived on a meagre annual allowance.

Aside from excursions to various religious orders in Britain and a handful of foreign assignments, Reynolds spent most of the next decade based in London. He did not own a permanent home but took temporary rooms at places such as the Liberal Club in Whitehall and Lincoln's Inn in Holborn. He continued with journalism and was still writing about Russia for the *Daily News* in 1911, despite returning from the country. There were other diversions. In that year he and Munro, who had both been in thrall of the Russian ballet in St Petersburg, hosted a reception for Sergei Diaghilev's ballet troupe, including its star Vaslav Nijinsky, during its first tour of Britain. Guests at this exotic event were required to speak French, as that was the only other language the Russians could speak. It was a sensational meeting of cultures. At one point Munro's sister, Ethel, found Nijinsky cowering under a table. 'It is the devil!' he cried to her, pointing in panic to an Aberdeen Terrier sitting nearby. He had never seen the breed before.[55]

Part of the reason Reynolds had returned to Britain was to capitalise on the unique experiences of his time in Russia. However, the book ideas he pitched to publishers did not meet with immediate success and he soon found he was missing life as a foreign correspondent. In 1912 he left for a second overseas assignment, this time reporting on events in Berlin for *The Standard*, forerunner to the *London Evening Standard*.

It was the first time he had lived in Germany. The country was 'exceedingly prosperous and enjoying the fruits of a peace, which, except for conflicts with rebellious natives beyond the seas, had not been interrupted for more than forty years', Reynolds wrote. 'There was work for all and German merchants and manufacturers were exporting their goods to the end of the earth.'[56] Reynolds may have arrived in Germany at a prosperous time, but he viewed Berlin as inferior to other European capitals. 'Berlin in 1912 had the air of a provincial city. It lacked the movement and animation of London and Paris, and the charm, which age has given to those cities, was absent.'[57] Despite this verdict, Reynolds enjoyed his time there, perhaps relishing the slower pace of life. 'In summer, the innumerable trees in broad streets compensated for the lack of beautiful buildings. The wheels of life went slower than in London and jolted less.'[58]

He arrived in Berlin early in February 1912, a few days before the British Secretary of State for War, Lord Haldane, arrived in the city to negotiate with Germany about a naval agreement between the two countries. Britain was prepared to yield to some of Germany's colonial demands in Africa if Germany would recognise Britain's dominance of the seas. The mission ended in failure. Rather than striking a deal, Haldane's visit only underlined the differences between the two countries. The chances of a future war had increased.

Reynolds passed his days reading, socialising and writing in the coffee houses of Berlin. He was at home in these centres of information and discussion, which he described as clubs without subscriptions. 'For the price of a mug of beer or a cup of coffee one could sit in them by the hour and read the newspapers of all the capitals of Europe, which the proprietors provided for their guests.'[59] Reynolds's favourite coffee house was the Café des Westens, 'a haunt of the intelligentsia, of poets and writers, artists and socialist members of the Reichstag.'[60] There he struck up a friendship with Rupert Brooke, who went on to become one of the great poets of the First World War with poems including 'The Soldier'.

> If I should die, think only this of me;
> That there's some corner of a foreign field
> That is for ever England

Brooke was in Berlin to research his dissertation on Elizabethan drama in the Prussian state library. One day Reynolds was sitting beside Brooke in the Café des Westens when the young student turned to him with glee and said: 'I have made this café famous.' The reason? Brooke had just penned his classic pre-war poem 'The Old Vicarage, Grantchester', in which he nostalgically dreams of England. A line at the top of the poem dates it to the 'Café des Westens, Berlin, May 1912'. It includes the famous lines:

> God! I will pack, and take a train
> And get me to England once again!
> For England's the one land, I know,
> Where men with Splendid Hearts may go

Brooke made a strong impression on Reynolds, who later described the encounter in his final book, *When Freedom Shrieked*.

> With his mop of yellow hair and a complexion as clear as a girl's, heightening, not diminishing, the impression of physical and intellectual strength that he made, Rupert was bound to attract attention anywhere. Set among the shallow scribblers and debaters of the Café des Westens, he was a god indeed.[61]

Reynolds's time in Berlin for *The Standard* was brief compared with his *Daily News* years in St Petersburg. His departure in the summer of 1912 was caused by the belated success of his attempts to find a publisher. Mills & Boon, a small British firm formed just two years earlier in 1910, commissioned him to write two books. The publisher came to be known for romantic fiction for women, but in its early years it published a broader range of books. Reynolds signed agreements to write one novel, *The Gondola*, and a non-fiction account of his time in Russia, *My Russian Year*. The latter was a factual account of Russian life, part of a Mills & Boon series of books including titles such as *My Parisian Year* and *My Sudan Year*. The price of slotting into this series was the book's misleading title, which unfairly shortened Reynolds's experience of life in Russia from six years to one.[62]

In August 1912 he moved to Ettal, a village in the Bavarian mountains, to write his books. Reynolds worked in the guesthouse of the Benedictine Abbey, at the centre of village life. There he found the quiet that he sought. In 1913 he returned to Britain, where the books were coming to market. *My Russian Year* made the greater impact. Reynolds kept a binder of newspaper and magazine reviews and collected forty-one in total from a wide range of publications, titles as diverse as the *Sunday Times*, *Punch*, *Tatler* and *Indian Daily News*.

A slim volume running to 165 pages, *My Russian Year* describes conditions in Russia with details of its customs, religion, food and drink, town and country life. The book was well received by the *Morning Post* – perhaps no surprise given that its review was written by Munro, who was keen to vouch for the book's veracity. 'An entertaining and instructive picture of twentieth century Russia… The general charm of treatment is matched by the accuracy of the details.' Other, perhaps less biased reviews, appeared in all the main papers. The *Times Literary Supplement* said it was 'conversational, easy and eminently readable … a truthful and impartial picture of ordinary Russian life'.[63] The *Daily Telegraph* called it 'by far the most comprehensive account of Russian life yet given to English readers … The flavour of his humour is delicious.'[64] The left-wing *Manchester Guardian* was also impressed. 'We have rarely come upon such an interesting and well-balanced account of modern Russia. Mr Reynolds has seen his Russia with eyes unclouded by passion, though they are often twinkling with humour, and occasionally dimmed by tears.'[65]

Reviews of the second book published by Reynolds in 1913, *The Gondola*, are harder to find. The novel follows the exploits of Richard Venning, who travels across Europe in pursuit of the affections of an Italian countess, 'Contessa Della Casa'. Written in a richly comic tone, it contains such sections of flamboyant prose as:

> The enchantment of the mountains enthralled Venning. The sky was a brighter and more luminous blue than he had ever seen it, and the sun, just risen above a snowy peak, threw trails of rose and saffron flowers on the opal surface of a frozen lake, stained the heights beyond crimson, and turned the snow by the roadside to crystal.[66]

The novel begins in the Swiss alpine setting of St Moritz, a stop-off on Venning's journey to Venice as part of a European tour. While there he attends a masquerade ball and meets the countess, but does not immediately win her affections. More of Venning's adventures across Europe are recounted, including several scenes set in St Petersburg, until the book's finale in Poland, where he is ultimately successful in his pursuit. Unlike Reynolds's subsequent books, which are serious in tone and offer factual accounts of his time abroad, *The Gondola* is something of a romp. Its comic style reveals, more than any other evidence in surviving books and letters, Reynolds's sense of humour. Here one can possibly detect the influence of his friend Munro, who may have emboldened him in this style of writing.

A lack of modesty shines through in Reynolds's description of Venning, who at one point is referred to as 'exceedingly handsome and probably an adventurer'.[67] He is pious, on one occasion reprimanding an English couple attending a church service in St Petersburg for criticising the Catholic practice of applying ash to foreheads on Ash Wednesday. While still in Russia, Reynolds has Venning refer to the 'silly tricks' of the suffragettes, indicating a somewhat illiberal attitude to the campaign for votes for women.[68] Reynolds's love for Poland shines through, as it does in all four of his other books. 'Were I not an Englishman, I would be a Pole,' Venning declares at one point.[69] In one passage the countess, who is Polish, bemoans the 'unjust' influence of Germany, Austria and Russia on her country.[70]

———

His books published, Reynolds found another way to capitalise on his time in Russia. Early in 1914 he began working as a lecturer specialising in the country for the Cambridge University Extension movement, which offered courses on different subjects at locations throughout Britain. The publicly funded movement started in Oxford in the 1880s before spreading to Cambridge and other universities, with the aim of disseminating knowledge from the country's academic centres to the wider public.

In January 1914 a series of adverts appeared in the *Devon and Exeter Daily Gazette* promoting a course of classes on 'Modern Russia', beginning on 23 January. The first one was free and a full course of eleven cost ten shillings and sixpence. Three days before the first talk the course was advertised in the newspaper's 'City Chat' column:

In view of the entente cordiale existing between this country and Russia, and the increasing interest in Russian art and Russian literature, the subject of the course should arouse wide interest, and the lecturer would seem to possess the qualifications necessary to give it a special interest. He was for over five years St Petersburg correspondent of the Daily News, and has had rare opportunities of contrasting Russian life with life in other countries for he subsequently acted as Berlin correspondent of the Standard, and his recent novel, The Gondola, shows an intimate knowledge of Venetian life ... His lectures ought to be particularly interesting, and, in spite of the academic auspices under which they are to be given, entertaining.[71]

Reynolds's lectures took him around the country, to cities ranging from Newcastle, Middlesbrough and Scarborough in the north-east to Exeter, Hastings and London in the south. Topics covered in the lectures, each of which was followed by a discussion, included Russian history, its political scene and religion. It was satisfying work that suited Reynolds well. Yet he had little idea that his nascent career as an author and lecturer on Russia would soon take on a new significance.

———

Reynolds was in London during the fateful summer of 1914. British politicians had grown increasingly disturbed by the expansionist intentions of the German Kaiser and the assassination of an Austro-Hungarian prince in Sarajevo provided the unlikely spark for a war that would change Europe irrevocably.

Munro was a spectator in the House of Commons on the day that Foreign Secretary Sir Edward Grey stated Britain's position, and war became inevitable. That evening Munro met Reynolds and two friends for dinner at a restaurant on the Strand to discuss the momentous events. He said the strain of listening to the speech was so great that he 'found himself in a sweat'.[72] Munro had insisted on walking to the restaurant from Westminster at great pace – the start of his drive to be fit enough to fight in the war. 'He was determined to fight,' said Reynolds. In the weeks that followed, Munro was 'condemning himself for the slackness of his years in London and hiring a horse to take exercise, to which he was a little addicted, in the park.'[73]

While Munro enlisted, Reynolds stayed behind in London. Just a couple of years younger than Munro, he did not share his friend's desire – which many felt ardently in the patriotic wartime atmosphere – to head to the front. A war memorial at Pembroke College records how narrowly Reynolds avoided being part of the generation ravaged by war. He studied at Cambridge between 1892 and 1895, leaving when Kaiser Wilhelm II's reign in Germany was just seven years old and a continental war seemed an unlikely prospect. Pembroke's memorial cloister lists the names of 300 college members who died in the First World War. Around a third of the men who joined Pembroke between 1911 and 1917 had died by 1919.[74]

The war was a difficult period for Reynolds. He lost friends in the trenches. A country and a leader he much admired, the Russia of Nicholas II, succumbed to revolution. Polish lands were again subject to foreign aggression. When war broke out and the lamps went out all over Europe, to use Foreign Secretary Grey's famous phrase, Reynolds was occupied with his lecturing. During 1914 and 1915 he continued to travel across Britain delivering lectures on Russia, which attracted more interest than ever given the country's new status as a wartime ally. For centuries viewed by Britons as a mysterious far-off land with a strange language and odd customs, Russia was now fighting the same fight against the deadly Hun.

Reynolds's enthusiasm for Russia, already evident from *My Russian Year*, made him an ideal teacher to inform the curious about their new allies. He spoke effusively about them. 'Our confidence in the Russians rests partly on their bravery and courage,' he told an audience in London in March 1915, 'but above all, on the fact that throughout their history they have always displayed a great spirit of self-sacrifice in times of national crisis.'[75]

He took the message around the country. 'If our friendship with Russia, which [is] so warm at present, was to last, it must be based on sincerity, truth and forbearance,' he told an audience in Scarborough in September 1915.[76] The next month he spoke in Middlesbrough. As well as loftier subjects such as religion and Anglo-Russian relations, Reynolds focused on day-to-day life in Russia to a surprising degree of detail. During a London University lecture in March 1915, he 'gave interesting particulars with regard to the cost of the living of the peasant classes of the country, basing his figures on personal observation'.[77] A typical Russian household, said Reynolds, may spend about sixteen pounds a year, with heating costing two pounds, lighting sixteen shillings, furniture one pound, tax fourteen shillings and men's clothing nine pounds. 'The women were expected to provide their own clothes, weaving themselves.'

Reviews in the provincial press suggest Reynolds's lectures on Russia were warmly received. Strong feelings existed about the importance of the lecture scheme during the war. 'It is impossible to over-rate the good which the University Extension movement has effected in the spread of education in the last twenty years,' said a September 1915 editorial from the *Newcastle Journal*. 'This is one of the reasons that makes us hope that in whatever other direction the present government may seek to economise in the present crisis, they will not adopt the penny-wise and pound-foolish policy of cutting down the grants to the universities.'[78]

Reynolds had more than his lectures to keep him busy in the early months of the war. He remained a regular contributor to various national and provincial newspapers ranging from the *Daily Mirror* to the *Birmingham Gazette*. The witty and playful style of his earlier writing was gone, replaced by a serious tone more suited to wartime. How else to deal with such subjects as the death of Miss Cavell, the British nurse executed by Germany for helping allied soldiers escape from Germany in 1915, or the perils faced by his Polish friends, witnessing unthinkable bloodshed and tragedy on the war's eastern front? These were dark days and Reynolds did his bit by drawing attention to the plight of the suffering.

One of his articles was titled 'My Friend the Squire: A Memory of a Manor House in Poland'. Memory it was, since the forest-dwelling squire in question had seen his homeland 'swept by flame' during the war, in the words of Reynolds. 'Now the voices are silent. Now the manor-house is deserted. Now the wild things have fled. Now the forest is withered in the breath of war.'[79] Another article, 'A Menaced Polish City: Recollections of a Visit to Vilna', drew attention to the centuries-old town of Vilnius, the capital of modern-day Lithuania. It was a similarly impassioned account of a place and people in danger.[80]

Reynolds's campaign to spread awareness of eastern lands extended beyond his lecturing and newspaper articles. His one-man propaganda effort to improve perceptions of Russia developed in 1915 with a new edition of *My Russian Year*. 'The unity of the Russian Empire at the present time is as perfect and as sublime as that of the British Empire,' he wrote in a new foreword. 'Racial animosity has disappeared. The disputes of politicians have ceased. Terrorists crave the privilege of fighting the enemies of Russia. Wrath at the wicked aggression of Germany and love of the holy Russian land have united throne and people.'[81]

He wrote two more books during the First World War: a second on Russia, titled *My Slav Friends*, and *The Story of Warsaw*, published in 1915.

The Story of Warsaw is a picture book and just sixty pages in length, with most of the space taken by photographs. It was billed as 'a popular account of the famous medieval city with its beautiful buildings. A vivid description splendidly illustrated with 68 unique photographs. An excellent idea of the city will be gained from this book, of most exceptional interest at the present time.'

Reynolds adopted a stridently anti-German tone in the book. 'Has any town in Europe suffered more terrible calamities or seen more bewildering changes [than Warsaw]?' he asked.[82] 'No Prussian occupation, not even if it were to last as long as the Prussian occupation of 1795, can permanently ruin the fortunes of a city favoured by nature and made famous by the genius of its citizens,' he wrote.[83] The book goes on to give a short history of Warsaw and introduce its main landmarks, several of which were later destroyed by bombing in the Second World War. The book was reviewed reasonably well in *The Spectator* on its release in the summer of 1915, but did not seem to make much of an impact.[84]

The other book he released during the war, did. *My Slav Friends*, published a year later in 1916, struck an even more ardently pro-Russia tone than *My Russian Year*. Reynolds was candid about the book's objective: 'I have at the moment no higher ambition than to convince the reader that the Russians are very much like ourselves,' he wrote.[85] There is an 'essential unity of the British and Russian peoples and the solidarity of their aims'.[86] The book was also published in the US, suggesting an attempt to influence public opinion there. America, still neutral, was not to join the war until 1917, but the British government was desperate to change this. Encouraging international support for the Russian alliance was an important aim until the Bolshevik Revolution in 1917.

A reviewer in the *New York Times* shrewdly observed that Reynolds's book amounted 'almost to propaganda'.[87] This is not far from the truth;

it may well have been officially sanctioned as part of Britain's secret war effort. The Liberal Party politician Charles Masterman turned his hand to propaganda during the First World War as head of the War Propaganda Bureau, known to insiders as the Wellington House Operation. He commissioned books and pamphlets by well-known authors including Arthur Conan Doyle and John Buchan to influence public opinion overseas. The unit was responsible for the 'Report of the Committee on Alleged German Outrages', which sparked global anger with its revelations of the atrocities committed by German troops in Belgium.[88] Some of its more extreme claims, most notably that German troops had bounced Belgian babies on their bayonets, were disputed in the years that followed. But the impact of the propaganda was undeniable and helped turn international opinion against the Kaiser and his army. Officially sanctioned or not, the publication of *My Slav Friends* was in line with the objectives of Masterman's Wellington House Operation. Reynolds's work during the first half of the war, designed to improve perceptions of Russia and its people, had another impact. It brought him to the attention of a secret department of Britain's emerging intelligence infrastructure that wanted to make use of him.

———

The UK's oldest spy agencies – the Security Service for domestic espionage and Secret Intelligence Service for overseas – are known widely by their more prosaic labels MI5 and MI6. This is a legacy of the First World War, when both were sections of the Directorate of Military Intelligence, itself a part of the War Office. MI5, MI6 and the Government Communications Headquarters (GCHQ), which provides signals intelligence, are the three spy agencies remaining in 21st-century Britain. Forgotten are the other divisions of military intelligence, since disbanded or subsumed into other sections of the British state, which fought the country's espionage battles between 1914 and 1918.

There were nine in total, from MI1 through to MI9, which handled all manner of issues, from military ciphers and postal censorship to the positioning of submarine cables.[89] The seventh section, MI7, dealt with press and propaganda in the UK and overseas. Part of its remit was the study of foreign newspapers in enemy and neutral countries to detect hostile propaganda. For this a skilled team of translators was required and the multilingual Reynolds was perfectly suited to the task.

The subsection undertaking this work was called MI7(d). Reynolds started in 1916, viewing it as another way to contribute as the horrors of the war intensified. The team of translators worked in a small office located just off the Strand in Watergate House, part of the Adelphi buildings, a neoclassical terrace designed by Robert Adam. Working in such grand surroundings was a welcome fillip for Reynolds in light of his eighteenth-century architectural tastes.

Through his work at MI7 he made a lifelong friend of Ronald Knox, the theologian and later author of detective fiction, who began there in the summer of 1916. Knox took just a few weeks to acquire enough knowledge of the Norwegian language to be useful – a skillset that, 'as far as can be known, was never of the smallest use to him in later life', his biographer Evelyn Waugh drily noted. Though Knox was born sixteen years after Reynolds, the two men had a great deal in common. Knox was also brought up an Anglo-Catholic and was ordained in the Anglican church before converting to Catholicism. His time with MI7 coincided with the period immediately prior to his conversion in 1917, a time marked by doubts and uncertainty about his faith. Reynolds, who had been through a similar process, was ideally placed to support Knox at this time.

While Reynolds, Knox and the other translators at MI7(d) served a significant purpose, the most important part of the unit was section (b), which dealt with the creation of propaganda to be distributed to foreign countries. Lieutenant-General George Macdonogh had served as an officer in France until the end of 1915, when he was recalled to London to serve as Director of Military Intelligence in the War Office. His time in France had alerted him to the possibilities of using propaganda to undermine the confidence of the German army and he was behind the creation of section (b) in March 1916. Captain A. J. Dawson, a journalist, author and staff officer working in military intelligence, was attached to MI7(b) and 'instructed to prepare a plan for obtaining continuous supplies of articles about the work of the army, so far as possible without cost to the country'[90] – in other words, to build a specialist team of propaganda writers.

That summer an appeal went out to British fighters overseas. Those with literary experience were invited to apply to work for a new section in London. The lure of a break from the trenches was greatly appealing and some thousands responded before a small team of officers was selected to conduct the work. For the remainder of the war the section, whose numbers averaged about twenty, produced reams of written and pictorial propaganda, some of it printed in allied newspapers and some dropped behind enemy lines. Efforts included *Le Courrier de l'Aire*, a weekly newsletter published in French and dropped by aeroplane over Belgium, and a 'Weekly Letter to Soldiers' distributed to British troops at home and abroad.

MI7(b) was a small unit of writers but it contained a remarkable array of talents. Its ranks included A. A. Milne, the creator of Winnie the Pooh, the humorist J. B. Morton and Cecil Street, another member of MI7 who later turned his hand to detective fiction, writing the Dr Priestley novels. So secret was the work of MI7 that few outside the small department's walls knew what its writers were up to. Macdonogh himself felt in the dark. 'I don't know what MI7 are doing but I do know there is no section that could land me in a worse mess,' he once remarked.[91] All of MI7's documents were destroyed as soon as the war ended because of the potential embarrassment that could be caused if information about its underhand methods got into the public domain.

Some evidence survived. Captain James Lloyd, one of MI7(b)'s writers, kept copies of 150 articles, which were discovered in 2013 during a house clearance in Wales. The cache contains a copy of the striking first issue of *The Green Book*, a small satirical magazine created by the writers of MI7(b) just after the war, which they intended to use to stay in touch. It is full of poems and prose, in-jokes and dry observations about their wartime work. 'In MI7(b), who loves to lie with me, about atrocities, and Hun Corpse Factories,' rhymes Milne on one page, while on the next Lloyd writes about how it might feel, decades hence, to explain his wartime duties to his grandson.[92]

In Lloyd's piece his grandson says that he has heard Lord Northcliffe was behind the propaganda efforts of the First World War. This was a sensitive issue for the men of MI7. The owner of the *Daily Mail* had indeed been involved in propaganda, but the way he and other press barons took credit for it publicly after the war was a source of sourness for MI7, whose efforts remained entirely secret. Lord Northcliffe occupied a powerful position during the war, with his ownership of the upmarket *Times* and populist *Mail*, which he founded in 1896, giving him a unique influence in political circles and wider society. Vigorous reporting by *The Times* on the military 'Shell Crisis' had been a major factor behind the collapse of Herbert Asquith's government midway through the war.

After turning down a seat in Cabinet, Northcliffe became the Director of Propaganda in Enemy Countries in February 1918 and oversaw efforts at Crewe House, which was responsible for distributing leaflets behind enemy lines in the last year of the war. It was important but, with the war ending sooner than expected, short-lived work. It certainly does not appear to merit the praise received two years later on publication of *Secrets of Crewe House: The Story of a Famous Campaign*. 'MI7 did the real thing and, as with Secret Service, kept it completely dark,' one of its staff, Colonel W. E. Davies, wrote to the war's official historian in 1943. But MI7's band of talented writers, who socialised at the Authors' Club once their work was done, could not compete with powerful self-publicists such as Northcliffe and Lord Beaverbrook. It has taken many years for some of the secrets of MI7 to emerge and most remain concealed more than a century on.

Reynolds was a fervent supporter of the country's propaganda campaigns in the war. 'The word propaganda has an evil sound today and is being degraded to a synonym for the act of passing off false news and lying statements for truth. Its history is noble,' he later reflected.[93] However, not working for the central section of MI7, he had a more nuanced view on the contributions made by the press barons. 'Lord Northcliffe's propaganda during the war had been to make facts known with the help of the machinery at his disposal,' he said, continuing:

> The material required was supplied by the Germans and was immensely superior to that which they could use themselves... They could not point to Cologne Cathedral in ruins or the state-library of Berlin in flames to set off against the destruction they wrought at Rheims and Liege. No Germans had to flee into foreign countries, rousing the pity and exciting the indignation of the people in whose land they found refuge by accounts of their suffering at the hands of British soldiers or Belgian or French soldiers. All the cards were in our hands, and Lord Northcliffe played them with such skill that the anger of his opponents was still alive long after the war.[94]

Like almost everyone in the country, Reynolds lost friends and acquaintances in the war. Rupert Brooke met his end in 1915 after a mosquito bite became infected while he sailed on a troop ship towards the Gallipoli landings. A ten-minute walk from Reynolds's old college at Pembroke is King's College and its stunning chapel, home to a memorial commemorating fallen soldiers including Rupert Brooke. 'War robbed England of him,' wrote Reynolds later. 'But the thoughts with which he faced that ordeal remain in the treasure-house of our literature and in the hearts of those who knew him.'[95]

Reynolds was hit harder by a death in the trenches. He was more than a year in to his work with MI7 when, in November 1916, he received terrible news from the front. Munro had suffered an arduous two years since enlisting in August 1914. He had refused a commission as an officer and served as a corporal and later lance sergeant. In the final months of 1916 he had contracted malaria. On 11 November, after hearing an offensive was imminent, he felt the lure of battle and discharged himself from hospital. Ancre was the scene for the last big British offensive of the Somme. Three days after leaving hospital Munro was in the trenches in the early hours. A troop nearby lit a cigarette, revealing their position. 'Put that bloody cigarette out!' barked Munro. His own head was exposed above the trench-line and seconds later a sniper's bullet found its target. In an instant, Reynolds had lost one of his closest friends. He became increasingly depressed working for MI7 during the remainder of the war. He continued to monitor foreign newspapers and helped where he could as Britain and her allies moved towards victory – but he struggled to come to terms with the death of Munro.

-CHAPTER IV-
WEIMAR GERMANY

Reynolds was growing restive in London, and the signing of the Armistice in November 1918 represented an opportunity for him to travel again. MI7 was disbanded that month and his time working in the secret war effort was over. The conflict had clipped his wings, trapping him on the British Isles when his natural instinct was now to venture overseas. Aside from his own inclination to travel, he had a pressing need for fresh perspectives to sustain his career in journalism. With his lecturing, books and wartime articles on Russia, he had milked his unique experience of that country dry. Of the Bolsheviks he knew little. The post-war environment represented a changed world and Reynolds needed new experiences to match.

One destination stood out above the rest: Poland. Reynolds loved the country, its people and its Catholic nature. The country had suffered at German hands in the war, but its conclusion had led to the long-awaited return of a united Poland at the heart of a restored and protected *Mitteleuropa*, or central Europe. It was a glorious rebirth for the country and Reynolds wanted to witness it first-hand.

He went to Warsaw to file reports for his old paper, the *Daily News*, and spent a lot of time touring through Poland and neighbouring countries to view the after-effects of war. In Vienna he noticed how faces were cadaverous after years of undernourishment. 'They looked as if they were made of wax,' he wrote.[96] He gave tins of corned beef to servants, who reacted 'as if they had been presented with caskets of jewels'.[97] Sardines and lemons, brought in by the Italians, appeared to be the only foodstuff available in quantity in the Austrian capital.

It was a similar story in Poland. He gave half a pound of chocolate to a friend in Warsaw and was incredulous when she ate it all at one sitting. 'She had not tasted chocolate for four years,' her husband told Reynolds afterwards.[98] In the years after the war there remained substantial resentment in Poland at Germany's actions during the fighting. Reynolds was particularly incensed by stories of how Polish church-bells had been stolen by Germany. He wrote an account of arriving in Warsaw before the war, alone and tired, and desiring to attend a church service on a Sunday morning: 'All the bells of all the churches were calling men to prayer. I went into the cathedral where the men were listening to a sermon,' he wrote. 'Presently the choir began to sing the creed in the mother-tongue of Europe to music I had heard in England and in France, and I did not feel lonely any more.'

He compared this to when he returned to Warsaw after the Armistice. The city was silent on Sunday morning. No bells rang out. He asked a bystander what had happened to them.

'The Germans took them away,' was the reply.

'Why?'

'To make them into cannon.'[99]

This period travelling made a strong impression on Reynolds. In the years that followed, a strong anti-German feeling emerged in his writing. His admiration for the Poles and love of their culture meant he felt their troubles all the more deeply. After working for a propaganda unit producing material that was not always factual, it was quite something to see and hear first-hand what the 'evil Hun' had really been capable of during the war.

At this time three of Reynolds's four siblings were back in Britain. His youngest brother Ronald had returned abruptly from tutoring in Russia because of the Bolshevik Revolution, joining his two sisters. The middle brother, Leslie, was in Rome, where he had been studying at Beda College in preparation for the Catholic priesthood. But his health was failing.

Kathleen was the second of five Reynolds children.

The middle child Leslie was intensely religious, like all the Reynolds children, and was studying for the Catholic priesthood in Rome when he died in 1919.

Ronald was the youngest son and later worked as a tutor in pre-revolutionary Russia, following Rothay to the country.

Marjorie (second from left) was the youngest child. During the First World War she helped care for blinded soldiers at St Dunstan's (the charity is now called Blind Veterans UK).

He had been a sickly man for several years and died in the eternal city in May 1919, six months after the end of the war. His death was marked by a small notice in the Catholic newspaper *The Tablet*.[100]

———

Just as Reynolds's knowledge of Russia proved a useful asset professionally, his newly inflamed anti-German sentiment was not without its advantages. Soon after his travels in Europe, Reynolds was seeking the stability of a permanent job. Making use of the contacts he had made during the war, he got in touch with Lord Northcliffe. The ageing press baron had an interesting offer for him: to head up an office for the *Daily Mail* in the German capital. Reynolds's age, experience and fluency in the language made him an attractive prospect for the paper, although his liberal politics and sophisticated interests jarred with its right-wing, populist outlook. That said, his time travelling in Poland meant he had few qualms about writing for a newspaper that, in the immediate aftermath of war, was no friend to Germany.

For Reynolds the appeal of regular, paid work as a foreign correspondent was too great to turn down and he gladly accepted a job with the third newspaper of his career. There was just one problem. The *Daily Mail* did not have permission from the German authorities to have a correspondent living in Berlin. Reynolds thought he had little chance of even getting permission to enter the country, let alone stay there. Lord Northcliffe and his newspapers were hated in Berlin because of their role in Britain's wartime propaganda campaign. Lord Northcliffe, however, did not expect a problem. 'They may turn you out of Berlin,' he flippantly remarked to Reynolds shortly before he left. 'But I hardly think they will dare.'[101]

It was March 1921. Reynolds went first to Cologne, in the west of the country and still under British occupation three years after the end of the war. It was part of the Rhineland region between Germany and France, which Germany had been required to demilitarise under the Treaty of Versailles. Reynolds heard tales from British soldiers of their callous treatment at German hands while being held as prisoners of war. The first article in the *Daily Mail* to carry his byline, sent from Cologne, had a suitably uncompromising headline: 'What No Hun Can Understand.' Reynolds reported on German surprise at the manner in which British officers walked around the city. They were baffled that leading members of the winning army did not demand any signs of deference from the people of Cologne. Reynolds remarked on how polite the soldiers were to everybody. He suspected that the Germans thought the British had short memories and were forgetting about the war. Yet their subsequent invitations to dinner and dances were refused by the British occupiers. Why the apparently contradictory approach? 'It is our duty to forgive our enemies,' and treat them well, Reynolds writes. But 'thank heaven, we are not commanded to make them our bosom friends!'[102]

In Cologne he received permission to venture deeper into the country. His journey was smoother than expected, and Reynolds soon arrived in a Berlin he did not recognise. The city seemed unclean, shabby and grey and there was no sign of any military, whose uniforms had brought some colour to the streets when Reynolds had been there before the war. The people, however, struck him as cheerful. 'I found everywhere not merely courtesy, but friendliness and cordiality. It was as if the nation had chosen to forget that there had been a war and that Germans and English had ever been enemies.'[103]

Reynolds had made it to Berlin, but needed permission to stay. He went to the Ministry of Foreign Affairs for an appointment with the relevant official, Dr Muellerheimer. It did not start well. The German was surprised to find a representative of Lord Northcliffe in Berlin and asked how he had made it so far. Reynolds gave an evasive reply, but need not have worried. Dr Muellerheimer, who went on to become a friend, decided not to make an issue of it and allowed Reynolds to stay. The new unspoken German policy of cordiality had worked in his favour.

Soon after his arrival Reynolds had a scoop that revealed Germany's friendly attitude was not fuelled by geniality alone. A confidential official document, which 'a happy wind blew' onto his desk, said the country must 'methodically rectify the picture of Germany' held by people overseas. 'We are regarded by the world as poor, tasteless, egotistic, mean, dishonest, rude, stupid and raw people; our fatherland as unfruitful, of ugly aspect, politically gone to ground; our wares as rubbish.'[104] This self-image gave rise to some overbearing attempts by Germans to ingratiate themselves with foreigners.

Reynolds was sitting in the bar of the Hotel Adlon in Berlin one evening when he was subjected to just such an attempt. The Adlon was one of the main venues in which international visitors to Germany congregated between the wars. 'Of course you hate the French,' said the man Reynolds was talking to. 'You see your culture and French culture as utterly different; whereas English culture and German culture are the same, and therefore we ought to be friends.' A few days later a different German said exactly the same thing to him in a separate incident. He soon heard from the French ambassador that the Germans were using precisely the same line to visitors from France, but in reverse.[105] There was calculation, it transpired, behind the cheerfulness.

The official stance of friendship towards foreigners was not adopted by all Germans. In April 1921, Reynolds attended the funeral of Augusta Victoria, the last German Empress. The grand event was held in Potsdam rather than Berlin for fear that it may stir resentment towards the former imperial family in the capital, just three years after Kaiser Wilhelm II had abdicated in humiliation. Boys from a local school attended, prompting a German observer sitting behind Reynolds to remark loudly on how healthy they looked *in spite* of the enemy blockade.[106] The wartime blockade had been carried out by Britain and its allies between 1914 and 1919 in an attempt to stop food and other supplies reaching the enemy Central Powers. It had not been forgotten.

Overall a general attitude of friendship made life easier for Reynolds in his early years in Germany. And not all of it was forced. 'The pleasing qualities of the Germans were to the fore during the first years after my return to Germany,' he reflected.[107] He reported on a visit by Ramsay MacDonald, leader of the Labour Party, who lectured in the Reichstag and was shown the countryside surrounding Berlin by the socialist Prime Minister of Prussia. Such a welcome to a socialist politician would have been unthinkable in the autocratic and militaristic days of the Kaisers. The Weimar Republic was Germany's attempt at democracy, the model of governance adopted long before by Britain. Reynolds was supportive of Germany's move towards a more modern form of government, but maintained an anti-German tone in his reports.

The bloody and brutal years of the war could not be forgotten, as Reynolds's dispatch from Cologne had made clear. The tone of his articles in his first few months was stridently, at times crudely, condemnatory of Germany and its people. 'It is a tragedy to see German women trying to look like French women,' he reported during a fashion week in Berlin in March 1921.[108] The next month, in the article mentioned above headlined 'The Bells in Berlin', he described an idyllic Sunday morning scene in the capital, before his mood darkens as he angrily remembers how German troops in Warsaw had removed bells to make cannon during the war.[109] In June he filed a report headlined 'Those "Starving" German Children.'

'There are many people who eat too much,' he sternly observed. '*There is plenty of food in Germany.*' Though he admitted that some were still struggling to feed themselves three years after the war, the general message was that the country had far more food than was realised abroad.[110]

In September 1921 Reynolds went again to Warsaw. He travelled by train to the city, which he had not been able to do since 1905. 'The tedious crossing of the border was a romance,' he wrote, describing how 'the lands which a Prussian King stole' were now part of a free Poland. However, his ensuing article for the *Mail* had a warning that would be proved prophetic by the events of 1939. Some voices in Germany were clamouring for the return of these lands. 'We shall not rest until we are again in possession of our Polish provinces,' he heard a politician tell a public meeting. Poland must be protected, Reynolds wrote. Her survival 'depends particularly on England'.[111]

The first president of Weimar Germany's newly established republic was Friedrich Ebert. A tailor's son, he led Germany's Social Democratic Party and had a central role in the creation of the Weimar constitution, which brought parliamentary democracy to Germany. He served from 1919 to his death in February 1925. 'There was not a better, more patriotic and more hard-working man in the country than the president,' said Reynolds. 'But he had no grip on the nation. He was rarely seen or heard. His modesty made him shrink from publicity.'[112]

Reynolds felt that Germany needed a more forceful personality to lead a successful recovery after the war. Ebert's leadership reflected what Reynolds saw as the 'drab' nature of Weimar Germany in its early years, with confidence low and food shortages still common in the wake of war. Though critical of German militarism, Reynolds thought the country had swung too far the other way. 'Soldiers in fine uniforms on prancing horses, the flash of scarlet liveries in the streets, were no longer seen. The men of the Republic were grave, disliked pomp,' he wrote.[113]

'They ought to give the president a military household, like the French president,' said a diplomat one day to Reynolds, who concurred.[114] There was one politician in Weimar Germany who recognised the need to restore Germany's self-confidence. Reynolds viewed Dr Gustav Stresemann, who was named Chancellor in August 1923, as the most able of the men who served Germany in the post-war years. Like several of the Weimar Chancellors he did not last long in office, but he served as Foreign Minister until 1929 and was hugely influential as the country progressed in those years. Stresemann understood how important displays of pageantry were to a country's mood and self-belief. He made this clear at a briefing with Reynolds and other foreign journalists, in which he used the Catholic church as an example. If Catholic clergymen 'attain eminence, the church clothes them in garments whose splendour emphasises their authority,' he said.[115] The state should do the same.

But the lack of pageantry was the least of the Weimar Republic's problems. Extremists on both left and right in Germany had plagued the republic in the early years after the war and centrist politicians struggled to assert control. Economic recovery was made more difficult by the terms of the Versailles Treaty, which was designed to extract full punishment from Germany after her defeat in the war. This was an ongoing source of bitterness for segments of the population. Though exhausted by war, Germany had not seen an enemy army occupy sizeable chunks of territory and some thought the surrender was premature. This led to the 'stab-in-the-back' myth, that politicians and civilians at home had betrayed the army by signing the Armistice. This theory would fuel the rise of extremist parties during the decade.

That rise may not have been possible had Weimar enjoyed the long-term economic success and recovery that at times it looked capable of achieving. At the start of the 1920s, however, such progress seemed far off. The hyperinflation crisis was a particularly damaging economic episode that Reynolds witnessed first-hand. Germany's currency had been weakening since 1921 but a new crisis at the start of 1923 worsened matters considerably. Germany had not been sending overseas the amount of coal and other raw materials required by the Versailles Treaty, and in January the French army marched into the Ruhr region to take control of the lucrative mining district. Germany initiated a policy of passive resistance in response, refusing to aid the occupiers, and printing money to pay the inoperative workers.

This caused 'an inflation of the debased currency of so extravagant a nature that the rate of exchange for foreign currency ran into astronomical figures,' said Reynolds. 'Fortunes melted away. People who had lived in affluence found themselves beggars, while others ingeniously increased their wealth. It was a disconcerting and fantastic period.'[116] As someone living in Germany but paid in non-German currency, Reynolds was one of those who could live exceedingly well for next to nothing. On one occasion he enjoyed 'an excellent luncheon in the restaurant of the Hotel Bristol, one of the best in Berlin, for exactly fourpence halfpenny, including drinks.'[117]

For the first and only time in his life, Reynolds was rich. 'In 1923 I became a billionaire, and more, a multi-billionaire, when the banks paid 16,500,000,000 marks for one English pound, if they happened to have the cash to pay with in their tills. Their difficulty was to get sufficient notes to pay their customers.'[118] He then heard from an Australian lady visiting his office that foreigners could get even more for their currency if they exchanged it at the 'black bourse' rather than at the bank. 'An extra six and a half billion marks on every pound was a very pleasant addition to my income,' Reynolds wryly remarked.[119]

It was not to last. Stresemann ended passive resistance in September 1923 and the monetary crisis was soon resolved by a new currency. But they were fantastical days indeed. Reynolds reflected on the period with an article headlined 'Alice in Hunderland (Or, First Steps to German Finance)'.[120]

The crisis was over, for now. Yet throughout this turbulent period in German history extreme parties waited in the shadows, poised to pounce when the opportunity arose. Reynolds thought the 'genius' Stresemann was the best of the Weimar politicians, but he also knew that populist parties were quietly gathering strength, capitalising on the republic's inability to inspire its citizens. 'Where there was enthusiasm, it was not for the republic, but for socialism or nationalism, for communism or Catholicism,' Reynolds said.[121] His interest in the popularity of extreme parties led him to track down a man, then of little consequence, who would come to shape Germany's future.

-CHAPTER V-
'A MESMERIC STARE'

O ne of the men drawing followers with his extreme views was a black-haired Austrian in Munich who had been captivating beer-hall crowds with his angry tirades. He had fought for Germany in the First World War and viewed the Armistice and Treaty of Versailles as betrayals. His supporters roared support and smashed their glasses together as the man, whose name was Adolf Hitler, accused weak politicians in Berlin of stabbing German troops in the back. His embittered speeches in the Bavarian capital proved popular and in 1921 he became leader of the National Socialist German Workers' Party.

Hitler turned thirty-two that year. He was virtually unknown in Britain. Readers of *The Times* had been informed of his existence by a short article in October 1920 reporting that 'the National-socialists of Bavaria are emulating the Italian Fascisti'. But it was a brief report, and British newspapers paid him little attention in the first years of his political career. It was more than a year later before he was first mentioned in the pages of the *Manchester Guardian*.[122]

Around this time a young student called Daniel Binchy, the future Irish ambassador to Berlin, was travelling in Munich and chanced upon one of Hitler's speeches. It made such an impression that he kept a detailed note of what he had witnessed. 'Here was a born natural orator,' Binchy wrote of Hitler. 'He began slowly, almost hesitatingly, stumbling over the construction of his sentences, correcting his dialect pronunciation. Then all at once he seemed to take fire. His voice rose victorious over falterings, his eyes blazed with conviction, his whole body became an instrument of rude eloquence.' Binchy was entranced:

> As his exaltation increased, his voice rose almost to a scream, his gesticulation became a pantomime, and I noticed traces of foam at the corners of his mouth. He spoke so quickly and in such a pro- nounced dialect that I had great difficulty in following him, but the same phrases kept recurring all through his address like motifs in a symphony: the Marxist traitors, the criminals who caused the revo- lution, the German army which was stabbed in the back, and – most insistent of all – the Jews.[123]

It was a message that would become familiar. But despite some provincial success, Hitler remained virtually unknown elsewhere in Germany and internationally. Binchy had happened upon him by accident. The idea at the start of the 1920s that Hitler would one day lead Germany was laughable. Yet he continued to attract supporters with his message. Kurt Ludecke was one early convert. 'He was holding the masses, and me with them, under a hypnotic spell by the sheer force of his conviction,' he wrote. Ludecke was a useful fundraiser for Hitler in the 1920s.[124]

By 1923 Hitler's status as a rising star in Munich had led to a small amount of outside interest, though he was dismissed as irrelevant by most. A *Times* reporter who saw him speak in May of that year noted his growing support but did not regard him as a serious contender for power nationally. 'Adolf Hitler has been described recently as one of the three most dangerous men in Germany. This is probably a rather flattering estimate of the little Austrian sign-painter,' the dispatch read. 'Nevertheless, the Hitler party today has to be reckoned with as one of the most important factors in the political situation of Bavaria.'[125]

'Childish, childish,' was the verdict on Hitler from an unnamed diplomat whose opinion had been sought by Reynolds. In October 1923 Reynolds had an assignment in Munich and knew he would have some spare time on his hands. He was travelling to interview Eugenio Pacelli, a leading Catholic dignitary who would later be named Pope Pius XII.[126] Discussing ecclesiastical matters was a great pleasure for Reynolds, but could not alone justify the expense of a trip from Berlin to Munich.

He decided he would try to track down Hitler, or as Reynolds described him, the 'hothead of whom people were talking'. As a journalist, Reynolds was used to pursuing leads and interviews even if there was only a slim chance they would lead anywhere. 'It hardly seemed a waste of time to go and see him,' he wrote.[127] The meeting took place in the office of the *Völkischer Beobachter* newspaper of the National Socialist movement, which Hitler, as leader, edited. Without making an appointment, Reynolds found the office in a small house in a street he described as dismal. Gingerly he stepped through the front door of the building and ascended a nondescript staircase leading to a narrow passageway. Halfway along it was a small room where two of Hitler's young supporters were talking. Reynolds thought they looked like dishevelled colonial soldiers. The two men, facing each other across a desk, looked up at their surprise visitor.

Reynolds explained the purpose of his visit. He was in the city for another appointment and thought, since he had some extra time, it might be interesting to meet Hitler. The pair were in no hurry to introduce the unexpected guest to their leader, who was working in a room at the end of the passageway. The office doubled as the headquarters of Hitler's storm troopers; rifles and machine guns were stacked up in a corner of the room. Reynolds was struck by the spirit of revolutionary enthusiasm, which reminded him of times he had spent among angry revolutionaries in Russia before the war.

While they waited for Hitler, the men talked. One of them had a pale and mild appearance that concealed an angry disposition. He informed Reynolds that 'international Jewish capitalists' were a grave danger to the world. Even the British Empire was not safe from its tentacles. He fervently stated his opposition to American loans to Germany, fearing that his countrymen would become the slaves of Jewish capitalists.

His storm trooper comrade passionately attacked the government of Berlin. 'You cannot have a rebellion,' he said, 'unless you clear out one quarter of the nationalists. We shall find enough trees in Germany to hang all the socialists and democrats who have betrayed Germany.'[128] Reynolds thought he talked like a madman, but was also fearful. He thought he seemed a dangerous madman, one who could possibly commit assassinations or other atrocities.

Reynolds was kept waiting for forty-five minutes until the word came that Hitler was ready. He was nervously led to the end of the passageway. The door was opened and Reynolds had his first glimpse of Hitler, attired in a similar fashion to his men. He said nothing as his visitor approached. 'He stared at me straight into the eyes,' Reynolds wrote. 'I thought that was a game two could play at so I stared back. We stared until it became ridiculous and until at last he sat down, and I sat down.'[129]

It was Reynolds's first experience of Hitler's stare, which he later described as mesmeric. Hitler's eyes were frequently commented on by his visitors (once they had left his intimidating presence). Reynolds felt that the manner in which Hitler stared at people in his presence was almost an attempt at hypnotism. It set the tone for a tense meeting that lasted more than an hour.

Reynolds started by asking for Hitler's opinion of the government in Berlin, and what type of system he wished to see. Hitler dismissed the question by saying the form of government in Germany was unimportant for National Socialists.

'It is not a question of republic or monarchy,' he said, 'but of delivering Germany from the men who have betrayed her.'

Hitler then moved on to the recently ceased policy of passive resistance in the Ruhr region.

'Never should passive resistance have been abandoned. We blame the German government for yielding to the French. It is clear that we could not have prevented the French from holding the Ruhr, but before we gave in, every mine, every factory, and every furnace should have been destroyed. Poincaré [the French Prime Minister] should have had the deathly triumph which Napoleon had when he saw Moscow in flames.'

Reynolds noticed how Hitler's voice rose during moments of passion. It was almost as if he was addressing a mass meeting. He struggled to interrupt as Hitler continued his diatribe. The invective was stinging. Reynolds felt it was useless to ask Hitler what he would have done to provide for the inhabitants of the Ruhr. He waited for Hitler to calm down before asking him a more general question about the aims of the Nazi movement. What did it hope to achieve?

Hitler looked up in surprise. 'You cannot expect me to answer a question like that.' He explained that the German people were crying out for a saviour, citing Benito Mussolini's rise to leadership in Italy the year before.

'If a German Mussolini is given to Germany,' he said, 'people would fall down on their knees and worship him more than Mussolini has ever been worshipped.'[130]

Reynolds persisted without success in his attempts to obtain clear answers from Hitler. Then, as abruptly as he had been shown in, the meeting was over. Reynolds was led away. As he walked through Munich to the train station he reflected on his meeting. He was not impressed by Hitler. 'I went away thinking no more of the encounter than it had given me the chance of seeing an odd type of unbalanced fanatic,' he wrote.[131]

At the station, Reynolds rang the office in London to pass on his report. 'I am afraid that the truth is that neither Hitler nor his followers have any plan. All I heard from them was the denunciation of other people and diatribes against the evils of the parliamentary system,' Reynolds reported to *Daily Mail* readers the next day. 'Whatever his idea is, he does not possess the genius to play the hand of [Mussolini]. When I left the headquarters I felt as if I had left a madhouse.'[132]

Reynolds returned to Berlin from Munich. He was struck by the difference between his two meetings that morning. 'It was an extraordinary change to go from that dignified intellectual presence to the little insignificant Austrian tub-thumper.'[133] Reynolds would scarcely have believed then that Pacelli would go on to be pope, yet his other meeting that morning would prove more interesting in historical terms.

For a small-town demagogue, whose influence did not extend beyond Bavaria, Hitler was remarkably blunt and graceless with his visitor from a well-known newspaper in London. Reynolds found the conversation markedly one-sided. 'It is extremely difficult to have a conversation with Adolf Hitler because when once he begins to speak he addresses an individual as if speaking to a public meeting. You can't get a word in edgeways,' he later remarked.[134]

Though his reputation did not extend far beyond Germany in those days, Hitler had evidently started to believe in his own greatness. Even his own followers were commenting on his egomania. In 1923, one of his associates said Hitler had 'megalomania halfway between a Messiah complex and Neroism'. His biographer Ian Kershaw believes Hitler's confidence in the interview with Reynolds is evidence that he may have been starting to view himself as a great man who could one day assume national leadership. When he talks of a German Mussolini, it is not difficult to imagine who he sees in the role.[135]

Hitler, however, was no *Il Duce*. Munich, let alone Germany, was out of his reach. His organisation was amateurish, poorly organised and he himself lacked sound judgement. Less than a month after receiving Reynolds, Hitler marched his followers into the centre of Munich to mount their botched coup, the Beer Hall Putsch. A handful of Nazis and police officers died in the fighting before Hitler and his associates were arrested. It was an abysmal failure to seize power in Munich.

As so often, however, Hitler managed to grab victory where seemingly there was none. He used the publicity surrounding his trial the next year to spread his message and gain more attention nationally. More Germans heard his embittered and extreme ideas and a growing minority were won over, boosting the reach of his movement. Hitler served just over a year in prison and used the time to write *Mein Kampf*, which became another crucial instrument for spreading his message.

At the time of his trial, however, Hitler's stock was low internationally. While there was sympathy for General Ludendorff, a hero of the First World War who had thrown his lot in with Hitler, the leader of the revolt was broadly regarded with contempt. For most Germans, wrote Reynolds, it is 'unutterably painful to see the once idolised general arraigned on the terrible charge of high treason, along with Adolf Hitler, a political adventurer and demagogue of the worst sort'.[136]

Back from his Munich assignment, Reynolds continued to file reports illuminating for readers at home the details of life in Germany. Extremism may have prospered on the fringes of national life, but from the hyperinflation crisis until the final year of the 1920s, Weimar Germany was largely a story of progress. The economic development in the republic was slow but real, while culture flourished.

Six years after the end of the war, Reynolds was still warning readers that some Germans viewed the conflict as unfinished business. In one article he told of meeting a policeman who revealed they had been trained to use machine guns and throw grenades.

'Whatever have policemen got to do with hand-grenades?' Reynolds asked.

'But we're not policemen,' his interviewee responded. 'We're really soldiers, and when the war with France comes the whole hundred and fifty thousand of us will go straight in.'[137]

Periodically painting Germans as villains was part of his job as the *Daily Mail*'s man in Berlin. That is not to say it was untrue that some in the country wanted another war with France – many did. But Reynolds also recognised that life in Weimar Germany was improving for many. People were moving on and looking to the future. 'The masses of the people were not perpetually harping on the loss of the French and Polish and Danish provinces that had been taken from them and given back to their lawful owners,' he wrote.[138] There was a widespread realisation that progress was being made.

Bitterness about how the war had ended gnawed for some, but for many others it represented a fresh start. 'The war had ended in defeat; but at any rate people were free to follow their peaceful occupations, and no German was haunted by the fear of receiving the announcement that father or son or lover had been killed at the front,' Reynolds reflected.

Culture and the arts flowered in Weimar Germany and Reynolds loved being part of it. 'There was new life in painting, in music, in the theatre. The palace of the Crown Prince in Unter den Linden, which was the property of the state, became the home of a fine collection of works of the French impressionists.' The pioneering Bauhaus arts movement, which had far-reaching consequences for design and architecture, was born. Reynolds saw progress all around. 'Young men flocked to the universities of Germany, and many foreigners were attracted to them by the high reputation for learning of their professors... New writers were coming to the fore. Erich Maria Remarque's *All Quiet on the Western Front* took the country by storm.'[139]

Reynolds took Arthur Collins, the playwright and stage manager of the Drury Lane theatre in London, to see the new Berlin opera house. Collins was suitably impressed. There were great advances in ballet, a passion for Reynolds since his time in Russia, as German and foreign groups toured the country. He met Cécile Sorel, a French comic actress, at a party given by Max Reinhardt, the Jewish director whose work would be banned under the Nazis. 'The great thing in life is experiment,' Sorel told Reynolds on one occasion. Reynolds later observed that the actress had 'caught the spirit that animated the artistic life of Berlin' during the Weimar years.[140]

Reynolds was enjoying himself. In one report on the availability of food in Germany, he is diverted from his serious theme by describing an evening of dancing spent with a friend named Jane. 'We went to a great hall with people drinking at little tables, and we jostled against jolly young clerks and shop-girls to an excellent jazz-band.'[141] In another article he describes an evening with Jane, the only person Reynolds ever wrote of in a romantic sense, in which she questioned him about German customs.

'Tell me,' said Jane, as the pair had coffee after dinner. 'Do all Germans hold each other's hands when they sup in a restaurant?'

'All,' Reynolds replied, seizing the chance. 'It is a very beautiful German custom, and as we are being thoroughly German tonight–'

'No, I won't,' Jane replied sharply. Reynolds frowned.

'Well, not until we're in the taxi,' she added.[142]

His accounts of evenings spent with Jane are notable for being the only articles he ever wrote that referenced a girlfriend. He had a wide circle of friends throughout his life but never seems to have settled with a long-term partner. His private life remains a mystery and whether he preferred the company of women or men is unknown. He was a discreet and private individual. One thing is certain: the nightlife in Weimar Germany was vibrant and Reynolds, who turned fifty in 1922, had a full appetite for it. 'In Berlin one big ball followed another. I once went to three in one night; a grand ball in the immense halls of the Zoological Gardens, a masquerade ball of artists and actors, and the Rhineland ball… Germany was no gloomy land in the years of restored prosperity.'[143]

The economy improved. Though there was turbulence in the years after 1918, culminating in the hyperinflation crisis, from the middle of the 1920s Reynolds was reporting on an improving picture, so much so that Germany was becoming a fierce competitor to Britain in global trade. 'Germany with increasing frequency beats Great Britain in open competition,' he wrote in 1925.[144] Reynolds reported on how Germany's shipbuilding industry was depressed, but in a good position to win orders ahead of other countries because it could fulfil orders more cheaply. He supported this assertion with the example of a German manufacturer which signed a contract to build five motor-ships for a British firm. Its price was £300,000 cheaper than any British rival and it could do the work more quickly.

In a series of articles in 1925 about the country's powerful industrialists, entitled 'The Masters of Germany', Reynolds was warning of a coming trade war between Britain and Germany. He did offer some reassurance for worried readers at home. He wrote an article asserting that shoe-sellers in Berlin viewed British products as superior. 'For elegance, distinction, fashion, there is no comparison,' he was told by one. 'After hearing from most of my German acquaintances that the British Empire has collapsed and that England is definitely done for,' Reynolds said, 'I felt that the pleasure of discovering that we can beat the world at cobbling was worth the extra money.'[145]

By 1928 the progress of Germany's recovery was sufficient for Reynolds to write a series of articles exploring 'Why Britain Loses Trade'. The newspaper struck a worried tone in an article promoting the series. 'It is remarkable that in recent months we have been losing in the world markets to Germany and other European countries.' Concerned that its readers were not aware of just how much danger British business faced from overseas competitors, the ever-patriotic *Daily Mail* 'instructed its special correspondent, Rothay Reynolds, an expert in the languages and life of Middle Europe, to carry out a careful investigation'. His conclusion was ominous. 'Germans and other European people are able to beat us, even though it is generally admitted that British workmanship is the best.'[146]

Reynolds revealed how large German companies such as Siemens were dominating their industries and making leaps forward in science and engineering. Cheap labour and the use of machines – and women – to boost productivity were also given as factors that put Britain at risk of falling behind. The impact of the articles was such that an association representing British electrical and manufacturing firms was spurred to publish a response in the *Mail*. While Reynolds's articles were interesting, it said, they 'show a tendency to magnify the achievements of the German and Belgian manufacturers out of due perspective'.[147]

These articles not only revealed British fears of a German revival – they highlighted the progress being made by the Weimar Republic. The economy was still shaky but markedly healthier than in 1924 and earlier.

'Germany has been declared as a going concern,' said Seymour Parker Gilbert, who oversaw reparations payments, in the spring of 1929. Reynolds fully agreed with that verdict. 'Trade was booming. Germany was engaged in a neck and neck race with Great Britain for second place after the United States in the export trade of the world.'[148] The installation of Europe's first traffic lights at Potsdamer Platz in Berlin, rather than a junction in London, seemed to symbolise Germany's economic development.

The issue of reparations remained a point of contention between Western countries a decade after the war. The German economy had been boosted by American loans agreed in 1924 under the Dawes Plan, which restructured the agreements struck at Versailles. It had eased the repa-rations burden but made the German economy dependent on overseas loans and investment. The *Daily Mail*'s reporting on German industry, motivated by a fear that its success was weakening Britain's economy, was followed by an article in May 1928 headlined 'Why Germany Can Pay'. Reynolds reviewed a book, *The Mythology of Reparations*, which suggested that Germany was fully able to meet its post-war obligations and pay the money owed under the Treaty of Versailles and subsequent Dawes Plan. The book is 'certain to command widespread attention,' Reynolds wrote. 'It bears out the view consistently expressed by the *Daily Mail* that Germany can pay.'[149]

In August 1929, politicians from Germany, Britain, France and several other countries convened at the Hague in the Netherlands for a conference to discuss reparations. Despite the economic progress, German calls for a new deal and withdrawal of foreign troops from the Rhineland had grown. Reynolds was there to witness the conference, at which it was agreed in principle to implement the Young Plan, which restructured German debts again. He travelled back to Britain on the same boat as Chancellor of the Exchequer Philip Snowden and his wife. 'The restoration of the political and economic sovereignty of Germany is one of the great achievements of the conference,' Snowden said, words that Reynolds duly passed on to readers the next day. The train carrying British politicians and journalists was greeted in London by crowds singing 'For he's a jolly good fellow'.[150]

The reparations deal seemed to have removed another obstacle to Germany's recovery. The Weimar Republic, after such a volatile beginning, looked capable of enduring success. 'Money was being poured into Germany. All the world had such a high opinion of the ability and ingenuity of an industrious people that offers of money came from every side. Americans were hawking money in Germany. Anybody who could offer any sort of guarantee got money,' observed Reynolds.[151]

This flow of easy money was a key reason for the boom years of the Weimar Republic, the *Goldene Zwanziger* – Golden Twenties – of economic recovery. It also contributed to its downfall. At the end of October 1929, the Wall Street Crash sent shares tumbling in America and marked the start of an unprecedented economic panic. Foreign loans were recalled and Germany, as one of the biggest recipients of US loans, was plunged into crisis. It was a fateful period for Germany. Earlier in October its Foreign Minister Gustav Stresemann, the architect of Weimar's success, had died of a sudden stroke at the age of fifty-one.

Reynolds had seen him at the Hague in August and sensed that he was unwell. 'I had had the impression that the hand of death was on him,' he recalled.[152] He was correct. Stresemann's talents had been such that Reynolds thought the course of Germany's history might have been different if he had lived. Yet even the guile and craft of Weimar's master statesman may not have been sufficient to contend with the volatile years that followed. Unemployment soared as the violent economic impact of the Great Depression undid the steady progress achieved since 1923. Germany was a broken country and its mainstream politicians, whose success had kept the extremists at bay, were under pressure as never before. The mood darkened. On a visit to the Rhineland in December 1929 to witness the withdrawal of the British troops stationed there, Reynolds was struck by the blank expressions of the local population. 'They were faces of stone.'[153]

CHAPTER VI

RISE OF THE NAZIS

I n March 1930 the Centre Party's Heinrich Brüning was appointed Chancellor by President Paul von Hindenburg, replacing Hermann Müller of the Social Democrats. The bespectacled Brüning's academic background and serious manner were seen as the perfect remedy to the economic crisis engulfing Germany. But his financial reform policy ideas proved immediately unpopular and his parliamentary support in the Reichstag ebbed away. In July, Hindenburg invoked Article 48 of the Weimar Constitution, which authorised rule by emergency decree, but the Reichstag passed a bill to reject the attempt. An impasse had been reached and elections were called.

The September election was the first to be held in Germany for two years. A lot had changed. Hitler's Nazis had grown in prominence throughout the latter half of the 1920s and by the end of the decade had a membership numbering tens of thousands. They made their presence felt in the build-up to the elections, rowdily protesting and marching in the streets. Alarmed, the Interior Ministry issued a statement warning that Hitler's Nazis were attempting to 'bring about the overthrow by violence of the German Republic. The party and the organisations which it has created are so constructed that they can all be used as united and militarily disciplined fighting troops.'

The warning did not work. The National Socialists achieved an incredible electoral breakthrough, increasing their number of seats in the Reichstag from twelve to 107. Almost a fifth of electors voted for them. The Social Democrats, led by Otto Wels, retained their position as the largest party, taking a quarter of the vote and winning 143 of the 577 seats. But it was Hitler's night.

The next time Reynolds went to the Reichstag he had to fight his way through a mob shouting 'Heil Hitler!' Once he was inside the atmosphere was equally charged.

> Within the building there was the singular spectacle of these 107 men, all wearing khaki shirts and red armbands, blazoned with swastikas, marching to their places in a long file. Members of the moderate parties, among them women with white hair, looked bewildered as they saw the invasion of the house by men who might have been colonial soldiers.[154]

A few days after the election Reynolds reported on a rather abrupt change of heart by the government. 'After careful and critical examination of the political situation in Germany,' said the Interior Ministry's Dr Wirth, 'I can say that there is no sort of danger of rebellion in Germany.' The Nazis apparently posed no threat. Reynolds thought the change in view was motivated by a desire to placate worried overseas investors, who had been alarmed by the electoral breakthrough of Hitler and the far-right.

Reynolds saw first-hand how Hitler's supporters were behaving in the wake of their triumph. Joseph Goebbels, a senior member of the Nazi leadership, led a demonstration of 3,000 supporters in the heart of the capital. It was a show of force, designed to impress upon Berliners the strength of the Nazi movement. The election breakthrough was just the beginning of their bid to win power, Goebbels said. 'If this cannot be done in a legal way, then we shall try to do it in an illegal way.'

Joseph Goebbels laughs with Hitler. An early supporter of the Nazis, Goebbels served as the regime's Minister of Propaganda between 1933 and 1945. (Wiener Library)

Nazis in the audience were fired up. Police who attended the scene were derided as 'Zörgiebel's dogs', a reference to the socialist head of the Berlin police. At first the policemen withstood the abuse, but then the Nazis stepped up their insults. 'You will be the first to dangle from the lamp-posts,' they jeered. Reynolds looked on from a distance as the police charged the Nazi rabble and beat them with rubber sticks. Even Goebbels relished the fight and was among those hit by police.

Ten Nazis were arrested in the wake of the violence. Goebbels had the gall to follow them to the police station and demand an explanation for the police action. He was swiftly evicted from the building. Reynolds wrote a long report on the violence headlined 'Mob Jeers at Police' in which he expressed the hope that this 'teutonic fury will be restrained'.[155] His view was clear. He thought the Nazis posed a threat to order and stability and recognised that something had stirred in a sizeable portion of the German population. A fury had been unleashed. Their anger at how Weimar Germany had fared, worsened by the economic crisis, was real. In the National Socialists they had an outlet at the ballot box, whose growth in electoral terms was perfectly legitimate. But Reynolds was worried by the behaviour he witnessed in the wake of their advance.

Not all Germans shared the anger felt by those who voted for the Nazis. The more reasonable among them recognised the progress the republic had made and remembered how previous economic crises had been overcome. They were still in the majority, but support for Hitler was quickly growing.

One man who was a supporter of Hitler's efforts in Germany was Lord Rothermere, who had assumed control of the *Daily Mail* after the death of his brother Lord Northcliffe in 1922. Within days of the 1930 election he was prominently airing his views in the pages of his newspaper, proclaiming that Hitler and the Nazis were a force for good and deserved to be respected. 'They represent the rebirth of Germany as a nation,' he wrote. He praised the emerging party's success and called it 'the beginning of a new epoch in the relations between the German nation and the rest of the world.' The election, he predicted, would prove 'an enduring landmark of this time.'[156] Hitler took note of this rare overseas support and Rothermere had his reward – a scoop in the form of an exclusive interview with the man himself. It fell to Reynolds to conduct the interview with Hitler, just five days after criticising the violent Nazi mob. He was in an awkward situation, caught between the admiring glances of a rich and powerful media baron, who happened to be his employer, and a politician of dubious character, who surrounded himself with violent supporters.

But he had a job to do. The interview with Hitler was a real coup for the *Daily Mail* and Reynolds was under personal orders from Rothermere to make it a success. He spoke to Hitler on the evening of 26 September. It was the first time the two men had met in seven years. Hitler was exhausted. He had spent all day in a courtroom in Leipzig, giving evidence on his feet for more than two hours in the trial of two army officers accused of Nazi Party membership.

The first thing Reynolds noticed was that Hitler's face was dead white. Hitler started by talking about Lord Rothermere's article on the rebirth of Germany. 'I need hardly tell you that I have read Lord Rothermere's article with the keenest interest, and you will not be surprised when I say that I read it with the greatest astonishment. We Germans are not accustomed to find that people of other nationalities should understand what we have in our hearts.'

After this flattering opening, Hitler returned to a familiar subject: the supposed inequities of the Treaty of Versailles. 'What Lord Rothermere has made English people understand is that Germany must have the same rights as other countries after being twelve years in the penitentiary of Versailles,' he declared to Reynolds. He then turned to a second familiar topic, warning that communism would spread in Germany unless the country was treated fairly. 'If Europe decides to make Germany serve a life sentence, then she must face the danger of having an embittered nation, desperate to the verge of crime, in her midst. What that would mean a child can guess – Bolshevism.'

Reynolds brought up the violence of some Nazi supporters and the accusations that the party would try and seize power by force. 'People have tried to associate me with a mania for rebellion,' Hitler replied. 'I ask you: why should I instigate a rebellion when I have today 107 members of my party in the Reichstag and count on having double that number in the next Reichstag?'

Hitler quickly moved the discussion on to relations between Britain and Germany. 'The English and Germany,' he said, 'cannot remain enemies forever just because they fought against each other for four and a half years. … To have a strong party in Germany which will form a bulwark against Bolshevism is in the interests not only of England but of all nations. You have difficulties before you, and the time may come when German friendship is not without its value.'

The discussion ended with more praise for Rothermere. Reynolds's employer was an astute man, Hitler said, to have recognised the 'life and energy' of Germany. 'To have seized upon this outstanding fact shows that Lord Rothermere possesses the true gift of intuitive statesmanship.'[157]

The two men parted and Reynolds rang the office to give his account. *Daily Mail* readers the following day found the long article 'Hitler's Special Talk to the Daily Mail' dominating page nine. Hitler's comments were reported in the order laid out above. There were also comments, seemingly given as the opinion of Reynolds, sprinkled throughout the piece, which cast a favourable glow over Hitler. 'The moment he spoke I realised that there was in him a burning spirit that could triumph over bodily weariness,' he wrote, adding that Hitler spoke with 'great simplicity and with great earnestness'. He continued: 'I was conscious that I was talking to a man whose power lies not, as many people think, in his eloquence and in his ability to hold the attentions of the mob, but in his conviction.'

Caught between Rothermere and Hitler, Reynolds strayed from an independent line with glowing references to Hitler's 'conviction' and 'earnestness'. But most of the piece was taken up by straightforward reporting of what Hitler had to say. It was an unfiltered portrayal of Hitler's message

– a message that was two-sided. On one hand he was reaching out to Britons, flattering and responding graciously to Rothermere's support. But there was also an implicit threat: Germany had been crushed by Versailles and unless the shackles were lifted, Europe would suffer. He used the ogre of Bolshevism to fuel fears that Russian communism could spread unless his demands were granted in future.

'We know now what his idea of a settlement was,' Reynolds later wrote. Yet Hitler's comments about Bolshevism and Versailles were cleverly designed and set the tone for the type of overtures he would repeatedly make during the 1930s. Drawing a link between the strength or weakness of Germany and the spread of communism was his primary method of winning western opinion round to his regime.

In Britain there was a receptive audience. In the immediate wake of the Versailles Treaty, some said its punitive terms were storing up trouble for the future. The economist John Maynard Keynes was among those who thought that impoverishing Germany was hardly conducive to future peace. There was a growing feeling that Germany had been wronged by the treaty. Other countries became magnets for increasing resentment, notably the old enemy France and newly communist Russia. As Labour politician Hugh Dalton reflected later: 'Some became stupidly anti-French; others stupidly anti-Russian; others reverted to a sentimental pro-Germanism, based on some myth of special kinships or national resemblance, or in the sporting habit of a handshake after a fight.'[158]

The anti-Russian feeling should not be underestimated. Even later, when Britain and Germany were at war, the philosopher Bertrand Russell said there was 'no doubt that the Soviet Government is even worse than Hitler's, and it will be a misfortune if it survives'.[159] As communism put down roots in Russia during the 1920s, fears of its spreading rose. Rothermere was one of many vocal critics and Hitler had the nous to play on these fears. Portraying himself as a 'Bulwark against Bolshevism' was enough, almost until the end of the 1930s, to outweigh many overseas fears about his virulent anti-Semitism.

The *Daily Mail* was not the only paper in Britain giving a platform to Hitler. On 28 September 1930, the day after Reynolds's interview with him appeared, Hitler penned a comment piece for Lord Beaverbrook's *Sunday Express*. Headlined 'My Terms to the World', he informed the newspaper's readers that 'our aim, our purpose is to free Germany from political and economic conditions that mean slavery'.[160]

At the start of October, Lord Rothermere wrote another article, headlined 'My Hitler Article and its Critics'. His support for Hitler had, he said, 'shocked the old women of three countries – France, Germany, and our own'. Targeting his print rivals, whose views were taken far more seriously than his own, he continued: 'A new idea invariably produces this effect upon the pompous pundits who pontificate in our weekly reviews and those old-fashioned morning newspapers whose sales and influence alike sink steadily month by month towards vanishing point.'[161]

The *Daily Mail*, with its screaming headlines and sometimes extreme views, was regarded as a much less serious newspaper than more esteemed rivals such as *The Times* and *Manchester Guardian*. Both carried great influence at home and internationally, *The Times* within government circles and the *Guardian* on the liberal left. But the *Mail* could boast a readership that outnumbered *The Times* and the *Guardian*'s combined circulations several times over in the 1930s, selling about 1.6 million copies a day in 1937 – around eight times more than the circulation of *The Times*. For all its influence, the *Manchester Guardian* had daily sales to match its status as a regional newspaper, of between 25,000 and 50,000.[162]

Lord Rothermere did not believe the borders imposed by the Treaty of Versailles should be viewed as permanent. The 'old women' writing for other newspapers, he wrote, 'imagine that the hundred million Germans and Hungarians who make up the population of Central Europe will be content to remain forever artificially divided by unnatural boundaries fixed and forced upon them without their consultation or consent'. He had words of advice as well as support for Hitler and the Nazis. He advised them to cut out their anti-Semitism. Even though 'the Jewish race has shown conspicuous political unwisdom since the war', he was clear that 'Jew-baiting is a stupid survival of medieval prejudice'.

Reynolds was less convinced by Hitler than his boss. He may have portrayed him in a flattering light in his 1930 interview, but he knew that the Austrian firebrand was ultimately no solution to German problems. In the following months, as the depression sparked by the Wall Street Crash continued in Germany, Reynolds saw Chancellor Brüning as the right man to lead the country. The next summer he wrote a flattering profile of him that would no doubt have angered Hitler.

Reynolds called Brüning the 'Strongest Man Since Bismarck' in the headline. He asserted that those in close working contact with the Chancellor said he had more 'strength and determination' than any German leader since Bismarck. 'He is forty-six, and he lives as an ascetic. He works from early morning to late at night, and the only relaxation he allows himself is reading. He rarely goes into society and he rarely gives a dinner party.' Reynolds added that after being wounded in the war, Brüning rose to prominence and was elected to the Reichstag in 1924. Since beginning in politics, his 'profound knowledge of social and economic questions' helped him rise quickly to the leadership of the Centre Party.[163]

Yet more trouble was brewing. Economic conditions in Germany worsened and unemployment grew. The rise of the far-right alarmed overseas investors, who called in more of their loans. All levels of society were affected. With embarrassment, Reynolds was asked by one of his wealthy friends for small loans. Theatres and cinemas were almost empty. Shopping one day in one of Berlin's busiest stores, Reynolds found that he was the only customer.

Hitler's confidence grew. At the start of December 1931 he called Reynolds in to see him. 'There is not the slightest doubt,' he said, 'that the National Socialists will come to power in Germany. It may be soon and it may be in a year's time; but there is nothing to stop the march of the party, which I founded with six men, seven with myself, and has grown to so many millions.'[164]

A few days later Reynolds went to see Brüning, who by this time had picked up the label of 'Iron Chancellor'. He was defiant about the Nazi rise. 'It is very natural that extreme parties should grow in strength in such times as Germany has passed through,' he said. But he was also complacent. 'Half the success of the National Socialist party is due to hard times.'[165]

———

A presidential election was scheduled for March 1932. At the age of eighty-four, Hindenburg, the incumbent and frontrunner, had not initially wanted to stand. It was a sign of how effectively the extreme parties were picking up supporters that the ageing war hero, figurehead of the old, militarist Germany, had to be persuaded to do so by the mainstream parties. Chancellor Brüning went so far as to call it grotesque that opponents dared to stand against Hindenburg. He described him as 'the man who fought at Königgrätz, who saw the empire founded in 1870, who lived through the war and brought the army back from the field, and even then gave his services to the Fatherland for another seven years'.[166]

Hitler was his main opponent and continued to attract more support with his incendiary message. 'Hindenburg is today the candidate of the men who destroyed our proud army,' he declared. 'He is a candidate of the November criminals who have thrown the nation in the dust. He is a candidate of the Jews and war-profiteers.'[167]

'Germany stands at a parting of the ways,' Reynolds reported in a comment piece accompanying his main report before the election. Hindenburg 'stands for the conservation of the system which was established thirteen years ago, and the men who were revolutionaries and innovators then form the Conservative element in the country now'. Hitler, meanwhile, is a 'man of magnetic personality' who 'denounces the present system of government and proclaims his intention to smash it'.[168]

Though others were standing, Reynolds knew it was a contest between Hindenburg and Hitler, and so it proved. In the first voting round in March none of the candidates won more votes than all of the others combined, which was required to win the poll. A second election was scheduled for April, in which the only candidates standing were Hindenburg, Hitler and the communist leader Ernst Thälmann. This time it was simple: whoever received the most votes would win.

Sefton Delmer, the *Daily Express*'s correspondent in Berlin, had a unique vantage point from which to observe the next stage in the election. Alone among the British correspondents, he had been invited to accompany Hitler on an aeroplane tour of campaign stops ahead of the second vote. Delmer, who went by the name Tom, was Beaverbrook's protégé at the *Express*. He had been working as a stringer for British newspapers in Berlin in 1927 when the Canadian press lord gave him a job. Within a year he was heading up the paper's new bureau in Berlin, at the age of just twenty-four. He was young but hard-working and desperate to impress his master in London. Delmer's illustrious career with the *Express* would last decades.

In 1931 Delmer had a breakthrough during his attempts to make contacts within Nazi circles. He was introduced to Ernst Röhm, the head of

Hitler's storm troopers. Delmer described him as 'the jovial little soldier of fortune with the shot-up face and a reputation for sexual abnormality'. But he was well aware of his importance at that early stage. 'As chief of the storm troops, [Röhm] was the most powerful figure in the Nazi organisation beside Hitler himself.'[169]

At their first meeting, Röhm was keen to downplay reports of violence within his group. 'I know the storm troops have been a rough and rowdy lot in the past, my dear Herr Delmer,' he said, raising his glass. 'But from now on, you just watch! The men will be quiet and disciplined and orderly.'[170] This first meeting was followed by an invitation to meet Hitler in May 1931, when Delmer became the first Englishman to visit the newly built Brown House Nazi headquarters in Munich. It was quite an improvement on the small and dingy office Reynolds had visited in 1923.

Delmer was led into Hitler's room, where an expensive-looking Persian carpet covered a parquet floor and tall windows looked onto a big balcony and the street beyond. Hitler, wearing a white shirt with black tie under a double-breasted blue suit, was in a corner talking to his associate Rudolf Hess. 'The very first impression he made on me was that of a very ordinary fellow,' Delmer later said.[171] Soon Hitler and Delmer were left alone and the reporter struggled to make himself heard as Hitler got carried away in a vicious tirade against the French. 'Herr Hitler,' he interrupted, 'your Stabschef Major Röhm tells me that you are anxious to secure the friendship of Britain.'

This set Hitler 'off like a bomb,' Delmer wrote.

'I believe,' the Nazi leader said, 'that Britain's interests are similar to those of Germany, and that we can therefore cooperate with Britain as also with Italy.'[172] The piece Delmer wrote for the *Express* after this meeting, which reported that 'Germany is marching with great strides to join the ranks of the fascist nations of Europe', greatly pleased the Nazis.[173] Delmer had proven his worth to them and he quickly became the English journalist they trusted most in the early 1930s. Röhm became a trusted source, sharing gossip and news with him ahead of other reporters.

By April 1932 the relationship Delmer had established with the Nazis was strong enough for them to invite him to observe Hitler's election tour. Ernst 'Putzi' Hanfstaengl was Hitler's public relations officer with the foreign newspapermen (Goebbels and his Propaganda Ministry would later assume control of such matters). German-born with an American mother, Putzi had studied at Harvard and spent the First World War trying to look after his family's art business in New York. He had been behind the successful introduction of American methods of electioneering to Hitler's campaigns. He had based the highly choreographed parades of marching storm troopers on his memories of Democrats and Republicans marching in America with brass bands.

Putzi had organised Delmer's inclusion in the tour, which allowed the young reporter to observe Hitler at close quarters for long periods. He noticed how Hitler transformed from a confident, crowd-pleasing speaker in public to an awkward, sometimes surly, character in private. On the very first flight, Delmer wrote, Hitler 'just sat there, staring gloomily out of the window, his chin cradled in his right hand, wads of cotton wool in his ears'.[174] While others on the plane journey ate meat, drank alcohol and smoked, Hitler 'ate only vegetable dishes – usually an enormous plate of carrots, peas, asparagus, onions, leeks, sliced kohlrabi and potatoes, all mixed up together under a thick white sauce'.[175]

Others in the press pack thought Delmer was too close to the Nazis – that he had sacrificed his journalistic integrity by embedding himself so deeply with Hitler's campaign. He thought he was just doing his job. 'The truth was that I had realised the political importance and the human interest of Hitler's fight for the chancellorship a little earlier than some of my brethren.'[176]

On some occasions he almost certainly did get too close. After the campaign plane landed for Hitler to make a speech on 5 April, Delmer was one of the small group following the Nazi leader to the podium. But instead of watching the speech from the crowd he found himself on the stage sitting behind Hitler. 'I was up on the dais sitting on a hard chair with a huge swastika banner hanging down from the balustrade in front of me, and looking down into this crowd that had been waiting here for Hitler since the early morning.'[177] As a supposedly independent journalist, Delmer should have kept more distance, but struggled.

Some of Delmer's admiration for Hitler may have made it into the *Express*, but – like many British newspapers – it did not regard Hitler in 1932 as a major threat to global stability. He was widely seen as a right-wing populist who was unlikely to be around for long. However, headlines in the *Daily Mail* during the run-up to the re-election were far from understated. It was described as 'Germany's Fateful Election' and the 'Poll That Affects the World'.

Reynolds's reporting on Hitler strayed from an impartial line – the looming influence of Rothermere in London is again evident. 'His appeal to patriotism and to the hopes of youth is tremendous. There is so much misery in Germany that the appeal comes with tremendous force to those who are suffering, and many will vote for Herr Hitler on Sunday because they have come to the point where they would give a chance to any system which might make life better.'[178]

The line appeared as an emboldened paragraph in the *Daily Mail*. It is not hard to imagine Rothermere standing over a hapless sub-editor's shoulder as he went over the piece, directing which parts to emphasise. He would certainly have been in Reynolds's mind when he wrote it. Rothermere was a domineering press baron, the BBC journalist John Simpson wrote in his 2010 book about twentieth-century journalism, *Unreliable Sources*.[179]

He influenced the angle and content of stories and had ultimate control over the editorial line. Rothermere was just as inclined to exert his influence as his late, elder brother Lord Northcliffe – who is often seen as the archetypal interfering press baron. His rival at the *Daily Express,* the upstart Canadian Lord Beaverbrook, also had a tendency to interfere, which would become more pronounced towards the end of the 1930s. All three men were intensely political and used their newspapers to force their views on the British public to an extent that was unrivalled at the time. It was an unhealthy, unpopular approach that would cause problems for the *Daily Mail* and its reporters as the 1930s went on.

Hindenburg won the election with 52 per cent of the vote. Hitler took 37 per cent while just a tenth of electors voted for the communists. Hitler was now firmly installed as the anti-establishment candidate, his position made stronger by Hindenburg's advancing years and the unpopularity of most members of the political mainstream. When Brüning's government collapsed at the end of May 1932, he prepared to capitalise on the tumult.

———

Hindenburg and Brüning had fallen out after the latter had planned to break up the estates of some great landowners, a move that could have had an impact on the president. Brüning's government resigned. 'President von Hindenburg has accepted their resignation, and in his hands lies the fate of Germany,' Reynolds reported. 'What he intends to do no man knows, and for the present the ship of State is drifting in dangerous waters without a pilot.'[180]

Hindenburg replaced Brüning with Franz von Papen of the Centre Party. Short of support in the Reichstag, the new man had little chance of ruling successfully. After just days in office, he called elections for July. The build-up took place in an atmosphere of uncertainty and violence. There were clashes between the brown-shirted Nazi storm troopers – who had been banned by Brüning towards the end of his reign, a move reversed by von Papen – and Communist Party paramilitary. 'Once let loose, this horde of young hooligans began to attack political opponents with knives and pistols. From all over Germany came accounts of fighting in towns, of the sacking of trade-union or Socialist premises, of retaliation by opponents, of cold-blooded murder,' Reynolds wrote.[181]

There was a sense that those in power were losing control. Martial law was proclaimed, yet this did not stop the warring Nazis and communists. It was a chaotic, bloody time. As far as politics was concerned, there was only one story in town: Hitler. Could the Nazi leader build on his remarkable support in the presidential election? Rothermere sent Reynolds to accompany Hitler on a campaigning tour of East Prussia. The Nazis had regarded their invitation to Delmer to accompany Hitler during the presidential election as a success and extended the practice. East Prussia had been part of the German Empire on the Baltic coast and remained part of Weimar Germany under the terms of the Versailles Treaty. This was despite being cut off from the rest of the country by West Prussia, which had become part of Poland.

The journalists on the trip included Reynolds's friend John Segrue of the *News Chronicle*. The tour was an incredible insight into the levels of popular support Hitler was attracting in the provinces. One night the convoy of cars transporting Hitler and his campaign group, accompanied by a band of weary reporters, was travelling to a hotel after a day of speeches. Reynolds and the other journalists had listened to Hitler make the same speech six times in one day and were eager for a rest. The convoy flew through the darkness, enveloped by a black, forested landscape, before pulling over to refuel. Here Hitler had an encounter that made a lasting impression on Reynolds.

A small group of villagers were walking home from a local inn when they noticed Hitler and his group standing by their cars. One of Hitler's lieutenants moved to bring one of them forward, a bearded peasant who looked so old that Reynolds thought he may have fought against the French in the Franco-Prussian War of 1870.

Hitler's eyes, illuminated by the light of the nearby inn, seemed to shine bright as he looked down at the ageing peasant. 'You have lived in a mighty Germany; you have lived in a weak Germany; you will live again in a mighty Germany,' he intoned deeply. The man, who did not say a word in response, looked to Reynolds as if he had been put under a spell. He did not doubt that Hitler had won the vote of the man.[182] 'The old man was a convert in an instant,' Reynolds wrote.[183]

Hitler's message that he would restore Germany to greatness was underpinned by brutal attacks on the men who had led the Weimar Republic. In speech after speech he accused them of bringing misery to Germany, conveniently ignoring that the republic had been born in the most difficult of circumstances in the wake of the Great War. Reynolds later wrote of how he had witnessed Hitler repeat the 'patently false idea' that Weimar leaders had inherited a 'country in exemplary order'.

'What have they done with our Germany?' Hitler would scream emotionally at the crowds, tears forming as his voice rose. 'What have they done with that beautiful, flourishing, blossoming land?' Hitler made no reference to problems caused by Germany's devastating defeat in the war. To listen to him you would not realise there had been a war, Reynolds reflected. The Weimar politicians were to blame.[184]

Reynolds was impressed by Hitler's electioneering energy and endurance, but not the 'stupidity' of the voters he encountered. They 'applauded without discrimination whatever he said, good or bad, true or manifestly false'.[185] His emotional speeches seemed to overpower them. 'The sobs and indignation in Hitler's voice seemed to paralyse the reason of those who listened to him and to obliterate the most bitter recollections of want and suffering from their minds.'[186] At one rally Reynolds turned to a man behind him who was applauding vigorously and asked him what Hitler had said. 'I did not hear,' replied the man, continuing to clap.[187]

Yet this detail did not make it into the account that appeared in the *Daily Mail*. 'Hitler will go down in history as the man who has revived Germany's faith in herself,' Reynolds wrote in a page-lead article headlined 'Hitler's Triumphal Tour of East Prussia.'[188] A triumph it turned out to be. The July election of 1932 was another breakthrough moment for the Nazi Party. They won 230 seats, more than double their haul in the 1930 election. It made Hitler, who just a decade earlier had been a nonentity, the leader of the largest party in the Reichstag. A dictatorship in all but name already existed in Prussia, where von Papen had named himself Reich Commissioner to restore order after the invocation of Article 48. With Hitler firmly in the ascendant, it was a sign of things to come.

Chancellor Papen, who by this point had left the Centre Party, proved unable to rule with parliamentary support and ruled by emergency decree with Hindenburg's blessing. But with few members of the Reichstag supporting him, it was a short-lived tenure. Hindenburg recognised the situation was unsustainable and yet another election was called. The president was in an awkward position. The biggest party in the Reichstag was the National Socialists, whose leader was far too radical and extreme for the position of Chancellor. Hindenburg agonised over how to reflect the apparent will of the people and also provide a working government. Reynolds reported on the quandary facing not only Hindenburg, but the average German voter.

'Numbers of Germans – and this is a strange feature of this election – are at a loss to know how to vote. Formerly they voted for one of the moderate parties, and now that these have become powerless and are almost extinguished, they do not know what party to support.' There was also a fear, Reynolds reported, that many of those who voted for the Nazis in the summer would be 'disheartened' that they had not done anything with their power, and vote instead for the communists.[189]

The election did not clarify matters. The Nazis won a third of the vote and remained the biggest party, despite winning thirty-four fewer seats. Hindenburg named an adviser, Kurt von Schleicher, Chancellor at the start of December. Unattached to any party, the former army staff officer had played a quiet but influential role behind the scenes in Weimar Germany. Hindenburg was running out of options, but von Schleicher was widely seen as a good choice. 'One of the cleverest politicians in Germany,' was Reynolds's verdict in a profile introducing him to British readers. 'He has earned the reputation of being a man who pulls the strings behind the scenes. That is why many people will be glad to see him forced into the open and obliged to justify his policy.'[190]

The new Chancellor faced the same struggle to attract enough support in the Reichstag. Thrust into the limelight, von Schleicher was exposed. His actions in power displeased Hindenburg. 'The clique around Hindenburg began to think that this General whom they had placed in power was a dangerous man. He was making concessions to the Catholics and to the socialists. He would have to go,' Reynolds wrote.[191] In the background, Hitler moved against him by forming an unlikely partnership with von Papen, who agreed to serve under him as Vice-Chancellor. His agreement to do so was a crucial element in Hitler's bid for the chancellorship; faced with the plan, Hindenburg caved in. He saw von Schleicher's rule as unsustainable in the long term, and now Hitler, who had a popular mandate, was backed by a politician seemingly of the mainstream. He was sure that if Hitler, as many anticipated, attempted extreme measures as Chancellor he could be restrained or even ejected, as so many of his predecessors had been. The stage was set for Hitler to realise his dream of taking power in Germany.

-CHAPTER VII-
HITLER TAKES OVER

I t was 1933 – a time before dictators had begun to spoil the English weekend, as Ian Colvin, one of Reynolds's contemporaries in Berlin, later wrote.[192] After weeks of political chicanery, Hitler was appointed Chancellor of Germany on 30 January. Reynolds observed the dramatic scene as thousands of storm troopers and steel helmets – the latter being Himmler's feared *Schutzstaffel* (SS) – held aloft banners and waved flaming torches as they marched down Pariser Platz in the heart of Berlin.

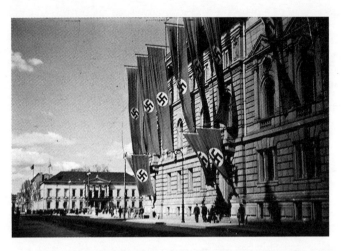

Flags emblazoned with swastikas hang from the front of the Reich Treasury building in 1937. (PA-1456 Thomas Neumann, The National Archives of Norway)

They strode in time to the warlike music of their bands. The national anthem, 'Deutschland über alles', was repeatedly played. Hindenburg stood at the window of his palace to take the applause of the multitude below. Undaunted by the cold conditions, the young crowds cheered and cheered at the old man who had put their leader in power.

They marched on towards the Chancellery, where Hitler stood on a balcony in his brown party uniform, lit up by a spotlight. He held his arm aloft in a triumphal Nazi salute. At just forty-three years of age, he had taken a huge step towards his goal of becoming Germany's ultimate leader. Hindenburg and his associates thought they had his measure. 'Hitler has been well wrapped up in cotton wool,' one of them told Reynolds.[193] One of his German friends was similarly nonchalant. 'We shall wait and see what they can do, and if we don't like them, then there will be a little *putsch* and we shall get rid of them.'[194]

For Sefton Delmer of the *Express*, Hitler's election seemed to vindicate the efforts he had made to spend time with the Nazi leadership. 'I must confess that I was even a little pleased at the way things turned out. I felt the satisfaction of a prophet of doom who sees his promised catastrophe come true.' His colleagues in the press pack did not see it this way.[195]

The stock market reacted well to the move. Businessmen saw Hitler as a leader who would be able to keep the communists and more volatile elements of the working classes in check. Yet the tone of life in Germany seemed to blacken as soon as the Nazis took power. One episode was a chilling harbinger of the horrors awaiting the country's Jewish population. Reynolds was on the Unter den Linden during a parade of schoolchildren organised to celebrate Hitler's triumph. Every few yards along the procession stood Nazi supporters who called out 'Judah!' to which the children responded '*Verrecke*' – in effect calling for their death.

The children were instructed to reply *Verrecke*, but the effect was no less sinister. At one point a group of ten- and eleven-year-old girls stopped before Reynolds and shouted the word 'in a thin treble with the glee of children who are allowed to make a noise, and were clearly unconscious of the meaning of what they said'. He was shaken by the experience.[196]

On 1 February another election was called for early the following month. It was the German electorate's chance to have their say on a Hitler chancellorship. Would they support Hindenburg's move or would the election precipitate another change? The build-up was fraught with more violence as storm troopers marauded the streets. Anti-Jewish sentiment rose. Ordinary citizens were forced by officials attached to the new regime to join demonstrations against the Jewish population. Reynolds was amazed to witness one such rally on a cold winter day. 'There they were, standing in thousands on the quay and yelling as ferociously as if they intended to rush through Berlin, murdering every Jew in the capital, instead of going home to eat cold sausage and to grumble at having been forced to tramp for miles in the cold.'[197] Reynolds did not think the vast majority of Germans bore any hatred towards Jews. He harshly attributed their convincing display of hatred to a lack of character. 'They were exhibiting themselves in a repulsive and barbarous demonstration, because their souls were the souls of serfs and they had not the courage to refuse to do an evil deed.'[198] It was not just the Jews who were targeted. Meetings of Social Democrat and Centre Party supporters were violently broken up by gangs of brownshirts.

'In less than a month Germans had lost freedom of the press, freedom of speech, freedom of assembly,' Reynolds later wrote. People quickly became fearful of discussing sensitive issues on the phone in case they were eavesdropped by the newly formed secret police unit, the Gestapo.[199] Germans would surely not respond to these restraints, bullying and intimidation by giving the regime further support in the election. But Hitler had another card to play.

It was the evening of 27 February and Reynolds was in a back room of his flat listening to the radio. His building lay on the Schiffbauerdamm, a road on the northern bank of the River Spree. It followed the bend of the river and many residents, including Reynolds, had views of the great glass dome of the Reichstag on the other side of the water. He was disturbed by a phone call from a friend. She had bumped into her hairdresser in the street and been told the Reichstag was on fire. This friend thought Reynolds might be interested to know. He dashed to the front window. 'Great flames were darting up from the roof of the Reichstag,' he observed. 'It was a terrifying and magnificent spectacle.'

He rang London at once to speak to his friend Douglas Crawford, the *Daily Mail*'s foreign editor. 'So they've done it another way,' was the Scotsman's response. Reynolds had previously told him the Nazis may orchestrate a bogus attempt on Hitler's life as a desperate act of election propaganda. After the call he went to the window to see the flames rise still higher, despite the efforts of the firemen present. He left to get a closer look but met a cordon of police. They would not let him through despite his press card. 'We are not even allowing members of the Reichstag to approach,' they said. 'There is a danger of the building collapsing.'[200]

Other correspondents had dashed to the scene. Delmer of the *Express* had been tipped off slightly earlier than Reynolds; he received news of the fire from one of the petrol station attendants near the Reichstag. His journalistic initiative had paid off; Delmer had given his card to several attendants and asked them to ring if anything interesting happened. He arrived at 9.45 p.m. and quickly ran into Douglas Reed of *The Times*, who had managed to get inside the building before being thrown out again by Hermann Göring, one of Hitler's closest allies. 'Beaten by that staid old slow coach, *The Times*!' Delmer thought bitterly.[201]

As fire engines continued to arrive, Delmer was making his way around the perimeter, taking down eyewitness accounts from bystanders. Suddenly a pair of large black Mercedes cars pulled up at the scene. His luck was in. Hitler swiftly disembarked from one of them and marched through the cordon towards the burning building. Delmer glided behind in his slip-stream. 'Without a doubt this is the work of communists, Herr Chancellor,' Göring remarked to Hitler. 'A number of communist deputies were here in the Reichstag twenty minutes before the fire broke out. We have suc-ceeded in arresting one of the incendiaries.'[202]

Hitler did not need to hear any more than that. He turned to Delmer: 'You see this building, you see how it is aflame? If the communists got hold of Europe and had control of it for but six months – what am I saying! – two months – the whole continent would be aflame like this building.'[203] His narrative for the outside world was established. 'If this is the work of communists,' Hitler warned Reynolds, 'they shall be crushed.' Sure enough, a young Dutch communist named Marinus van der Lubbe was found to be responsible.

Reynolds's first report on the fire was published the next day and named van der Lubbe as the alleged perpetrator. After the accused had been taken to the police station, Reynolds had stayed at the Reichstag and interviewed the policeman who had arrested him. Apparently van der Lubbe had been found wearing only his trousers and immediately confessed to starting the fire.

In the days that followed, theories spread that the fire had in fact been the work of the Nazis. It seemed almost too convenient for Hitler's party that the communists should so clumsily undermine themselves in the eyes of the electorate just six days before the election. Hitler's campaign played on fears of communism, which grew after the attack. He was furious at suggestions of a Nazi plot and called Delmer in. 'I could have that com-munist who was caught in the Reichstag hanged from the nearest tree!' he screamed. 'That would dispose forever of this vile slander that he was an agent of ours.'[204] Almost a century on, his guilt has still not been proven. Writing in 1939, Reynolds was sure that van der Lubbe, who was guillotined for the crime in 1934, was not responsible. He called it a cock-and-bull story.[205] Delmer, writing in his 1968 memoir, thought van der Lubbe alone was responsible – but that his fanaticism was so great it would be unfair to blame this on the wider communist movement.

Irrespective of culpability, the Reichstag fire sowed seeds of doubt in German minds. Their mounting distrust of Hitler and the ugly behaviour of his supporters was totally overshadowed by renewed fears of the communist threat. The Nazis responded by persuading Hindenburg to sign a decree permitting martial law in Germany. 'The police are given the right to raid every home in Germany,' Reynolds reported. 'The postal and telephone services are no longer secret, and scores of other public rights are withdrawn.'[206] Many Germans were frightened by this development, but felt that perhaps it was necessary. Maybe Hitler was in fact the man needed to restore order and prosperity in Germany. In the election on 5 March, support for the Nazis rose. The party won 288 seats and 44 per cent of the vote.

The *Daily Mail* welcomed the result in an editorial. 'In Germany the elections have brought some relaxation of tension in the Fatherland. Herr Hitler has won his majority cleverly. If he uses it prudently and peacefully, no one here will shed any tears over the disappearance of German democracy.'[207]

With the Reichstag building a burnt-out shell, Germany's politicians convened after the election at the Kroll Opera House. 'It was the most beautiful of the modern theatres of Berlin, with panels of polished wood and a pale roof with touches of colour in a fantastic pattern,' observed Reynolds, who had thought the old Parliament building ugly. He was present as Hitler and other leading Nazis took their seats in the new Parliament for the first time, shortly after the fire. It felt an odd experience. 'It was strange to be in this theatre, which one had thought of as a place where the cares of the day could be forgotten, for so grave a business as a meeting of legislators.'[208] A huge red banner emblazoned with a Nazi swastika dominated the stage. Hitler, wearing his familiar khaki shirt and breeches, entered and exchanged salutes with his fellow party members. At this stage the Nazi salute was performed only by members of the party, but it would soon be pressed onto the German population as a general greeting.

A couple of days after this meeting the new Parliament met again and the ruinous Enabling Act was passed. The legislation allowed Hitler and his government to make and pass laws without any input from the Reichstag. Hitler needed a two-thirds majority of votes to pass the law and packed the Kroll Opera House with Nazi guards and supporters to intimidate those present. It was a fevered and unpleasant atmosphere. Reynolds was sitting in the fourth or fifth row of the stalls for the momentous occasion.

'When I arrived to attend this sitting, I found the Kroll Theatre more like a barracks than a parliament-house,' Reynolds later recorded. 'In the hall, on the staircase, in the foyer and corridors were posted Nazi Black Guards.' Before entering the building he had been patted down by security men, a practice he was not used to. Their greatest fear was an 'assassin with a bomb or a revolver in my pocket,' Reynolds said.[209]

Also present was Vernon Bartlett, a British journalist who had done some work for the BBC. Later in 1933 he started working in Berlin as a correspondent for the liberal *News Chronicle* newspaper. 'The orchestra stalls were crowded with Nazi deputies in uniform, with a block of sullen, dark-coated socialists on their right,' he wrote. 'At one moment during the debate Hitler looked up as though he were listening intently to some faint noise. I wondered if he could hear – as I could in my faint gallery – the shouts of thousands of young Nazis who were waiting outside. "We want full powers for the Government," they yelled.'[210]

The communists were virtually banned from the meeting, but the Social Democrats and Centre Party could have formed enough opposition to put down the motion. The latter party was persuaded not to by concessions on religious interests granted by Hitler. 'The Centre Party had to look at the question before them from every point of view,' Reynolds later wrote. 'And its leader did not know, as Mr Chamberlain should have known six years later, that Herr Hitler was a liar.'[211]

The motion passed and Hitler was now poised to dominate Germany. 'The German parliament, guardian of the liberties of the German people, ceased to exist,' Reynolds recalled.[212] The one man who could have blocked the law, President Hindenburg, did not. He was elderly, hidden away in his East Prussia country estate, too feeble and reliant on poor advice from his courtiers to obstruct Hitler's path.

The thuggish behaviour of Nazi supporters outside the Kroll Opera House was one part of the 'Brown Terror' that swept the country in the weeks before and after the March election. Hitler's supporters felt emboldened by his ascent to the chancellorship and vindicated by his victory in the subsequent election. 'For the terror as a whole the regime is responsible,' Frederick Voigt reported in the *Guardian*. 'Although it has ebbed it has not ceased. There are continual raids by Brown Shirts; there were at least two in the "Norden" quarter of Berlin on Tuesday. Arrests are being made the whole time. Prisoners are continually being shot "while trying to escape," and dead bodies are continually being found.'[213] This report was published on the very day the Enabling Act was passed. It was an early example of the *Guardian*'s probing and revealing reports on Germany – reports that would make life dangerous for its correspondents based there in the 1930s.

During the first two months of Hitler's chancellorship Reynolds realised just how difficult his employer's politics would make his job. He was well aware of Lord Rothermere's pre-existing admiration for Hitler, which had coloured the *Daily Mail*'s coverage of Germany since the Nazi breakthrough in 1930. But now that Hitler was actually in power, Reynolds expected Rothermere to demand a more critical, questioning approach. This instruction was not forthcoming and the newspaper continued to take a firmly pro-Nazi line.

A first taste of this came when the *Mail* reported on the passing of the Enabling Act. While the *Mail* did not mention the aggressive atmosphere, which made opposition to Hitler virtually impossible, the *Express* reported on the storm troopers shouting warnings at politicians. 'Chancellor Makes Listeners Tremble While Storm Troops Shout Threats Through Windows' ran its headline. Reynolds had witnessed it – as his later account in *When Freedom Shrieked* proves – but the *Mail*'s coverage fell short. 'The *Express* has caught the menace of the Nazi regime, while the *Mail* has deliberately chosen to ignore it,' was the verdict of BBC journalist John Simpson in his later history.[214] He claims Lord Rothermere was to blame. 'The *Express* presented a far more realistic picture of the Nazis than the *Mail* did, because it was less cluttered with its proprietor's preconceptions.'

Reynolds's experience was a sign of things to come. Hitler's early treatment of the Jews presented a stark example of how Rothermere would order his paper to cover unfolding events in Germany. It is difficult to determine how much of what appeared in the *Mail* stemmed from dispatches sent by correspondents, as opposed to subsequent interference by Rothermere and his editors in the London newsroom. But during the Jewish Boycott came clear evidence of proprietorial interference in London.

With other journalists in Berlin, Reynolds had been reporting on the mounting tension between the Nazi authorities and the country's Jewish population. Nazi supporters were further emboldened by the passage of the Enabling Act and the country, it seemed, was now theirs to dominate. The 'Brown Terror' focused increasingly on Germany's Jewish population, a minority that represented about 1 per cent of the country. Storm troopers were sent to intimidate Jewish shop-owners and businesses, and to dissuade Germans from going inside. The violence towards Jews led to an international outcry. Hitler and his associates purported to be beyond angry at what they saw as 'propaganda' spread by Jews abroad. They accused 'international Jewry' of spreading deliberate lies about the Nazi regime to damage Germany. Increasingly vehement language was used. The great physicist Albert Einstein, who happened to be a Jew, had left Germany in December 1932 after Nazi intimidation. In March 1933 Reynolds asked one of Hitler's associates if he would be allowed to return. 'What would England do to British subjects who abused their country abroad?' was the cold reply.[215]

The Nazi response to what they called 'atrocity propaganda' – rather than plain truth – was their boycott of Jewish businesses in Germany. It would begin on Saturday 1 April. On 27 March the *Daily Mail* printed a report by Reynolds carrying an official statement. 'All the reports of the mishandling of Jews are barefaced lies,' said Hitler's spokesman. Reynolds's report also carried comments from Hermann Göring, who had hosted a group of foreign correspondents at his official residence. 'The government is shocked, indignant and indeed speechless at the reports which have been written abroad about Jews in Germany,' he said.

Göring then offered a statement that is chilling in its detail. He denied authorising any violence, but revealed a familiarity with methods of torture. 'There is not a man in Germany whose finger nail has been hacked off or who has had the lobe of his ear pinched off, and all have kept their sight.'[216] The words of Göring and Hitler's spokesman are reported without judgement by Reynolds. Objective journalism, perhaps, but other news-papers printed reports that gave a fuller idea of what was going on. The *Manchester Guardian* reported on 1 April from Dusseldorf that 'all the lead-ing Jews of the city have been deprived of their passports, thus preventing them from leaving the country'. German newspapers were being ordered not to employ any Jews. Non-Jewish employees of Jewish firms were being encouraged to ask for two months of wages in advance. 'Black placards with yellow spots' were to be placed on all Jewish shops during the boycott. It was a blunt and revealing report by the *Guardian* that gave no prominence to the meaningless Nazi platitudes and excuses.[217]

The easy ride given to Hitler on the Jewish question by the *Daily Mail* gives away the malign influence of Rothermere. A few days later, Reynolds reported on Hitler's response to the boycott. Yet his article, which appeared on 3 April, headlined 'Germany's *Jewish* Boycott', is not exactly what he had filed to his editor in London. Goebbels had authored a violent dia-tribe against the Jews in *Der Angriff*, the newspaper he founded in 1927 to spread his hateful Nazi messages. Reynolds quoted from the article in his report on the boycott and ended by saying: 'The *Angriff* says: The boycott was carried out in a way worthy of the German people.' Reynolds said he had written this as 'an ironical end' to his dispatch, intended to give some idea of the ridiculous pitch of the comments issued by Nazi officialdom.

It did not appear that way in the paper. The words 'The *Angriff* says' were omitted, totally altering the meaning of the piece. 'The statement appeared as my considered opinion,' Reynolds later wrote.[218] He did not directly accuse Lord Rothermere or any other individual at the *Daily Mail* of doctoring his copy, but the change in meaning was such that it led *Der Angriff* to subsequently report: 'The Berlin correspondent of the *Daily Mail* says that the boycott was carried out in a way worthy of the German people.'

It was a clear early example of the restrictions Reynolds faced working for the *Daily Mail* in Berlin. He was forced to walk the tightrope between Rothermere's overbearing influence and his own journalistic integrity. In many cases, as with his reporting of the Jewish Boycott, this was impossible and he fell short. Only later was he able to reveal his true thoughts about Hitler's early attacks on Germany's Jewish population. 'I found myself in a mood of extreme depression, to which my nature does not incline me,' he wrote in 1939. 'I was beset by a sickening feeling, as if I had been in contact with something unclean from which I must be purged.'[219]

Reynolds's reporting peers in Germany shared his sentiment. Bartlett was in Berlin to monitor the boycott and was moved to tears. 'If its object was to preach hatred, it certainly succeeded,' he wrote. 'I came back to my hotel so overcome with shame that I almost wept.'[220] Their humanity meant he and other correspondents could not help but intervene in what was going on. Bartlett was almost beaten up after going to the defence of a Jewish flower-seller who was being rebuked by half a dozen storm troopers for not closing her shop. They turned on him, and calmed only when he showed them his official papers. 'My cowardice came back and I hurriedly produced my passport to prove I was a foreigner.'[221]

Readers in Britain had to look to the *Manchester Guardian* and elsewhere for the truth of the boycott. The *Mirror* also emerges with credit for printing a critical telegram from Commander Oliver Locker-Lampson, a Conservative MP and supporter of Hitler: 'The decision to discriminate against the German Jews has had a most damaging effect upon the good feeling for Germany which was growing stronger... This action against the Jews is making the work of myself and other friends of Germany almost impossible.'[222] Germany's treatment of the Jews drew public opprobrium in Britain. In May 1933, Dr Alfred Rosenberg, Hitler's minister for Germans abroad, laid a wreath at the foot of the Cenotaph on Whitehall, in honour of the Great War dead. It was removed in protest and thrown into the Thames.

Eric Gedye, who had a long career reporting in Vienna for the *Daily Telegraph*, observed in 1933 that masses of ordinary Germans were willing to shut their eyes to the dangers facing Jews and socialists because of their belief that Hitler could unify and strengthen the country. He described the mood he encountered: 'If a few Jews and socialists have lost their jobs and had their ears boxed, are you really going to concentrate on abusing us for these unimportant incidents and overlook the glorious national awakening?' Yet as early as 1933 Gedye saw that the abuse accompanying Hitler's rise to power went beyond boxed ears. In an eyewitness piece for a magazine he described the 'brutal beatings, killings, suicides of dismissed intellectuals, the lacerated backs, cripplings and ruined existences which have marked the triumph of Hitlerism'.[223]

In a book published before he started at the *News Chronicle*, Bartlett summed up the conflicted emotions of many Germans and overseas observers. A general sense of economic optimism competed with unease about the increasing Nazi persecution of Jews and other minorities. 'Some are so impressed by the enthusiasm that is everywhere evident that they look upon the ill treatment of Jews, social-democrats, communists, and pacifists as an inevitable, if unpleasant, feature of a revolution,' he wrote. 'Others are so revolted by accounts of this ill treatment, and so alarmed by photographs of uniformed storm troops marching in excellent military formations past some Nazi leader, that they believe war to be the great ambition of the National Socialist movement.'[224]

Most British journalists working in central Europe in 1933, including Gedye and Bartlett, were clear in their conclusions and perceived Hitler as a tyrant in the making. Bartlett did not think that Hitler wanted war immediately, but believed he may well do in the future. Gedye was alert to the hypocrisy at the heart of National Socialism from the start. He took pleasure in exposing it. 'This movement, which claims to be the very essence of Germanism, has so far grown great by studying and copying other countries. From Sanskrit comes its Swastika badge, from Imperial Rome its fascist salute, from Mussolini its dosing of its victims with Castor oil.'[225]

This analysis was clear-eyed and not borne of the virulent anti-German sentiment that coloured the reports of some correspondents. Gedye had lived for seven years in the occupied German territory of the Ruhr after the war. While reporting for *The Times* on developments in that region and the Rhineland, he had pointed out that Germany's punishment after the war may be storing trouble for the future. 'I did what was possible in that capacity to make people at home realise the intolerable – and from the standpoint of British self-interest, dangerous – treatment to which a great nation of sixty millions was being daily subjected.'[226] He saw the argument from all sides, but knew there was no justification for Hitler's brutality.

Some Britons outside the press pack sounded early warnings in 1933. The ambassador in Berlin, Sir Horace Rumbold, was a grizzled veteran of Britain's diplomatic service. Eton-educated, in common with so many members of the country's ruling elite, he had enjoyed a long and brilliant career, working across the world in postings ranging from Cairo to Tehran, Vienna to Tokyo. A smartly turned-out man with a pale face and neat moustache, Rumbold had started his Berlin posting late in the 1920s. He had hoped to see Brüning succeed, believing his success to be the best way to keep extremists in Germany at bay. He was approaching retirement age when Hitler came to power in 1933 and immediately recognised the threat posed by the country's new leader and his supporters.

Two months after Hitler took the chancellorship he made his views clear in a letter to Lord Vansittart, the most senior civil servant in the Foreign Office. Hitler's government was characterised by 'a mean spirit of revenge, a tendency to brutality, and a noisy and irresponsible jingoism,' Rumbold wrote. The rise of the Nazis had led many writers, artists and political activists to leave Germany, creating a 'kind of vacuum,' he said. 'Whatever may have been the shortcomings of the democratic parties, they number among their following the intellectual life of the capital and nearly all that was original and stimulating in arts and letters.'[227]

Rumbold had read *Mein Kampf* and identified the threat posed to Germany's Jewish population. Many at this early stage had not read Hitler's tome of political hate, even so-called experts on Germany such as the historian John Wheeler-Bennett.[228] Rumbold did not believe foreign opinion overseas had quite realised the extent of the hatred towards Jews borne by Hitler and the Nazis. He presciently expected Hitler to take further action, beyond the Jewish Boycott, and in time thought he could even try to expel Jews from Germany.

Why did Rumbold think this? He had seen at close hand the measures Hitler was imposing on Jews and others. As early as April 1933 he was warning senior government figures in London about the establishment of concentration camps. These were not yet the factories of genocide they would become in wartime, but just a few months into Hitler's chancellorship he was using them as centres for Jewish oppression. During one of Rumbold's meetings with Hitler in May 1933, he was on the receiving end of a tirade about the Jews and their supposed fermentation of anti-German sentiment abroad. 'It would be a mistake to believe that anti-Semitism was the policy of his wilder men whom he has difficulty controlling,' Rumbold concluded.[229] He had done his research. After taking the effort to read *Mein Kampf*, he knew the policy stemmed from Hitler directly.

In June the ambassador reached the age of retirement and was forced to leave Berlin. He was perceptive to the end, describing Hitler, Göring and Goebbels as three 'notoriously pathological cases' in his last dispatch to London. 'One looks in vain for any men of real worth' among the Nazi leadership, he wrote.[230] Few others had yet reached this conclusion. In an unfortunate twist it was Lord Vansittart, the senior British diplomat who was another early and persistent critic of Hitler, who forced Rumbold to leave his post. He was in charge of enforcing the retirement rules and did so punctiliously, despite the quality of Rumbold's work in Berlin. Even Vansittart's admiring biographer, the journalist Ian Colvin, recognised this as a mistake. 'Every rule ought to have its exceptions,' he wrote in a rare piece of criticism in *Vansittart in Office*.[231]

The diplomat partly made up for this lapse by continuing the often lonely work of warning against Hitler in the years to come. Vansittart never held the view, popular across London from the clubs of Mayfair to the boardrooms of the City, that communist Russia posed a bigger threat than fascist Germany. 'Hitlerism *is* exceedingly dangerous,' he wrote in a pointed memo to Sir John Simon, the Foreign Secretary, in 1933.

> Russia has been too incompetent a country to be really dangerous, even under Bolshevism. But Germany is an exceedingly competent country, and she is visibly being prepared to external aggression. I do not think that anything but evil and danger for the rest of the world can come out of Hitlerism.[232]

In a separate memo that year Vansittart said that Hitler had a psychological obsession with Austria and predicted he would attempt to annex the country.

Another man who was early in identifying the threat posed by Hitler was Brigadier Arthur Temperley, Britain's military representative at the League of Nations. He did not mince his words in a memorandum which warned that Hitler was like a mad dog that must be locked up or destroyed. Germany 'is powerless before the French army and our fleet,' he wrote. 'Hitler, for all his bombast, must give way.' This was forwarded to the

Cabinet by Vansittart in 1933 but it had no impact. MacDonald and his government were in no mood to take pre-emptive action against Hitler.[233] Later the *Daily Telegraph* would make use of Temperley's perceptive qualities in its anti-appeasement coverage.

Meanwhile in Berlin, Reynolds found an atmosphere of fear and suspicion taking hold. One day he had a clergyman friend to visit. 'You have a telephone there,' his guest exclaimed, before throwing his coat over it. 'They may have put a microphone in it, and the Secret Service may be listening to our conversation.'[234] That was as early as 1933. But most Germans were oblivious to the fate awaiting their country – many thought they would be able to give Hitler an opportunity, and eject him if he failed. 'We shall give them a chance, and if we do not like them they will have to go,' was the general mood Reynolds encountered.[235] It was to prove a naive hope.

-CHAPTER VIII-

NIGHTS AT
THE TAVERNE

Reynolds was part of a close-knit community of foreign correspondents who met most nights to share experiences and compare findings.
Their regular haunt was the Taverne, an Italian restaurant in the middle of Berlin, where British, French and American correspondents had a
Stammtisch, a table permanently reserved for them in the corner. It was
run by a fat German man named Willy Lehman and his slim Belgian wife,
and was a haven for the foreign reporters during the 1930s as the Nazi
oppression grew.

Most of the reporters working in Berlin shared Gedye and Bartlett's
critical attitude towards Hitler. One of the correspondents Reynolds
mixed with was William Shirer, the American broadcast journalist whose
reports of life in Nazi Germany and 1930s Europe had huge audiences in the
US. Shirer recorded details of the era in his famous diaries of the pre-war
years. The Taverne 'has become an institution for the British and American
correspondents here, helping us to retain some sanity and affording an
opportunity to get together informally and talk shop – without which
no foreign correspondent could long live,' he wrote. The correspondents

relished the chance to gossip and hatch plans – the table was usually full from about 10 p.m. until three or four in the morning.[236]

Rothay Reynolds pictured in the 1930s smoking a cigarette,
immaculately dressed as ever.

By 1933, Reynolds was twelve years into his time as Berlin bureau chief. His young assistant Ralph Izzard, who had joined him two years earlier in 1931, would be present for nights at the Taverne. Izzard had started studying forestry at Queen's College, Cambridge, pursuing a passion that his father, Percy Izzard, had written about at length as the *Daily Mail*'s agricultural and horticultural correspondent. The elder Izzard's columns during the First World War had been read avidly by fighters at the front, who soaked up images of a bucolic England as a respite from the grim reality of life in the trenches.[237] In 1931, Ralph Izzard travelled to the Black Forest in Germany to examine foresting techniques. That was the end of his studies – he used his father's friendship with Douglas Crawford, the *Mail*'s foreign editor, to secure a position with the paper as an assistant in the Berlin office. He was just twenty-one. On occasions, G. Ward Price, the *Mail*'s roving star reporter, would also drop by, though his closeness to the emerging fascist movement in Britain did not make him popular with other correspondents at the Taverne.

Norman Ebbutt of *The Times* had been a correspondent in Berlin since 1927 and his experience was much valued by Shirer and others. He had left school at the age of fifteen to travel and learn languages overseas before working for British newspapers. At the age of thirty-three, he was appointed chief correspondent for *The Times* in Germany. He loved the artistic culture and freedoms of the Weimar Republic and developed strong contacts within the German government and church. By the early 1930s he was, alongside Reynolds, one of the most respected British correspondents working in the country. He had spotted the Nazi menace early. Halfway through 1932 he attended a Nazi meeting addressed by Hitler, Goebbels and other Nazi leaders. He told his friend, Frederick Voigt of the *Manchester Guardian*, that it had made him feel 'physically sick'.[238]

Ebbutt was a well-built man prone to bouts of illness. He wore thick spectacles and would quiz his sources while sucking on a long pipe. His network was particularly deep in the German church, meaning he was well-placed to provide penetrating reports of changes affecting Christians living in Nazi Germany after Hitler took power in January 1933. Ebbutt's reports drew praise for their seriousness and accuracy and did not pass unnoticed in Berlin, where English-speaking Germans increasingly read *The Times* for news of events in their own country.

His reports on the struggle between Christians in Germany and the Nazi leadership were a cause of great displeasure to the German government. In April 1933 Leo Kennedy, a journalist at *The Times*, had lunch in London with Baron de Ropp, one of his German political contacts. He heard from his source that Hitler and his Nazi associates read *The Times* 'minutely' but did not let the German press feature information reported in the newspaper because it was too 'candid'. This was welcome, if frustrating intelligence – Ebbutt and his *Times* colleagues in Europe were evidently doing their job if their reporting was considered too truthful for the Nazis to stomach. Kennedy was troubled, however, by the news that German newspapers were not allowed to pick up *Times* reports. He noted in his diary that night: 'I must try to write just favourably enough to Hitler to get him to allow the articles to be quoted in the German press.'[239]

Kennedy's initial reaction – that content in the newspaper should be tweaked to pacify Hitler – was a harbinger of controversies over *The Times*'s reporting of Germany later in the decade. During the lunch meeting he also heard from de Ropp that Ebbutt had become a target for the Nazis as a result of his rapier-sharp reporting and criticism of their rule in Germany. 'De Ropp said that the Nazis had got their knife into Ebbutt, metaphorically speaking, owing to his opposition to their movement. He said they would not dare to do him any outward visible damage – but that if they were given the chance they would certainly get him run over by a motor-car, or otherwise accidentally done in.' Kennedy was shocked. 'I must warn Ebbutt, but carefully, because the poor fellow is already much shaken by his experiences. (He is over here in England, resting),' he wrote in his diary.[240]

It was a stark warning that Kennedy passed onto his colleague. The Nazi reputation for brutality was already rising – Hitler's demagoguery gave a voice and confidence to thousands of thuggish supporters. The prospect of returning to Germany, where intimidating bands of storm troopers roamed the streets, was not an appetising one for Ebbutt as he recuperated in England in the spring of 1933.

His friend Voigt had joined the *Guardian* in 1919 and been sent to Berlin the following year. He had cut his teeth as a foreign correspondent under the *Guardian*'s famous editor C. P. Scott and remained based in Berlin throughout the Weimar era. Voigt had been resolutely critical of Hitler as the Nazis edged closer to power and moved to Paris a few weeks before Hitler was made Chancellor in January 1933. But he continued to report closely on German affairs in partnership with his replacement in Berlin, Charles Lambert. Their coverage of the Jewish Boycott and Brown Terror caused outrage among senior Nazis, who dismissed the *Guardian* as a 'dirty communist rag'.[241] Even in France, Voigt was not judged to be safe; there were fears the Gestapo had marked his card because of his anti-Nazi dispatches. He abruptly left France for London in December 1933 after the French Foreign Office passed on their knowledge of plans for an attack on his life.[242]

For Lord Beaverbrook's *Daily Express*, the swash-buckling Sefton 'Tom' Delmer had been a sensation in Berlin. But in March 1933 he too was told to move to Paris. 'Tom, you are the best foreign correspondent this newspaper has ever had. I want to build you up as a great world reporter,' Beaverbrook told him (according, it must be said, to Delmer's own memoirs).[243] Delmer finally left in September and was replaced in Berlin by Philip Pembroke Stephens, who would soon make his name with reports very different in nature to those sent by Delmer. Selkirk Panton and Noel Monks, a pair of Australian reporters, also sent dispatches during the 1930s for the *Express*, which had more foreign correspondents than any other paper at this time.

Reynolds's friend John Segrue reported from Berlin for the liberal *News Chronicle*, another paper that had a large number of reporters posted overseas. Bartlett would play a prominent role in the paper's reporting on Germany after joining Segrue in Berlin later in 1933. Bartlett never forgot his first meeting with Hitler, an interview in the chancellery days after he took power. He found Hitler to be 'quite amiable, but with nothing terribly impressive about him'. As with so many of Hitler's visitors, Bartlett remarked on his eyes. 'The only exception was his large, brown eyes – so large and so brown that one might grow lyrical about them if he were a woman.' Hitler was 'a little fuller in the face, and a little wider in the moustache' than Bartlett had expected.[244]

The Labour Party-supporting *Daily Herald* had Wallace King as its Berlin correspondent, while wizened former communist William Ewer wrote popular articles as its diplomatic correspondent in London. At the other end of the spectrum, the fervently right-wing *Morning Post* had Karl Robson as its man in Berlin. A close friend to Ebbutt, Robson's articles would sting the Nazis repeatedly in the following years. In 1933, Ian Colvin, a journalist who would rise to prominence later in the decade, was working for the paper.

The *Daily Telegraph*'s correspondent in Berlin between 1933 and 1938 was Eustace Wareing. A young Oxford graduate, Hugh Carleton Greene, joined him permanently as his assistant not long after finishing his degree in 1933. Noel Panter was the paper's correspondent in Munich. The reporters of the *Sunday Times* and *Observer*, being published once a week, made less of an impact in these years – the influence of these newspapers was felt more heavily in the realms of opinion. For this reason James Garvin, the long-standing editor of *The Observer*, W. W. Hadley, the *Sunday Times* editor, and Herbert Sidebotham, who penned the latter paper's much-read foreign affairs column 'Scrutator', are the most important names in relation to how those newspapers covered events in Germany.

With all of Britain's major newspapers having at least one correspondent permanently based in Berlin, the reporters' table at the Taverne was rarely quiet. Reynolds enjoyed socialising in this way. It brought back memories of times spent in the Café des Westens before the First World War. Often, however, there was unwelcome company. The Gestapo were all too aware of this meeting-place of foreign reporters, many of whom they were desperate to expel – something they would do with increasing regularity as the years went by. The harder the Gestapo men monitoring the reporters tried to lurk furtively in the shadows, the more they stood out in such a convivial environment. At other times they were merely sent to intimidate and made no effort at stealth.

On the first night of the Jewish Boycott the group had another kind of unwelcome guest – a representative from Germany's Ministry of Foreign Affairs. The representative had been sent to the Taverne to persuade the journalists to report the events in the best possible light; 'smoothing us down,' as Reynolds described it. In the twenty-first century, this person would have been called a spin doctor.

'There are times, I think, when a correspondent should be a diplomat,' the man said to Reynolds.

'I am a simple reporter,' Reynolds replied in non-committal fashion, not wishing to engage him.

Reynolds later wrote: 'His purpose was obvious and he evidently hoped that I should be induced to write a wishy-washy account of the day's proceedings, which would not make too bad an impression on the British public.'[245]

From the earliest days of the Nazi regime, attempts were made by senior members of Hitler's team to silence the foreign press. A few days after the Reichstag fire, Göring invited the foreign newspaper journalists based in Berlin to meet him. Rumours were flying about that communist leaders were being secretly murdered by the Nazis. After annoying the reporters by organising the meeting on a Saturday – the one day off for daily newspaper journalists – Göring arrived fifteen minutes late. Though he was yet to move permanently to Berlin, Vernon Bartlett was present for the meeting. He described how Göring began an attack against the foreign press unlike any he had ever previously witnessed. He informed those present that he knew 'not only what they sent in their telegrams and telephone messages, but also what they wrote in their private letters'. Bartlett was incensed and amazed by what he heard. 'I found it difficult to sit through the whole address.'[246] He was relieved not to be part of the group of journalists taken by Göring to see some of the more prominent communist prisoners to prove they had not been murdered.

Such clumsy attempts at persuasion would later look the height of sub-tleness compared to the crude tactics deployed by Joseph Goebbels and his Ministry of Propaganda. As the 1930s went on, his grip on the domestic press in Germany tightened. Every morning and afternoon Reynolds had all the German newspapers sent to the *Mail*'s Berlin bureau. They were laid out for him in a row, which shortened as the years went by and various publications were banned. Goebbels was at the heart of the Nazi operation to control the press and served as Reich Minister of Propaganda throughout their time in power. He bullied German newspapers into adopting certain positions and used *Der Angriff* to spread anti-Semitic hatred and lies about the truth of life in Germany.

'Soon one began to notice that the (German) newspapers which rem-ained were suspiciously alike,' Reynolds wrote. 'Joseph Goebbels had got to work and was giving orders to editors, who did not dare disobey, because they found by experience that disobedience was punished by confisca-tion or by suppression, the duration of which depended on the minister's caprice.'[247] Newspapers received orders from Goebbels about which events or speeches should be given prominence in the next edition. Defying these orders could result in arrest or worse.

'Identical opinions were expressed in the leading articles of newspapers that had previously been distinguished by the difference of their views. This artificial harmony was produced by summoning the leader-writers to the Propaganda Ministry to receive orders,' Reynolds wrote.[248] As early as the summer of 1933, the *Telegraph*'s Eric Gedye saw the reality clearly. 'There is no significant press left in Germany except the Nazi press.'[249]

It was not just in religious matters that informers feared for their lives. Sources speaking to Reynolds almost always made the same kind of request: 'I beg you not to let anybody know that you heard this from me, or it might get around and I should be arrested.'[250] It became perilous to be a journalist. Many members of the British press were expelled, whose stories we will hear. 'The house of one of my colleagues who was subsequently arrested, was watched; it became unsafe for persons desiring to give him information,' Reynolds recalled.[251] 'Our profession became dangerous… We were courted on the one hand and intimidated on the other.'[252]

Reynolds and the other foreign correspondents did not rule out anything when it came to Goebbels. Though he could be charming on occasion, he was widely regarded as a vicious figure. 'Dr Goebbels is a slender little man whose club foot kept him out of the war, and, by so doing, made him more violent and more bitter than he ought to be,' Bartlett wrote.[253] Goebbels's control of the domestic press revealed not only his love of power but also his total disregard for the role of a free and impartial media.

Soon after the Nazis came to power Goebbels moved against Edgar Ansel Mowrer, a correspondent in Berlin with the *Chicago Daily News*. He was one of the earliest reporters to warn of the dangers posed by Germany's move towards extreme politics. He published *Germany Puts the Clock Back* around the time that Hitler took power. It was an uncompromising portrayal of Nazi aggression and malice, 'particularly disliked on account of the frankness with which he informed the American public of ugly deeds in Germany,' according to Reynolds.[254] Once the Nazis took power their retribution was swift. The government informed Mowrer that it could not guarantee his safety, meaning that he would not be protected if attacked by storm troopers.

Mowrer wisely decided to leave the country later in 1933, but not before further riling the German authorities. A Nazi official was sent to the train station, where a large number of foreign correspondents had gathered to bid Mowrer farewell, to check he boarded the assigned train to remove him from the country.

'When are you coming back to Germany, Herr Mowrer?' the official asked in a goading voice.

'Why, when I can come back with about two million of my country-men,' Mowrer responded. He firmly believed that war would come and his country, the US, would be involved.[255] After Berlin he had a short-lived stint in Japan running his newspaper's Tokyo bureau before moving to Paris, from where he continued to report on Europe. Mowrer was awarded the Pulitzer Prize for his early reports on Hitler. He was the first foreign cor-respondent expelled from Berlin but many more would follow.

With the German press enfeebled, the foreign correspondents in Berlin became important points of contact for those wishing to know the truth about life in Germany. After losing her seat as a Labour MP in the early 1930s, the radical left-wing politician Ellen Wilkinson travelled to Germany to report for the feminist magazine *Time and Tide.* 'Some tribute ought to be paid to those pressmen who, in danger of physical violence… and equally in danger of their jobs on certain papers,' she wrote, 'managed to get the ghastly truth over to the world.'[256]

The journalists in Berlin knew there was a gulf between their perception of the Nazis and the impression held by the outside world. At a lunch at the British Embassy in April 1933, Douglas Reed, who was then a junior correspondent with *The Times,* was keen to make his views known to other guests including the Labour politician Hugh Dalton, who had travelled from London. Dalton found the embassy staff and its guests to be 'all very anti-Nazi'. He recorded Reed's view that 'British opinion didn't yet begin to realise the truth about the Nazis. The Nazis spoke of their "revolution," but power was handed to them on a silver tray.' Reed painted a grim picture.

'Private executions were still going on and the wiping out of old grudges. In the concentration camps, just opened, things were pretty bad.'[257] Reed and the other reporters felt ardently they should do all they could to get the truth out before it was too late.

The writer Storm Jameson said in her memoirs she preferred to find out from correspondents first-hand – rather than their newspapers – what was happening in Germany and Europe. 'The after-dinner gossip of foreign correspondents is the best in the world,' she said. 'I was listening to Harrison Brown [a freelance correspondent], who had come back from Berlin with evidence – at that time new and barely credible – of what Hitler planned to do with the Jews living in Germany. I was still [in 1933] naive enough to think that he had only to lay it before the editor of *The Times* to blow away for good every hopeful illusion about the Nazi regime.'[258]

Jameson later felt she could not trust her copy of *The Times* – or any other newspaper – to provide the real story of life in Germany. She may have guessed that correspondents had to write carefully, and sometimes misleadingly, to avoid falling foul of Goebbels and being expelled from the country. But there was more than that. As her final sentence suggests, she did not necessarily trust the editors and proprietors in London to faithfully relay what their correspondents in Berlin were reporting. The journalists meeting at the Taverne faced varying degrees of interference from their newspaper masters. The reasons for this were complex and varied from paper to paper. They formed the background to battles between reporters in Berlin and their bosses in London throughout the 1930s.

———

Lord Rothermere had been running the *Daily Mail* for more than a decade when Hitler took power in Germany. After a series of battles in the 1920s, his firm grip on the paper was established. His time in charge follow-ing the death of his brother in 1922 had been full of controversy. In 1924 the *Daily Mail* had published on its front page the forged Zinoviev letter, which spread unfounded fears about the spread of communism in Britain. Rothermere did not mind – many believed the letter cost the Labour Party victory in the election held only days afterwards. His hatred of communism was all-consuming and became a key element of his attitude to foreign affairs, and support for Hitler, in the 1930s.

Two years after the Zinoviev affair, Thomas Marlowe, who had been editor of the *Daily Mail* for twenty-seven years, left after arguments with Rothermere. Other senior staff left at that time, allowing Rothermere to assert himself on the newspaper and influence content. His style of manage-ment was different from how Lord Northcliffe had run the paper; though both interfered, Rothermere tended to back managers over journalists.[259] 'The day-to-day production of the paper was carried on under the system of bullying and insult,' observed one newly hired sub-editor towards the end of the decade.[260] A circulation battle with the *Daily Express*, led bril-liantly by Lord Beaverbook, ensued in the following years.

The two press barons dominated the popular press and followed Lord Northcliffe's lead in using their position to influence those in power. Rothermere was shameless in his attempts. One early instance occurred in 1922. Three years earlier, his son Esmond Harmsworth had been elected to a Conservative seat in Parliament at the age of nineteen. He was the youngest member of the House of Commons, known as 'the baby of the House'. Rothermere told Andrew Bonar Law that the support of his news-papers would be withheld unless Esmond was given a position in Cabinet – a threat ignored by the Prime Minister.[261]

Before the general election in 1929, Rothermere tried a similar trick. He refused to support Stanley Baldwin, the Conservative leader, unless Baldwin promised to provide him with the names of eight of the ten members of Cabinet he planned if elected. Baldwin replied: 'A more preposterous and insolent demand was never made on a leader of any political party. I repudiate it with contempt and I will fight that attempt at domination to the end.'[262]

At the start of the 1930s both Rothermere and Beaverbrook were passionate believers that the British Empire should form a free trade area and impose high tariffs on imports from elsewhere. This put them in conflict with Prime Minister Ramsay MacDonald, who had formed a minority Labour government after the 1929 election, and Baldwin, who favoured more protectionism. In 1930, Rothermere allied his United Empire Party with Beaverbrook's Empire Free Trade Crusade and the two parties agreed to fight by-elections together on the issue.

This incensed Baldwin further. On 17 March 1931 he delivered his famous tirade against the press barons at the Queens Hall in London. 'Their newspapers are not newspapers in the ordinary acceptance of the term, they are engines of propaganda for the constantly changing policies, desires, personal wishes, personal likes and personal dislikes of two men,' he thundered in a speech partly written by his cousin Rudyard Kipling. 'What the proprietorship of these papers is aiming at is power, but power without responsibility, the prerogative of the harlot throughout the ages.'[263]

Even so unruffled a figure as Clement Attlee later called Beaverbook 'the only evil man I ever met'.[264] The reason these proprietors so infuriated politicians was the power they wielded. Though unelected, they could influence events greatly in Britain, which seemed to undermine the principle of its centuries-old parliamentary democracy. It was not just Rothermere and Beaverbrook – the power of the press in 1930s Britain was amply demonstrated when the major newspaper proprietors conspired to suppress news of the controversy surrounding King Edward VIII and Wallis Simpson in 1936. On that occasion, the politicians were delighted to be assisted by the pressmen. Media outlets in America and the rest of the world were reporting on the scandal engulfing Edward, who wished to marry the divorced American socialite, for months before the British press. Owners of newspapers clubbed together with Prime Minister Baldwin and other high-ranking members of the government to ensure that not a word about the growing controversy was reported. Incredibly, it worked, and when newspapers finally reported news of the crisis in December 1936, it was to the shock of virtually the entire nation.

Hitler's rise to the chancellorship in Germany was greeted with predictable delight by Rothermere. He had courted the German leader since his election breakthrough in 1930 – and now his support would continue. In July 1933, on one of the many trips he made to 'Naziland' to witness events first-hand, he wrote an editorial headlined 'Youth Triumphant'. After declaring fascist Italy to be the best-governed country in Europe he said he was confident of seeing similar results achieved by Hitler. 'There has been a sudden expansion of their national spirit like that which took place under Queen Elizabeth. Youth has taken command,' he wrote admiringly.[265]

In 1933, Rothermere met Hitler for the first time, in an introduction brokered by the mysterious Princess Stephanie Hohenlohe, an Austrian princess and suspected German spy. The pair struck up a friendship and Rothermere would visit Hitler at Berchtesgaden three times later in the decade. On 7 December 1933 the enamoured press baron received a letter from the dictator, who thanked him for supporting Germany in withdrawing from the League of Nations just weeks before. 'A policy that we all hope will contribute to the enduring pacification of Europe,' Hitler wrote.[266] The strengthening friendship between the pair coloured the *Daily Mail*'s coverage of Germany during the first half of the decade. Compared to Rothermere, Beaverbrook interfered less in matters of foreign affairs in the early 1930s. He invested in a network of foreign correspondents and strongly backed them. Only towards the end of the 1930s did he interfere significantly in *Daily Express* coverage of Germany.

There were differences in how the other major newspapers were owned and managed. The influential Astor family had controlling interests in both *The Times* and *Observer* and in 1933 both newspapers had long-standing editors who reigned supreme. Establishment man Geoffrey Dawson, whose love for his home county Yorkshire was second only to his love for the British Empire, started his second spell as *Times* editor in 1923, while the irascible James Garvin had edited *The Observer* since 1908. Both were larger-than-life figures whose presence was felt on every page of their newspapers. While disputes over foreign reporting at other papers were more likely to arise between staff and ownership, at these two it was more likely to be between editor and staff.

The *Daily Telegraph* was owned by a peer, Lord Camrose, who was generally unlikely to interfere. His paper stood out from *The Observer* and *Times* in the 1930s by having editors who were much more averse to interfering with the work of its correspondents. Lord Kemsley, who owned the *Sunday Times*, occupied the other end of the scale. He took an increasingly active interest in Britain's relationship with Germany as the decade progressed and this approach did not leave the newspaper's content untouched.

The *Manchester Guardian* was unique. It had been transformed into an influential liberal newspaper during the 57-year editorship of C. P. Scott, who died in 1932. After this his sons devised the Scott Trust, which was intended to provide a sound long-term financial footing and free the paper from the whims of a proprietor. The trust began in 1936. The most influential leading figure at this time was William Crozier, who took over as editor in 1932. He mainly backed his foreign correspondents, though there were conflicts over some of the paper's reporting and its positions on several issues as the 1930s went on.

The Labour Party-supporting *Daily Herald* had been majority-owned by Odhams Press since the start of the 1930s, with the Trade Unions Congress retaining a substantial minority stake. There were disputes at the paper, which boasted a high circulation, over how closely their policy positions should mirror those of Labour. Towards the end of the decade, Odhams owner Lord Southwood would be one of the press barons the government tried to influence when it came to the reporting of Anglo-German relations. This caused consternation among staff.

The *News Chronicle* was a liberal newspaper owned by a pair of Conservative-minded peers, the Cadbury brothers. Sir Walter Layton ran the newspaper on their behalf and there would be tension over Germany between these three men and the paper's editor, Gerald Barry, and his loyal staff.

The correspondents at the Taverne often discussed how their newspapers were owned and managed back in London. They were well aware that prejudices at home may colour their work. Bartlett touched on some of the contradictions in his book about Germany in 1933. 'Papers,' he said, not mentioning the *Daily Mail* by name, 'which were most bitter against Germany at the Peace Conference are the only ones which sing praises of the Storm Troops.'[267] Editors and proprietors would support and aggravate their reporters in Berlin in equal measure for the rest of the 1930s.

As 1933 progressed the international furore surrounding the German boycott of Jewish goods faded a little. *The Times* was representative of mainstream British opinion with an article in September, penned by Ebbutt, which asserted that much of the 'shouting and exaggeration' in Germany was just 'sheer revolutionary exuberance'. Germans who had 'felt themselves to be the only true patriots are enjoying the sounds of their own unrestrained voices'.[268]

Many in Britain wanted to see if Hitler could succeed in turning around

Germany's economy and curing unemployment. The clampdown on Jews was ugly, but if Hitler could provide a stable government and restore Germany's confidence, they thought maybe it would be justified to turn a blind eye. Levels of anti-Semitism in Britain were lower than in Germany, but disdain for Jews was still far from uncommon. This limited the general sympathy felt for their plight, especially as few could envisage the depravity of Hitler's future actions against the Jewish population. Those who held serious concerns were invariably the same people who had taken the effort to read *Mein Kampf*.

A potential turning point for British policy towards Germany came in October 1933, when the German delegation walked out of the Disarmament Conference. This aggressive act defied international attempts at mutual understanding and reconciliation. It was one of the first reliable indicators, since Hitler had taken power, of the brazen, uncooperative and erratic path he would pursue in foreign affairs. At just the moment politicians in Britain could have chosen to unite against Hitler, they were distracted by electoral concerns. The death of the Conservative MP for Fulham East forced a by-election. The timing meant that rearmament would be a key issue for voters. The Conservative leader, Stanley Baldwin, did not mention it in his electoral message, but Labour claimed the Tories wanted war. Ramsay MacDonald had been disowned by Labour, meaning his National Government was reliant upon the support of Conservative MPs for its parliamentary majority. The Conservatives were vulnerable to attacks. Labour campaigned on the basis that a vote for its candidate was a vote for peace. It became an election about war and defence and Labour's campaign triumphed, overturning the Conservatives' huge majority.

It was an eye-opening moment for Baldwin, who served in MacDonald's government. In a meeting with the Foreign Office's Lord Vansittart he admitted it would be electoral suicide to campaign on rearmament and risk being seen as wanting war. 'Look at these East Fulham results,' he groaned.[269] In the months that followed, ministers handled the rearmament issue gingerly, in Vansittart's opinion, and were frightened of a voter backlash on the issue.

While politicians in Britain vacillated, foreign correspondents in Germany were confronted with the clearest evidence yet of their hazardous predicament. Noel Panter was the *Daily Telegraph*'s man in Munich. Just thirty-one years old, he had quickly developed a reputation as an informed and intelligent reporter respected by others in the British press pack. In October he attended a march of 20,000 storm troopers in Munich, an event infused with militaristic fervour. He described it for *Telegraph* readers in these terms, despite an instruction from the German authorities that any military comparisons were to be avoided in reports.

Panter was arrested on 24 October, after which his flat was raided and his personal papers confiscated. He was held for more than a week, despite growing calls for his release by the British media and government. The Nazis were initially resistant to all diplomatic approaches, so great was their anger at his report. Rivals in the press lauded his bravery in daring to tell the truth about Nazi Germany. The report he wrote was 'a faithful and admirably written account of a very remarkable event,' wrote A. J. Cummings in the *News Chronicle*. 'The arrest of Mr Panter suggests a new development. It suggests that foreign journalists are to be subject to the same censorship and to the same penalties as the German press.'[270]

After more than a week in prison Panter was released and expelled from Germany. He was the first British journalist to be thrown out by the Nazis, and he crossed the border into Switzerland with huge relief on 3 November. 'I can hardly hope to convey to those who have not experienced it what it means to me in Switzerland tonight to be free from the eternal clicking of heels, fascist salutes and "Hail Hitlers" of Munich,' he informed *Telegraph* readers the next day.[271]

Panter's expulsion drew a flurry of comment and criticism in Britain but no wholesale change in approach. Germany continued on its aggressive path, leaving the League of Nations in December 1933. That month, Hitler greeted British enquiries about his storm trooper forces with a glibness that would become standard. 'Hitler assured me that the S. A. and S. S. might be compared to the Salvation Army,' said Sir Eric Phipps, the new British ambassador in Berlin. 'Here I regret to say I laughed.'[272]

Frederick Voigt of the *Guardian* ended the year in a gloomy mood. 'Grey depression, grey as the London fog,' he wrote in his diary in December. 'A whole world foundering before the onslaught of Hitler. Where there is understanding there is no will; where there is will, there is no understanding.'[273]

-CHAPTER IX-

'HURRAH FOR THE BLACKSHIRTS!'

Sefton Delmer's departure from Berlin for Paris in 1933 left a large hole in the *Daily Express*'s coverage of Germany. But the vacancy also represented a significant opportunity. Delmer's reports from inside Nazi circles had established his reputation as one of the better-known foreign correspondents – and he soon developed an ego to match – but had drawn criticism too. The wider press pack thought he was too close to the Nazis. Even if he did not support Hitler, rivals felt he was too quick to relish his meteoric success and the opportunities it afforded him as a journalist.

His replacement in Berlin was an Englishman named Philip Pembroke Stephens. Born in 1903, making him a year older than Delmer, he had reported from Paris and Vienna before being sent to Berlin. He trod a different path from his predecessor in Germany. While many other reporters in Germany became distracted and did not focus on the long-term consequences of the Jewish Boycott, Stephens made it a priority. He travelled widely in Germany and reported on events first-hand rather than relying on reports, which became increasingly unreliable as Hitler's grip on power tightened.

Stephens filed reports from cities including Hamburg, where he witnessed the consequences of the international boycott of German goods. The boycott had been designed to force Hitler to end his anti-Semitism by the use of economic pressure. Jews outside Germany would boycott German-made goods for as long as Hitler's regime continued to boycott Jewish-made goods. 'No town has suffered more from Hitler than this once wealthy city of commerce,' he wrote in one dispatch in May 1934. He was clear that Hitler, and not the international community, was to blame for the situation – which did not please the Nazis.[274] It was obvious where his sympathies lay.

The report from Hamburg earned Stephens a short stay with the Gestapo, who arrested him shortly after its publication. It did not intimidate him, however, and in the following days he sent dispatches with headlines including: 'Germany Pleads Poverty While Trade Booms' and 'Germany Dodging State Loan Obligations'. On 25 May he wrote a long article revealing just how dark life had become for Jews in Germany. Under the headline 'New Hitler Blow at the Jews', he described in grim detail the conditions facing Jews living in Arnswalde, a small German town that is now part of Poland. 'Unaffected by his arrest and imprisonment last week by the German secret police, [he] sends another vivid dispatch,' the *Express* wrote in an introduction to the front-page article.

'I have spent the past few days visiting districts where the Jews are reported to be suffering most keenly,' Stephens wrote. The tales he heard were bleak. 'Jew baiting has been brought to a fine art and cafés carry the slogan, "No Jews allowed here."' He reported that Jews in Bavaria were no longer allowed to use the public swimming baths and that synagogues and Jewish cemeteries had been attacked. German Jews, he wrote, are 'friendless, persecuted and told by Nazi officials "the best thing you can do is to die"'.[275]

Days after this article was published, Stephens was again arrested by the Gestapo. This time there would be no second chance. The Nazis charged him with 'Abuse of Hospitality' and he was given twenty-four hours to leave the country. When he was arrested, the police would not tell his wife where he was being taken. In a statement explaining his detention the Nazi authorities blamed 'constant misrepresentation of the peaceful efforts of the German government and frivolous and distorted reports'.[276]

The next day Stephens crossed the frontier to Belgium and rang the office in London to pass on a report describing his expulsion that made the front page of Saturday's *Daily Express*. 'I was locked up like a beast in a cage behind high wire netting. I was not allowed to telephone my wife,' he said. He had witnessed horrific sights during his short stay at a prison in Berlin. 'Grim photographs of murdered men with blood-stained faces distorted in death grinned at me from the walls.' It was a clumsy attempt to intimidate and threaten the reporter before he left, perhaps in the hope that it would dissuade him from writing about his expulsion.

It did no such thing. 'It is impossible to tell the truth, the real truth about Germany, and remain an accredited correspondent in Berlin,' he wrote. 'The life of a foreign correspondent these days is one long, uncomfortable thrill.'[277] Two days later he wrote another article questioning why he had been expelled. It would have made uncomfortable reading for the Nazis. 'Was it because I exposed the extent of German rearmament? Was it because I told the truth about Germany's financial condition? Was it on account of my article on the German Jews?'[278]

Stephens was the second British correspondent to be expelled from Germany, following Noel Panter. The intrepid reporter did not remain in Britain for long. Lord Beaverbrook valued Stephens highly after his expulsion, which set the tone for the *Daily Express*'s critical reporting on Nazi Germany during the middle part of the decade. He reported on many other major foreign events before dying in 1937 after being caught in crossfire while reporting on the Japanese invasion of China. He was not yet forty. Pembroke Stephens was one of 'the heroes of British journalism in the 1930s', according to John Simpson. 'It took courage to write openly about the behaviour of the Nazis in the streets. Most of the foreign correspondents in Berlin chose to ignore this as much as possible, and concentrated instead on the safe business of reporting political and diplomatic issues. Stephens was not that kind of journalist.'[279]

The reporting of the brave and perceptive Stephens stands out in this period because few other major newspapers in Britain were reporting so critically on the Nazis. There was certainly scant chance of articles of the type penned by Stephens making their way into Lord Rothermere's *Daily Mail*. While John Segrue provided some piercing reports on Jewish treatment for the *News Chronicle*, the *Manchester Guardian* was the main exception. Its robust reports on life inside Nazi Germany were commendable but not without risk: in the early years of Hitler's rule, the role of *Guardian* correspondent in Berlin was widely perceived to be the most dangerous and precarious journalism job in Europe.[280]

Midway through January 1934, and shortly before Hitler celebrated his first anniversary in power, Rothermere published his most bullish article to date on the fascist movement. His support for Mussolini and Hitler had led him to support a politician who was attempting to replicate their success in Britain. Oswald Mosley was a restless, aristocratic young man who had become disillusioned with mainstream parties in the 1920s. He had been an MP for both the Conservatives and Labour, but sought more radical solutions to the country's economic problems and set up the New Party in 1931. Rothermere was a fervent supporter of Mosley and that year offered to place the whole of his family's press at his disposal.[281] The pair had much in common. During a trip to Italy, Mosley came to admire the dictatorial rule of Mussolini. He fervently believed that strong and ruth-less action was required by modern politicians and the sleepy democracies that remained were not up to the job. Inspired by Mussolini, in 1932 he ditched the New Party for a new nationalist movement, the British Union of Fascists, founded on the model of Mussolini's Blackshirts.

The British Union of Fascists' commitment to youth and a nationalist spirit, as well as its focus on rearmament, appealed greatly to Rothermere. He closely monitored the development of the emerging movement and lent it further support. The *Daily Mail*'s leading foreign correspondent, G. Ward Price, was a close friend of Mosley. He helped develop a plan that would see Mosley and Rothermere go into business together producing cigarettes.[282] Staff at the *Daily Mail* started wearing black shirts to work in solidarity with their leader. A series of supportive articles started appear-ing in the newspaper, which reached a fresh high with 'Hurrah for the Blackshirts!'.

It was strident stuff. 'To cope with the grim problems of the present day the energy and vigour of younger men are needed,' Rothermere wrote. He called for 'the gigantic revival of national strength and spirit which a similar process of modernisation has brought about in Italy and Germany. They are without doubt the best-governed nations in Europe today.' Air-defence warranted a mention, as it did in so many of Rothermere's articles. 'In the vital matter of air-defence [Britain] has been allowed to sink from the foremost to the lowest position among the Great Powers.' But the appeal of fascism was the main message of the article, which concluded with a direct call for members: 'Young men may join the British Union of Fascists by writing to the Headquarters, King's Road, Chelsea, London.'[283]

Rothermere, Price and Mosley were a bellicose trio, confident in the righteousness of their cause and backed up by the huge machinery of the *Mail*. Price was especially pleased by the triumvirate. A *Mail* man through and through, he loved the paper's staunchly right-wing stance and the opportunities it offered him to travel and report from all over the world in his role as special correspondent. Now he consolidated his position by bringing his friend Mosley and employer Rothermere together in friendship.

Price first met Rothermere after Lord Northcliffe's death in 1922. He quickly established the same kind of relationship as he'd had with his previous employer – one of obsequious respect. 'What made it so agreeable an experience to tour the world with Lord Rothermere was his unfailing high spirits,' Price wrote. 'Whether at his villa in the South of France or crossing to the States in a transatlantic liner or making long motor tours on the Continent or walking on the moors near one of his favourite houses in the north of Scotland, he was always the embodiment of good humour.'[284] Such fawning helped establish him as the *Mail*'s most important foreign correspondent of the 1930s.

The British Union of Fascists signed up more members after Rothermere's article, but there was a problem. Just as Hitler and Mussolini's movements had violent tendencies, it did not take long for the ugly side of their British equivalent to emerge and indeed dominate. The problem simmered for months before the aggressive attitudes and fighting instincts of many young British fascists spilled into the open at the Olympia Rally in London in June 1934. Left-wing anti-fascist groups congregating outside to protest against Mosley were attacked. 'For over an hour before the meeting the crowds jostling one another outside Olympia numbered several thousand,' the *Manchester Guardian* reported. 'There were catcalls and booing and cheering, and in a scuffle one could catch sight of a yelling demonstrator being dragged off by the police.'

Inside the hall Mosley had put on a show designed to compete with the theatricalism of Hitler and Mussolini. 'There was a massed band of

Blackshirts, there were flags, the Union Jack, and the black and yellow flag of the British Union of Fascists,' the *Guardian* reported. Mosley 'kept his audience waiting while the band played patriotic marches and other tunes devised for the British Fascists'. He then took to the stage. 'Some people – they did not seem to be many – raised their arms in a fascist salute and others with less commitment, cheered.'

But then the booing began. Chants and shrieks came from one of the galleries. 'Blackshirts began stumbling and leaping over chairs to get at the source of the noise,' the report described. 'There was a wild scrummage, women screamed, black-shirted arms rose and fell, blows were dealt.' A new chorus rang out clearly above the chaos: 'We want Mosley, We want Mosley.'[285]

This was too much for Rothermere. These dark scenes of violence, and the movement's anti-Semitism, meant his support soon evaporated. The violence of the night signalled that a blackshirts movement was not the remedy to Britain's problems. Indeed, it could make them worse. Izzard, by Reynolds's side in the Berlin office, received a telegram from the news editor in London. 'The blackshirts are in the wash and the colour is running very fast,' it read. The message was clear. 'What it meant to us in Berlin was we were no longer so friendly with the Nazis as we were before,' Izzard said.[286]

Such a conclusion was premature. If Reynolds and Izzard thought their boss's discomforting experience supporting the fascist movement in Britain would curtail the *Mail*'s pro-Nazi attitude, they were mistaken. Fascism in Britain may have been short-lived, but Rothermere's admiration for Hitler and what the Nazis were achieving in Germany had deeper roots. He despised communism and viewed the rise of fascism in continental Europe as an unpleasant but necessary counterweight to the menace he saw rising in the east. Communism in Britain was his greatest fear. Bizarrely, during the 1930s he bought acres of land in Hungary as insurance in case the communists overwhelmed Britain.

Lord Rothermere was far from alone in his early support for Hitler. Many other Britons also viewed him as a man of action and vigour who could solve Germany's economic problems. He capitalised on a feeling in the post-war years that France had been too harsh on Germany at Versailles and instigated an agreement that callously reduced its enemy's chance of ever recovering. While the awkward French were blamed for the troublesome Treaty of Versailles, which was viewed less favourably with every passing year, the untrustworthy communists leading Russia were viewed as a threat to be kept under control. These prejudices created an environment that made it easier to support Hitler. He had not hidden his extreme views, but for many these were not considered a sufficient basis to oppose him.

In the first half of 1934 the grim reality of his situation was clearer than ever to Reynolds. Though the fascist movement in Britain would not last, Lord Rothermere had expressed his views plainly with his 'Hurrah for the Blackshirts!' article. Reynolds tried to report with balance on the Nazi regime, which was starting to demonstrate its brutal nature. But his press baron employer was utterly blind to its awful reality.

Fewer articles carrying Reynolds's byline appeared in the paper, the start of a sidelining process that continued for the rest of the 1930s. Other correspondents became more prominent in the reporting of German affairs as Rothermere seemingly lost confidence in the man his brother had sent to Berlin in 1921. The *Daily Mail* had little interest in the issues Reynolds was passionate about – most notably the growing Nazi pressure on the Christian churches in Germany, which rivals such as Norman Ebbutt of *The Times* reported in full.

Reynolds read the Italy-based publication *L'Osservatore Romano* to keep informed about the increasing religious persecution. 'The fact that I

- 'HURRAH FOR THE BLACKSHIRTS!'-

had to resort to an Italian newspaper to find out things that were happening in Germany shows sufficiently clearly the difficult situation in which the representatives of foreign newspapers found themselves in Berlin.'[287] Those in the church feared the consequences of talking to journalists, even those as supportive as Reynolds. One morning he was told that a German bishop in Berlin had been particularly critical of the Nazis in a sermon. Reynolds rang the church for a copy of the sermon, but was disappointed. 'It would do us great harm if it was discovered that we had given it to a representative of the foreign press,' he was told.[288]

Even if Reynolds had been able to file an article on the sermon to the *Mail* there is no guarantee it would have been published. He once described his job as 'to send my paper reports – which might or might not be printed'. As the 1930s wore on Reynolds became increasingly used to the latter. Other difficulties pressed as conditions for foreign correspondents in Germany worsened. 'When freedom went, life changed,' Reynolds observed. 'It was full of barriers, hindrances, inhibitions.' A colleague from the *Mail*'s London office visited him and remarked: 'It seems to me that what a foreign newspaper needs in Berlin is not a journalist, but a detective.'[289]

This was especially true midway through 1934 when Hitler achieved another milestone in his capture of total power in Germany. The brownshirted storm troopers led by former army officer Ernst Röhm had become a problem for the Nazis. Röhm had supported Hitler from the start and participated in the Munich Putsch of 1923. He had been appointed to lead the *Sturmabteilung* force in 1930 and the storm troopers had been an important part of the Nazi rise to power. But he over-played his hand, arguing that his storm troopers should take precedence over the German army. Hitler began to see the force, whose love of street violence had become almost embarrassing, as a threat. Hermann Göring and Heinrich Himmler,

Röhm's rivals at Hitler's immediate side, urged the Führer to remind him of his station.

Hitler went further than that. Even the cold-blooded duo of Göring and Himmler were shocked by the action taken by Hitler at the end of June. During the Night of the Long Knives he had Röhm and scores of other former supporters murdered in extra-judicial killings. Former Chancellor Kurt von Schleicher and his wife were murdered, while Franz von Papen was arrested. Hitler's personal involvement in the killing of Röhm was particularly shocking. He turned up at his hotel in Munich and passed him on to members of Himmler's SS, who killed him.

Reynolds and Harold Cardozo reported on the events for *Daily Mail* readers in a series of co-written reports beginning on 2 July. 'Herr Adolf Hitler, the German Chancellor, has saved his country,' read the first line of the first article. It set the tone, dismissing any notion that Rothermere's paper had become more critical of the Nazis. 'Swiftly and with inexorable severity [Hitler] has delivered Germany from men who had become a danger to the unity of the German people and to order in the state. With lightening [*sic*] rapidity he has caused them to be removed from high office, to be arrested, and put to death,' the report said.[290]

The events were described in blunt detail. Hitler 'roused the ringleader, Captain Röhm, Chief of Staff of the Brown Army and Reich Minister without portfolio, from sleep and caused him and his fellow conspirators to be arrested,' read the report. 'Röhm was put in a prison cell and a loaded revolver placed at his side. Whether from religious convictions or a hope that he might be reprieved at the last moment, he refused to take his life and was shot today.'

'"Clean-up" Completed' was the headline to the report by Reynolds and Cardozo the next day. They relayed the latest official Nazi statement: 'The task of cleaning up came to an end last evening and no further action

will be taken in this direction.'[291] Reynolds's reporting of the Night of the
Long Knives was a source of regret until the end of his life. He admitted to
accepting without challenge the official version of events, while the tone
of admiration in the report was no doubt inserted at Lord Rothermere's
behest in London. 'Reading over the dispatches that my colleague, Harold
Cardozo, who came from Paris to help, and I wrote at the time, I can see
how grossly we were deceived,' he later wrote. 'We were told, for instance,
that General von Schleicher, revolver in hand, had tried to resist arrest and
had therefore been shot down.' In fact, the former Chancellor and his wife
had been murdered in cold-blood.[292] Reynolds later concluded:

> The butchery of June 30, whether men were shot at their desks or
> shot after arrest, was murder. No enquiry was made as to the guilt of
> those who were slaughtered. They were not brought before a court
> of justice and were not allowed to defend themselves from the vague
> charge of conspiracy and treason brought against them.[293]

In the following days Reynolds was present inside the Kroll Opera House as
Hitler proclaimed himself the 'supreme court of the Reich'. Rows of men in
Nazi uniforms whooped, clapped and cheered their approval. Looking on,
Reynolds viewed the spectacle 'as the measure of Germany's degradation'.[294]

None of this went into the *Mail*. There was no room for such sentiment
in Rothermere's newspaper, which remained at this point a firm supporter
of Hitler's efforts to supposedly restore Germany to greatness. Reynolds
himself is not blameless. He accepted too easily the official Nazi line. He
later made his true feelings about Hitler's regime known, but kept quiet
at the time. It would have been a huge risk to voice his disdain publicly.
Not only would he have come up against Joseph Goebbels, the Reich's
Propaganda Minister, but also Rothermere in London. His livelihood

would have been at risk. In 1934 Reynolds turned sixty-two and was still enjoying life in Germany, despite the lengthening shadow extended by the Nazis. He had a wide circle of friends and was lecturing on subjects including the English monasteries at Berlin University. For a range of reasons, his and the *Mail*'s reporting fell short.

From the middle of 1934, Reynolds reported less and less on the main political events in Germany as G. Ward Price, the *Daily Mail*'s star foreign correspondent, took centre stage. Price was closely trusted by Rothermere despite their ill-fated flirtation with Mosley's fascist movement. His was usually the byline for the most momentous European events reported by the newspaper. From the middle of the 1930s he would often be the reporter who conducted interviews with Hitler, supplanting Reynolds despite the latter's position as Berlin bureau chief. In Nazi Germany, Price had the dubious honour of being the only foreign journalist trusted by Hitler. He was the only non-German who reported his words without prejudice, the dictator told Göring.

It was not an accolade in the eyes of his peers, who started to view Price as they had Delmer, but it helped him win access to the leadership. Price 'was welcomed to interviews in the Reich Chancellery in a more privileged way than all other foreign journalists,' the German historian Hans-Adolf Jacobsen wrote.[295] Yet that access bore a heavy price in terms of impartiality if you worked for the *Daily Mail*. Not only was Price beholden to Hitler for the interview rights he was granted, he was actively encouraged to pursue a pro-Nazi line by his employer in London. It was a cosy little set. Reynolds was not invited to Hitler's first major dinner party for foreigners in December 1934, but three of the guests of honour were Price, Lord Rothermere and his son Esmond Harmsworth (who within three years would be running the newspaper).[296]

Price got on better with Goebbels than other foreign correspondents at the time. 'He was by far the best orator of the Nazi Party and appealed with great success to the industrial classes of Berlin and the large towns,' Price wrote.[297] (He also noted that Goebbels was 'undersized, swarthy and notoriously lascivious'.) Good relations with the Nazi set and his newspaper's sympathetic reporting combined to help Price replace Delmer as the British reporter most trusted by the Nazis in the second half of the 1930s.

Like Delmer, Price was criticised after the war for being too soft on the Nazis in his reporting during this period. He strongly defended himself, saying he merely reported what the dictators Hitler and Mussolini had told him. 'This provided British newspaper readers with an opportunity to form their own estimate of the genuineness or falsehood of the declarations that they made,' Price wrote.[298] He admitted that he had greater access to the Hitler than other reporters. 'Since I reported his statements accurately, leaving British newspaper-readers to form their own opinion of their worth, I had many opportunities of observing him under different sets of circumstances,' he wrote. 'He appreciated having a foreign auditor for the long harangues in which he tried to justify himself and his policy.'

While the *Mail*'s reporting of the Night of the Long Knives was not a glorious moment for the newspaper, Delmer of the *Express* riled the Nazis with some commendably fearless journalism. The expulsion of Stephens, his successor in Berlin, had helped open his eyes to the ruthless nature of the Nazis and he was now more willing to stand up to the authorities in Germany. Following the events of 30 June, Hitler and the Propaganda Ministry had promised to publish a list of men killed in the purge. But a week later the list had not been published. Delmer chose to take the initiative. 'As Chancellor Hitler will not publish his list,' he wrote on the front page of the *Express* on 6 July, 'I have done my best to put together a provisional list of the dead. Forty-six men, it is already officially admitted, have been executed. But I am told that the true figure is now above 108.'[299]

The Nazis were incandescent at this. Two days after publication Delmer was issued with an expulsion order by the Gestapo. He defied the order and, with Beaverbrook's backing, told the Ministry of Propaganda he would be staying. He threatened to write more 'articles on everything I know about the purge' if he was forced to leave Germany. The British Embassy also made representations. It worked. German authorities chose not to enforce the order. Maybe Delmer's reputation as something of a friend to the Nazis had helped him – they may have regarded his report as an aberration rather than typical of the articles he wrote. But it was a brave correspondent who stood up to the Gestapo during those years, and Delmer deserves credit for his actions.

The *Daily Mail*'s sympathetic attitude towards Nazi Germany during the mid-1930s was shared by many in Britain. This culminated later in the decade when an influential group of aristocrats, politicians and media barons who congregated at Lady Nancy Astor's palatial country home became known as the pro-Nazi 'Cliveden Set'. But there were leading figures who took the opposite view. Banished from the front line of government, Winston Churchill was in the midst of his 'wilderness years' as Hitler's grip on power tightened. He was good friends with Rothermere, and the two were in total agreement on the importance of rearming and developing a strong air force in Britain. But Churchill mocked his friend for the *Daily Mail*'s friendship with Hitler.

During a lunch one day with Rothermere and Price, Churchill turned to Price and said he had been reading the *Mail*. 'I see that you've been over in Germany again, shaking the hands of your Nazi friends,' he said darkly – and only half in jest. Price fired back a churlish reply criticising

Churchill for how he had handled the Irish nationalists at the start of the 1920s, but the point was made.[300]

Churchill was close friends with Lord Vansittart, the hawkish Permanent Under-Secretary at the Foreign Office, and the two were fiercely distrustful of Hitler's intentions in Germany. Both men believed that Britain should be a stronger ally to France and Russia and not give way to Hitler. Vansittart struck up an unlikely close friendship with Russia's ambassador to Britain, Ivan Maisky, and the pair would often meet with Churchill.

Maisky was an easily recognisable figure in the gilded circles of London's diplomatic scene as a result of his beard, which though small and thin was highly unusual. As a member of the communist elite, he drew resentment from some in London society for the brutal way in which Russia's ruling family had been killed in 1918. Vansittart's indefatigable wife Sarita, who was at his side for countless official functions, gave Maisky short shrift when he compared the assassination to the deaths of Charles I in England and Louis XVI of France. 'But that was two centuries ago and more, and you killed the entire imperial family! Why,' she cried, 'you even killed their dog!'[301]

In 1934 Maisky and Churchill attended a dinner at Vansittart's grand home in Mayfair, during which Churchill summed up the basis of their agreement.

> I consider that the greater danger to the British Empire is Germany, and therefore now I am the enemy of Germany. At the same time I consider Hitler is making ready to expand not only against us but to the east, against you. Why should we not join forces to combat our common enemy?[302]

The British government did not see it this way and shied away from stronger ties with Russia throughout the 1930s.

Vansittart's attempts to foster closer ties with France met with a similar lack of success. He was acquiring a reputation for being a Francophile who detested the Germans. Even Stanley Baldwin remarked in private that Vansittart felt hatred towards Britain's First World War enemy. He was saying this in April 1934, a year before becoming Prime Minister. Baldwin was never a member of the 'Cliveden Set', which rose to prominence towards the end of the decade, but he shared their sense of inherent contempt for Vansittart's continuous warnings about Hitler and Germany. Vansittart was not put off and rightly believed he would be vindicated in the end.

'The foundation of Herr Hitler's faith is that man is a fighting animal,' Vansittart wrote in 1934. 'Pacifism is therefore the deadliest sin. Had the German race been united in time, Hitler argues, it would now be master of the globe.' Vansittart based his findings in part on an uncensored version of *Mein Kampf*, which had not been sanitised for English eyes. Few other leading politicians or civil servants went to such trouble, relying on the more palatable official translated version, and their perspectives were flawed as a result.[303]

As the sides in the British debate over Anglo-German relations took shape – a clash that would define the second half of the 1930s – Hitler moved to consolidate his power. The Night of the Long Knives had reined in the storm troopers and established his power over the army. On 2 August 1934 President Hindenburg died at his estate in East Prussia at the age of eighty-six. Just hours after his death, it was announced that Hitler would combine the roles of head of government and head of state and serve as Germany's Führer. He finally had the total power he craved.

-CHAPTER X-
A CONTESTED VOTE

The weeks leading up to the second anniversary of Hitler taking power in January 1935 were dominated by events in the coal-rich Saar region between Germany and France. Under the Treaty of Versailles, France was granted the right to exploit the German territory's resources as a reparation for the damage inflicted on its own coal-mines in the war. The Saar had been governed under a League of Nations mandate since the conflict, but this period was coming to an end. Voters were to be asked to determine their future in a plebiscite scheduled for 13 January. There were three options: for the region to remain independent under League of Nations authority, to return to being part of Germany, or to become part of France.

Reynolds and other reporters descended on the capital of the region, Saarbrücken, to report on the unfolding events. The vast majority of voters were German nationals and the result was widely expected to fall in Hitler's favour. But it was not that straightforward. 'Many of the Saarlanders, as many of the Austrians, are not very enthusiastic about accounts they hear of Nazi concentration camps, and the Saar has become one of the principal refuges for Jews, communists, socialists and others who do not like the atmosphere of Nazi Germany,' wrote the *News Chronicle*'s Vernon Bartlett.[304]

Banners adorned with Nazi swastikas dominate the front of the Berliner Dom ahead of a party rally. (PA-1456 Thomas Neumann, The National Archives of Norway)

There was huge international interest in the process, which was seen as a significant test of Nazi popularity at the ballot box. Tension increased as polling day neared, with violence breaking out between supporters of the German Front, which wanted the Saar to become part of Germany, and the United Front, which opposed Hitler. Impartial observers from other countries were enlisted to oversee the process and ensure voters were not intimidated, but there was controversy about their effectiveness. There was even conflict within the massed ranks of the press, with German reporters taking umbrage at the influx of foreign correspondents. When one of the Germans complained, a Dutch journalist sparked uproar by replying that Goebbels and his propaganda department needed only one press ticket between them.[305]

Ten days before the vote, Reynolds reported on growing conflict between rival groups. 'Political animosity is finding expression in increasing numbers of deeds of violence.' An array of weapons was used in a growing number of small-scale scuffles: 'Pistols, pitchforks, hammers, knuckledusters and steel rods.' Reynolds took a balanced view on competing claims. 'Accounts of such incidents are highly coloured by political feeling,' he wrote. 'There is no means of checking the accounts of disorders which pour in from both sides.' He expressed frustration with officials from the International Commission for failing to provide information. In particular he castigated their failure to comment on the injuries suffered by the founder of the Christian Miners' Trade Union.[306]

Reynolds remained even-handed two days later in reporting on the great demonstrations planned by both campaigns ahead of the plebiscite. He included an interesting detail about German Front supporters, who were under pressure to behave. 'The German Front has warned its supporters on no account to give the German greeting – which consists in raising the right arm and saying "Heil Hitler!" before voting.'[307] It is interesting to note that, early in 1935, the average reader in London was not assumed to know about the notorious Nazi salute.

Reynolds was as even-handed as he could be, given the ever-looming presence of Rothermere in London. Other reports provided a clearer picture of the reality on the ground. Supporters of Hitler and the Nazis were subject to some violence, but the intimidation and aggression they meted out to opponents was far greater than what they received. Among the British correspondents watching proceedings, Shiela Grant Duff's reports for *The Observer* were especially sharp and revealed clearly the difficult circumstances facing voters in the disputed territory.

'Jewish shopkeepers have been asked to hand over their voting cards to the *Deutsche Front* officials,' she reported on the day of the vote. 'Brutal attacks on supporters of the status quo continue in isolated places... As a newcomer enters a status quo eating house, frightened eyes turn inquisitively to the door.' She saw how much the election meant to the Nazis – it was ultimately a measure of Hitler's popularity. 'It is assumed by most people here that "love for Germany" will prove triumphant over "hatred for Hitler," which is the real issue in the Saar.' But she feared greatly for what would happen to the losing minority.[308]

Grant Duff was a remarkable woman, whose story deserves wider recognition. Her route into journalism was unique. She was brought up to regard war as the greatest evil, and became convinced while studying at Oxford that a second global conflict was inevitable. This was partly because of vivid dispatches from Berlin sent to her by a friend, Goronwy Rees, who was studying in Germany in the early 1930s:

> Here what seems a nightmare in London is the sober everyday reality: the betrayal and death of every human virtue; no mercy, no pity, no peace; neither humanity nor decency nor kindness: only madness, shouted everyday on the wireless and in the newspapers, spoken by ordinary people as if it were sober sanity: and sixty million people pleased and proud to be governed by a gang of murderous animals.[309]

Moved by such words, Grant Duff made a private commitment that she should pursue a career with one objective – to help prevent another war. At Oxford she sought the counsel of Professor Arnold Toynbee, who advised that the best way to stop war was to study the possible causes. 'The best way to do that was to work as the foreign correspondent of an influential newspaper,' he said.[310]

This advice took Grant Duff to the office of Geoffrey Dawson at *The Times*. She asked if the paper would employ her to work as an assistant in the Paris office. Dawson sent her to see a senior member of the foreign news department, Ralph Deakin, who explained that women were unable to work on the editorial side of newspapers as it would involve nightshifts alongside men. He riled her further by mentioning that if she happened to visit Paris she was welcome to send articles about fashion. She was incensed. 'To feel capable of stopping a world war and then to be asked to write fashion notes!' she wrote.[311]

Unbowed, Grant Duff travelled to Paris and tried to get a start in newspapers with the American press. She was introduced to Edgar Ansel Mowrer, the Pulitzer Prize-winning Paris correspondent of the *Chicago Daily News*. He was one of the earliest reporters to warn of the dangers posed by Germany's move towards extreme politics and had been forced out of the country by Goebbels soon after Hitler took power.

Mowrer took Grant Duff on as an unpaid assistant and in the months that followed gave her a dynamic introduction to the world of international journalism. He remorselessly poked fun at her English character and sensibilities. On one occasion he relished her shock when he told her that a lot of newspapers were in the pay of foreign powers. He said the French newspaper *Le Matin* was known as the Paris edition of Goebbels's *Angriff*. When she protested that nothing of the sort would ever happen in Britain, he recited a favourite rhyme.

> You cannot hope to bribe or twist
> The honest British journalist;
> But seeing what the man will do
> Unbribed, there's no occasion to.[312]

Her eyes were opened to the hypocrisy and fickle nature of some sections of the press. Mowrer also disabused her of notions picked up at Oxford that the French were the villains of the post-war period and Germany the victim of the Treaty of Versailles. 'Keep your eyes open and report what you see,' he advised her, 'and hope that the great democracies will wake up and realise what they have to deal with in Nazi Germany.'[313]

This advice stood her in good stead at the end of 1934, when *The Observer* found it did not have a correspondent to report on the historic events in the Saar. The connections Grant Duff had established in journalism helped her win the posting. She was consequently one of many reporters who congregated in the town of Saarbrücken at the end of December 1934 ahead of the vote. 'It was my first experience of the exciting and festive atmosphere which spreads over a town, and especially its main hotel where they drink and congregate, when it suddenly becomes the focus of top-ranking international journalists.'[314]

While reporting on events in the Saar, Frederick Voigt of the *Guardian* took Grant Duff under his wing. 'Patiently he talked to me and took me with him round the mining villages,' she wrote. 'He seemed to have contacts all over the Saar and to be known and trusted by simple people and by anti-Nazis who would have been afraid to talk to anyone else.' The two correspondents were shocked by the stories they came across. 'We heard at first hand about the sinister pressure and frightening intimidation which was being brought to bear on the local population. Every street, village and factory had its local [Nazi warden] spying on its inhabitants and whispering about the fate they could expect if they voted against the fatherland.'[315]

The international authorities were no help. Their failure to assist the local police in identifying trouble-makers and reluctance to deploy any military force to maintain order were roundly criticised by the non-German journalists. 'This sort of talk considerably annoyed the British authorities,' according to Grant Duff. 'For English journalists to hold such views was considered "disloyal," "unpatriotic," and "thoroughly objectionable." It was in His Majesty's officials abroad that one met the nearest approach to the attitudes of the *Deutsche Front*.' The British and American journalists argued fiercely for a greater peacekeeping force to ensure opponents of the Nazis were protected. All appeals on the issue were rejected. It was not just the Nazis who viewed the journalists present as nuisances – the senior British members of the international force seemed as keen as Hitler's supporters to complete the vote as soon as possible.

Snowfall overnight meant the Saar region resembled a German Christmas card on the day of the vote – a seemingly 'innocent, friendly, happy' scene, observed Grant Duff.[316] But the situation at polling booths was far from relaxed. 'Outside the polling stations stood not the cheerful, neutral faces of the British tommies "keeping the peace" but the stern faces of the local Nazis,' she reported.[317] In the end, nine-tenths of voters opted for the Saar to become part of Germany again. It was a huge win for Hitler, but hardly a fair victory. Grant Duff relayed to readers that it was not as clean and straightforward a triumph as the victors would have the world believe.

In the months and years that followed, Grant Duff remained a friend of the United Front supporters in the Saar who opposed Hitler, many of whom fled to France. 'That day the face of the Saar changed. A great plague of spiders – the dreadful Nazi swastikas – descended everywhere. Whole streets were filled with them. The green garlands which had hung so decorously amid the snow were suddenly replaced by these tawdry flags.'[318]

Reynolds returned to Saarbrücken two months after the vote to report on the region's formal handover from international authorities to the Nazis. His otherwise straight report veered from an independent line in a stirring second paragraph. 'For all Germans, whether they be Saarlanders or inhabitants of the most distant provinces, this reunion is the return of a child to the mother from whom it has been cruelly separated for fifteen years.'[319] In the same article he relayed local reports – officially denied – that Hitler himself would attend the handover ceremony. Of course, he was never going to miss the event and flew in, supposedly at the last minute; 'Herr Hitler's arrival came as a complete surprise to the Saar,' Reynolds reported the next day.[320] Hitler paraded around the town taking the Nazi salute from his gathered hordes of supporters.

Reynolds interviewed Hitler and reported his words to readers in Britain. 'This day should be a lesson to those who believe that they can rob a nation by terror or force of its character, who believe that they can tear out a piece of a nation and steal its soul,' the Nazi leader declared. 'Blood is stronger than any paper documents. By the plebiscite you have eased my task extremely, which is to make Germany happy.'[321]

The celebrations culminated in a large fireworks display and a torchlit procession led by the Nazi storm troopers. Grant Duff was present for Hitler's speech and the ceremony. As she noted down his words she was surrounded by storm troopers, who aggressively questioned her motives. Only after showing her British passport and press card, and receiving some assistance from a local policeman, did they leave her alone. The message was clear: the Nazis were in charge of the Saar region now.

In contrast to most of their correspondents in Berlin, British newspapers still did not view Hitler as a threat in 1935. Most took him at his word when he said he had peaceful intentions. After the Saar plebiscite, *The Times* printed an article penned by a pro-German friend of the editor Geoffrey Dawson. Hitler 'has said explicitly to me, as he has also said publicly, that what Germany wants is equality, not war; that she is prepared absolutely to renounce war,' it said.[322] His word was enough.

Hitler was emboldened by victory in the Saar. On 12 March he announced that Germany would be re-starting conscription in breach of the Treaty of Versailles. He also publicly announced plans for the country's rearmament, a process he had secretly worked on since taking power in 1933. These aggressive steps were accompanied by a peace offer that many publications in Britain were taken in by. They took the easy route of believing that Hitler had good intentions rather than opting to criticise him for his actions. Norman Ebbutt of *The Times* saw straight through Hitler's combination of sweet words and malicious deeds. He encouraged the other reporters in Berlin to scrutinise Hitler and watch him closely. 'Ebbutt keeps reminding me to be very sceptical,' William Shirer recorded in his diary.[323]

Ebbutt's paper was not as critical as he would have liked. A line in Ebbutt's report that focused on how the development breached conditions agreed at Versailles was cut from later editions. A *Times* editorial was cautious rather than condemnatory.[324] It was an early sign of a tension between the reporter and his paper that would grow with time.

France and Russia responded to Hitler's bullish moves by agreeing the Franco-Soviet Pact in May 1935. Meanwhile, Jews in Berlin continued to face greater hardships. 'Many Jews come to us these days for advice or help in getting to England or America, but unfortunately there is little we can do for them,' Shirer noted sadly in his diary.[325] Hitler's announcements about conscription and rearmament breathed fresh fire into the growing debate about Britain's military firepower. Churchill and Lord Vansittart were at the vanguard of a group of senior figures arguing that the country must rearm to counter any possible threat from Germany. Attempts at disarmament in Europe earlier in the 1930s had failed, they said, and Britain must be prepared for the worst.

The pair were joined by the unlikely figure of Lord Rothermere, who in spite of his warm relations with Hitler was one of those arguing loudest for quicker rearmament, particularly in the air. Rothermere had continued to use his newspaper to publicly support Hitler in Europe: Hitler and

Rothermere had been exchanging compliments since the start of the decade and met for the first time in 1933. The relationship had strengthened since then and not been harmed by Rothermere's decision to abandon the fascist movement in Britain.

What Hitler did not know, however, was that while Rothermere's *Daily Mail* was talking up the Nazis in public, in private its owner was issuing drastic warnings about the threat Germany may pose. He described the Nazi leadership as dangerous and ruthless oligarchs in a letter to Neville Chamberlain, Ramsay MacDonald's Chancellor of the Exchequer, in October 1934.[326] In a separate letter that year he wrote to Lady Vansittart to say that he was cultivating a friendship with Hitler that may prove useful if relations soured. He said he would be more than happy to act as a go-between in talks between Britain and Germany. His double-handed approach to Hitler – to offer him support in public while offering warnings in private to British politicians – was curious. It may have been sincere. But it was also a way of covering his back in case it transpired his Nazi friends harboured malicious intentions.

He was apparently sincere in his offers to help Britain's leaders deal with Hitler. He sent copies of his letter exchanges with Hitler to Lord Vansittart, which undoubtedly contributed to the senior diplomat's keenly held views about Hitler. He made repeated warnings to the top of government about the lack of defences he perceived in Britain. He feared the country was vulnerable, particularly in the air. Like his friend Churchill, Rothermere loved flying and had a daredevil attitude to the new technology. He flew more than senior politicians – Neville Chamberlain did not step into an aeroplane until 1939. It was more than a personal passion – during the middle of the 1930s, Rothermere fought a national campaign in his newspapers to try and make the government spend more on its emerging air force. He sent warnings to Ramsay MacDonald in 1934 about the strength of German airpower. Whether the Prime Minister, who had been the first Labour politician to hold the role, was inclined to accept help from the owner of the newspaper behind the forged Zinoviev letter in 1924 can only be guessed at.

In other quarters, opinion was similarly mixed about Rothermere's efforts. They doubted his motives in corresponding with Hitler, even if the letters were secretly passed on. King George V's reaction to Rothermere's exchange of letters over an Anglo-German understanding in 1935 was cold. He and his courtiers found it to be a 'great surprise' that Rothermere was engaging in correspondence with Hitler.

For Rothermere the matter of air power was an obsession bordering on neurosis. He sent letter after letter to the country's leading politicians, both before and after the Conservative Party's Stanley Baldwin had won power in November 1935, to emphasise German air superiority over Britain. Chamberlain's response to one letter in October 1934 was typical of a government mindset that failed to recognise the importance of air power and did not believe the rumours about how quickly Germany was rearming. 'Aeroplanes at present do not bring us food or raw materials, and we must protect the trade routes,' he wrote. 'Armies are still necessary, if only to ensure us suitable locations for Air Forces.'[327]

On this, however, Rothermere was right. And some took notice of what he had to say. One of the most important people to listen to Rothermere was Churchill – yet he was in no position to directly affect the situation. This changed as the 1930s progressed and Churchill was able to draw on a wide range of informers to form a full picture of German rearmament. He became more influential as he was able to oppose the government's foreign policy on an informed basis. But even he was at times exasperated by Rothermere's dual approach to Hitler. 'I was disgusted to see the *Daily Mail*'s boosting of Hitler,' Churchill wrote to his wife, Clementine, later in the 1930s. Rothermere 'wants us to be very strongly armed and frightfully obsequious at the same time. Thus he hopes to avoid seeing another war. Anyhow, it is a more practical attitude than our socialist politicians. They wish us to remain disarmed and exceedingly abusive.'[328]

The more 'establishment' figures in government viewed the pair as irresponsible, trouble-making outsiders. A letter in 1935 from Lord Londonderry, the Secretary of State for Air, thanking Churchill and Rothermere for raising awareness about Britain's weakness in the air, rang hollow. 'Success was due to your being able to frighten the people of the country by giving them wholly exaggerated figures.'[329]

Rothermere did at least back his private pleas to government with some action. In 1935 he started the National League of Airmen, which aimed to increase air force strength, and made donations to the RAF. In 1936, the *Daily Mail* started a campaign – 'Arming in the Air' – which highlighted the newspaper's 'Warnings of Three Wasted Years' and argued for a larger air force. He then funded the development of a new breed of warplane, which he donated to the RAF – and which became the Blenheim Bomber.

'He combined awareness of the danger to Britain implicit in German rearmament with a belief that a rearmed Britain could be firm friends with a rearmed Germany,' concluded one writer in the *Sunday Times*. 'He saw Hitler as a sincere man who had defeated communism in his own country and whose programme was now to reverse the *Diktat* of Versailles.'[330]

Rothermere's balancing of support for Hitler in public with warnings in private set the tone for attitudes taken by newspapers throughout the 1930s. As we will see, others on the right, most notably *The Times*, were criticised for their pro-German reporting, yet argued for rearming far more than papers on the left, including the *Guardian*, even though that newspaper was much more vocal in its criticism of Hitler.

-CHAPTER XI-

RHINELAND

The Nazis celebrated their third anniversary of taking power in January 1936. They had achieved much in the first three years, consolidating their control over Germany and making territorial gains in the Saar. The *Daily Mail* greeted this landmark with more enthusiasm than other major British newspapers. 'The enemies who so persistently predicted [Hitler's] early fall have had to confess their complete want of foresight,' it said in a leading article. 'At the end of three years of power he is stronger than ever and more popular with his countrymen.'[331]

Ebbutt in *The Times* marked the anniversary with less fanfare. 'That three years of contact with hard realities have brought a certain amount of disillusionment to the party and to the country at large is not to be denied,' he wrote in a long article about Germany. 'Not everyone is so confident as the Storm Troopers who marched through the streets singing.'[332] Ebbutt's article reflected how he and the correspondents in Berlin were feeling. The mood was despondent. In February Ebbutt made his feelings clear to the American ambassador in Berlin, William Dodd. 'I only wish I could leave this country. Everything here is in such a condition and all of us newspaper people kept in such a state of mind that life is miserable.'[333]

Working under the constraints imposed by Goebbels's Propaganda

Ministry was taking its toll. The Nazi propagandist tried to keep foreign correspondents in as much darkness about what was going on in Germany as the wider population. In January, Shirer noted details in his diary about Goebbels's secret daily orders to the press. 'They made rich reading, ordering daily suppression of the truth,' he wrote. 'The German people, unless they can read foreign newspapers (the London *Times* has an immense circulation here now), are terribly cut off from events in the outside world and of course are told nothing of what is happening behind the scenes in their own country.'[334]

In February, Germany was scheduled to host the Winter Olympics in Bavaria and the Nazi regime started the year keen to show its best side to the world. 'The Nazis at Garmisch had pulled down all the signs saying that Jews were unwanted (they're all over Germany),' Shirer wrote in his diary. 'The Olympic visitors would thus be spared any signs of the kind of treatment meted out to the Jews in this country.'[335]

The newly built Messe Berlin exhibition hall, which hosted Olympic events in 1936, pictured a year later. (PA-1456 Thomas Neumann, The National Archives of Norway)

The *Manchester Guardian*'s Frederick Voigt was by this time the paper's diplomatic correspondent in London. This was a roving role that involved reporting and commentating on foreign affairs generally, but he continued to take a special interest in Germany. In the opening months of 1936, his coverage of events in the country was superior to reports sent by British journalists based in Berlin, who knew that over-critical reports would result in their expulsion. Voigt was nonetheless brave to continue his investigative work relating to Germany – the Gestapo had long before marked his card and there had been fears for his safety even when he was based beyond German borders in Paris.

'You are the channel through which practically all the damning exposures of what goes on in Germany gets into the paper,' his editor William Crozier wrote to him in January 1934. 'It must long ago have occurred to these people ... that if they could get rid of you they would stop off the supply of damning stuff to the [*Manchester Guardian*]. I hope, therefore, that you will distrust everybody and everything, and take great care not to be alone in lonely places.'[336]

Voigt had been born the son of a German wine merchant in Hampstead in 1892 and joined the *Guardian* in 1919. A year later he was despatched to Germany and spent the 1920s reporting on the rise and fall of the Weimar Republic. He had been deeply suspicious of Hitler from 1930 onwards and did his best to warn readers in Britain with sharp accounts of the Jewish Boycott and intimidation in the Saar. In February 1936 he wrote more articles of the kind that made Crozier fear for his safety. Under the headline of 'The "Opposition" in Germany', he reported on the dangers facing Hitler's political opponents:

> Their existence is one of extreme peril, of nervous tension, and drab
> poverty. Their self-set task is to create centres of action and resistance

for the day when general discontent shall take political form in Germany. They are a kind of 'Iron Guard' that is preparing to lead the revolt against one of the worst tyrannies of modern times. To be an active member of this 'opposition' is more dangerous than it was to be in the trenches. The casualties are very high; and, whereas a man who was wounded in the trenches would frequently be in kind hands, whether of friend or of foe, German political prisoners are often deliberately injured after capture by their foes.[337]

The vivid report ended with a swipe towards the reporters who chose to focus on the economic achievements of the Nazis. After referencing an unfair trial staged by Hitler's regime, Voigt concluded: 'It is such trials rather than the speeches of Herr Hitler, the new buildings, the motor roads, and the unemployment figures that tell the truth about the Third Reich.' He followed this report eleven days later with one which maddened the Nazis further, headlined 'How the "Gestapo" Works'. This was the first detailed account of Hitler's barbaric secret police force to be published. He describes its leader Heinrich Himmler as 'a man of great charm, an able organiser, and completely ruthless', and says the Gestapo is 'now one of the most efficient instruments of tyrannical power in the world'.[338] The piece describes how the Gestapo's organisational structure allows it to monitor the German population for signs of disobedience or disloyalty. It went beyond anything published in other papers at the time.

Voigt's elevation to diplomatic correspondent had been one of Crozier's first acts after assuming the editorship two years earlier. 'I think we can do with a little more of the spirit of Milton and Cromwell in respect of German topics,' Crozier had written to Voigt. 'As you and I think, I believe, pretty well on common lines as to what we could do and the duty of the *Guardian* to do it, I am looking forward to some interesting cooperation.'[339]

The pair shared a good working understanding on most topics, though an awkward fissure developed over German rearmament during the 1930s. Voigt was frequently nudging his editor on the issue and wanted the *Guardian* to take a firmer line in support of British rearmament. 'If we were not rearming, Germany would certainly prepare to attack France, leaving her Eastern plans until later on. If war is averted at all, it will be British rearmament that will have done it,' Voigt wrote to Crozier in February 1936.[340]

Voigt was a rare voice on the left wing of the newspaper industry in arguing for more rearmament. Together with the *News Chronicle* and *Daily Herald*, the *Guardian* was one of the newspapers most openly critical of Hitler and the Nazis in the 1930s. Yet these prescient warnings were not accompanied by calls for greater British rearmament until much later in the decade. It fell to papers on the other side of the political spectrum to make the case for rearmament. The right-wing *Morning Post* newspaper led the way. As early as January 1936, the paper began a defence campaign with a leading article on 'what the country is not told'.[341] Its reporter in Berlin, Karl Robson, had been clear about the possible long-term threat posed by Hitler, and his paper had strongly and clearly relayed the message. *The Times*, *Telegraph*, *Daily Express* and *Daily Mail* were the other right-wing newspapers calling for more rearmament in 1936.

On Saturday 7 March 1936 the *Daily Mail* started a competition: a 'money-prize contest' for ideas from readers on how the country could increase its number of military volunteers.[342] The timing of such discussion about defence was uncanny, for it coincided with an event that prompted European countries to dramatically reconsider their state of arms. On that Saturday, Hitler ordered his troops to march into the Rhineland territory between France and Germany in a clear breach of the terms of the Treaty of Versailles. The industrial region had been demilitarised since 1930, when international forces stationed there since the war had departed. But Germany was required by Versailles to keep military forces out of the region, which was similarly rich in resources to the Saar – but much bigger. This was Hitler's most brazen act of international defiance so far.

On the day of the invasion, politicians and diplomats in Britain scrambled to get information about German intentions. Would Hitler follow his move into the Rhineland with other territorial claims? Only one British man successfully got hold of Hitler in the immediate aftermath of the Rhineland invasion – and he was a journalist. When news of the troop movements broke in London, Price of the *Daily Mail* headed straight for the airport and took the first available plane to Berlin. In the evening he spent an hour with Göring and Hitler, who repeated their familiar arguments about the supposedly unfair terms agreed at Versailles. They claimed their country had a historic right to remilitarise the Rhineland. As ever, they sugared the pill of their aggression with an olive branch. Hitler offered to return Germany to the League of Nations. He also said he would sign a non-aggression pact with France and a separate air pact outlawing the use of bombs during war. Price returned to London the next day and briefed Lord Halifax personally, acting as an intermediary between the Nazis and the British government. He had better access than any other Briton in Berlin, even Ambassador Phipps. 'Hitler won't see *me*,' Phipps said to Price indignantly on one occasion.[343]

The timing of Hitler's 'Saturday surprise' in the Rhineland meant Britain's daily newspapers had more than a day to decide how to report on events. By the time readers picked up their papers on Monday, the initial shock of Hitler's action had subsided. Though some judged his actions harshly, many newspapers were satisfied that Hitler's subsequent words were proof that he and Germany wanted reconciliation, not war. The arch-appeaser Lord Lothian summed up the feelings of many Britons when he likened the action to Germany walking into its own back garden.

Hitler would have been gleeful at the *Daily Mail*'s verdict. 'Germany's latest stroke may be said, indeed, to have cleared the air. Like a fresh breeze from the mountaintops it has swept away the fog and shown exactly where she stands,' it said in an editorial on 9 March. 'This is a moment when it is most important to be aware of the Bolshevik trouble-makers.'[344] Almost all papers agreed that Hitler's offer of peace talks should not be ignored. William Ewer in the *Daily Herald* said to refuse the offer would have been to 'have bitten off our noses to spite the Führer's face'.[345]

Hitler's activity in the Rhineland caused a split in the newsroom of *The Times*, marking the start of a division among the paper's staff, which would soon widen. Colin Coote, a leader-writer, hoped that Hitler's action would be met with criticism from the influential *Times* comment pages. The task of writing the leading article fell to his colleague, Leo Kennedy. 'I rushed hopefully into his room expecting that this breaking of the Führer's own pledges would be castigated,' Coote wrote. Instead, he found Kennedy writing an article very different in tone, entitled 'A Chance to Rebuild'.[346]

The leader in *The Times* was ambiguous, mixing criticism of German actions with the open-ended conclusion that 'it is the moment, not to despair, but to rebuild'.[347] Yet Ebbutt saw straight through Hitler's offers of peace. 'The people at the head of this show are pure gamblers and do not care two buttons for the League of Nations, which was thrown in by Ribbentrop as a sop to British public opinion,' he wrote to Dawson in the following days. *The Times* correspondent knew the Nazis' lightning capture of the Rhineland was just the latest – and certainly not the last – expansion step planned by Germany. 'They are extremely formidable, and I do not believe for one moment that their ambitions will be satisfied by the settlement which may come out of the present negotiations.'[348] His paper's verdict on the Rhineland did not match this conclusion.

The *Guardian* thought Hitler had a case for his move into the Rhineland. 'For Germans to insist on defending their own territory with arms is not the same heinous moral offence, nor deserving the same penalties, as waging war, like Mussolini, on an unoffending country or preparing a base for an actual invasion.'[349] Italy was at the time fighting a colonial war in Abyssinia (modern-day Ethiopia), which had drawn international condemnation. The German action did not look so bad by comparison.

Only the *Telegraph* criticised the peace offer. 'Great Britain would herself in other circumstances have welcomed unreservedly the suggestion of Germany's return to the League [of Nations],' the paper asserted. 'But the actual circumstances are what they are – the flagrant repudiation of treaties, the assertion of glorification of overpowering military strength, and the promise of good neighbourliness.'[350] In his diplomatic correspondence column, the *Guardian*'s Voigt struck a similar line – and was more critical of the Nazis than his paper. The peace offer was 'cleverly attuned to the weakness of the collective system and is at the same time a skilful peace of demagogy,' he wrote a couple of days later.[351] Robson of the *Morning Post* was especially stinging in his criticisms of the Nazi leadership. He called Goebbels 'the biggest organiser of deception the world has ever seen'.[352] The Gestapo added this to their growing dossier on Robson and from this moment, his days in Berlin were numbered.

On 29 March, Germany held elections that the Nazis made into a vote on their action in the Rhineland. Remilitarising the strip of land between Germany and France had been wildly popular among Germans. Great cities such as Düsseldorf and Cologne had been brought back firmly under militarised German control. Ebbutt in *The Times* was especially perceptive in his article the day before the election:

The number of Germans who do not vote for Herr Hitler tomorrow is far short of the total which has misgivings about the present regime. Its work has been done at the expense of freedom, truth, and justice as these are conceived in the Western world, and some who feel bound to support the Führer tomorrow on the patriotic issue will do so in fear and trembling that they are delivering Germany over to a new wave of National-Socialist fanaticism.[353]

The Nazis were not confident enough to allow a free election. It was tarnished by voter intimidation and a lack of choice for electors; if you wanted to vote against the regime you had to deface the ballot paper. The official result was a backing of 98 per cent for the Nazis. The *Daily Herald* and *News Chronicle* delivered blistering criticisms of the outcome. The *Daily Express*, however, spoke in favour, setting the tone for its appeasing coverage during the rest of the 1930s. The newspaper's single aim at this time was to keep Britain out of another world war, meaning that foreign aggression or tyranny was seldom judged too critically. More surprising was the *Manchester Guardian*'s leading article, which asked: 'What other answer would the English people have made had they been asked, after a war which led to their disarmament, whether they maintained their right to fortify the coasts of Kent and Sussex?' But it did highlight shortcomings in the election process.

> The most serious aspect of the election is the proof [of] how a whole people, by a process based ultimately upon terrorism and carried through by every form of propaganda, may be gathered up and concentrated into a single, solid instrument in the hands of the dictatorship.[354]

Voigt continued to report without fear on worsening conditions inside Germany. A report on 1 April 1936 revealed how prisoners inside concentration camps were being treated – 'No Improvement in Germany', ran the headline. 'It grows more and more difficult to establish the facts about the Terror in Germany because the precautions taken to ensure secrecy have become much more elaborate,' he wrote. But Voigt gave several examples of the kind of punishment meted out to prisoners, many of whom were Jewish. Describing the flogging of one Jew, he wrote: 'After eighteen lashes he began to whimper. But the flogging went on until he lost consciousness.' Outside the concentration camps, Voigt wrote that the 'Terror' is now inflicted by the Gestapo rather than storm troopers. 'There are no legal guarantees for those who fall into the hands of the Gestapo… Many prisoners have been beaten to death, and many have died after lingering awhile as a result of their treatment at the hands of the Gestapo.'[355]

After receiving this dispatch Crozier wrote a glowing letter to his correspondent, telling him it would be in the next day's edition. 'No one but yourself could have got that for the paper. The S. S. know perfectly well that you are the author and, in general, are the most serious opponent of Nazi Germany in the English press, and, further, as you yourself know, they conspired against you in Paris.'[356] But all was not rosy between the pair. Voigt continued to want Crozier to use the *Guardian* to argue more strongly in favour of British rearmament. His strong convictions made him difficult to handle for the *Guardian*'s leadership. On at least thirteen occasions in 1936, Crozier either advised Voigt to tone down his diplomatic correspondence columns or refused to publish parts altogether.[357]

'I don't think you would expect us possibly to print the latter half of your article. I think you know that we have to make the best, and not the worst of this business of dealing with Germany,' Crozier wrote to Voigt on 18 March. 'Don't think that I am deluded about Hitler and his aims and methods, but I do think there is at least as much to be said for taking him at his word, or, if you like, calling his bluff, as for refusing to have any dealings with him at all.'[358] Voigt was overruled.

Newspapers on the right continued to shout loudly about the need to rearm. 'It is madness for Great Britain to remain unarmed when Germany and Italy are armed to the teeth and able at any moment to attack our vital interests,' the *Daily Mail* said on 7 July 1936.[359] Its star correspondent Price boiled this message down into a simple catchphrase: 'Negotiate – but arm.' *The Times* took up the message strongly. 'Everyone is agreed in these days that British foreign policy must have the backing of far greater strength to enforce it,' a leading article said on 6 July.[360]

Hitler had got away with his action in the Rhineland. There was no unified international response despite his clear breach of the agreement struck at Versailles. Following the election at the end of March, the 'Olympic Pause' commenced. As with the Winter Olympics earlier in the year, the Nazis made sure not to aggravate other countries in the months leading to the games in August. During this 'pause', there was a let-up in the ill treatment of the country's Jewish population, though those incarcerated in concentration camps beyond the public gaze were not so lucky.

Reynolds' sidelining at the *Mail* continued during this time, with Price taking charge of the paper's coverage of events in the Rhineland. Soon afterwards, Reynolds went away for several weeks. He took an increasing number of trips away from Germany from the middle part of the decade onwards. The increasing oppression was too much. 'To live in Germany during these years was to look on, powerless to help, while a friend was being slowly suffocated,' he wrote. 'To escape, if only for a time, and breathe free air became the aim of all.'[361]

Reynolds's job had previously restricted his chances of escape. But a unique opportunity arose in the spring of 1936 when the Nazi-designed

Hindenburg airship was making its maiden voyage across the Atlantic. He did not manage to get a ticket for the westward flight from Germany to the American town of Lakehurst in New Jersey, but he had a place for the return journey in May 1936. He could therefore extend his holiday by taking a more leisurely route to America on a transatlantic liner. This was his first trip to America. The return trip on the *Hindenburg* was the newly built airship's first eastward crossing of the Atlantic. There were over a hundred passengers aboard the gigantic drifting structure, more than half of whom were its crew. Alongside Reynolds were journalists from Germany, Britain and America as well as Nazi officials and diplomats and other specially invited guests.

The crossing took more than two days and was a triumph for Germany. During the Olympics in August, the airship was used to highlight Germany's recent technological achievements and it also made trips over Britain, emblazoned with Nazi insignia on its tail. It seemed to represent the stunning innovation and powerful personality of the Third Reich. Just a year later the *Hindenburg* dream ended in flames when the airship crashed in New Jersey, killing all on board, but it was a powerful propaganda tool for the Nazis in 1936.

The Olympics passed successfully in August. The *Guardian* was among the voices outside Germany calling for an international boycott of the games, but the campaign was not strong enough. The presence of sporting representatives from other nations in Germany was another victory for Hitler, seeming to validate his regime. He put on a show and presented to the world an image of a united and powerful Germany. Despite the friendlier face the Nazis demonstrated at the games, journalists continued to fear for their safety. This was a worry not just for correspondents living permanently in Berlin but also for visitors. Westbrook Pegler, an American sports reporter over for the games, expressed fears in 1936 of being snatched by the Gestapo as a result of his reports.[362]

The *Daily Mail* trio of Price, Rothermere and Harmsworth continued to press home the point that a strong Germany was essential to thwart the spread of communism in Europe. After the outbreak of the Spanish Civil War in 1936, which brought fears of a leftist revolution in that country, their anxiety rose. 'Although Bolshevism has made progress in France and Spain, Hitler's rearmament of Germany has confronted it in Central Europe with a new and formidable barrier,' Price wrote in September 1936.[363] In the same article he says Britain should remain neutral in the event of a European war between fascist and communist countries. But his sympathies were clear.

Later in September, David Lloyd George, the former British Prime Minister, used the pages of the *Daily Express* to write a long and glowing account of Hitler and Germany following a visit to the country. 'The idea of a Germany intimidating Europe with a threat that its irresistible army might march across frontiers forms no part of the new vision,' Lloyd George wrote. 'German hegemony in Europe, which was the aim and dream of the old pre-war militarism, is not even on the horizon of Nazism.'[364] Vansittart, Churchill and others in the emerging anti-appeasement brigade read the words with horror.

In October, Hitler's new appointment as British ambassador, Joachim von Ribbentrop, arrived in London. One of Hitler's closest and most trusted lieutenants, Ribbentrop had joined the Nazi ranks relatively late. He had been a successful businessman and was first introduced to Hitler in the late 1920s. The new man immediately caused a sensation by greeting King Edward VIII with a Nazi salute. So desperate was Ribbentrop to get his son into Eton that he canvassed the editor of *The Times*, Geoffrey Dawson. Finding no success there, he even asked Whitehall's chief opponent of appeasement, Lord Vansittart, for help. It was to no avail. The headmaster resisted all his efforts.

Ribbentrop would be an ambassador of a kind not seen before by polite society in Britain. Voigt criticised Ribbentrop from the start, calling him 'an ambassador who is only here by fits and starts, who is more concerned to teach this country what its policy ought to be than to inform himself what its policy is'.[365] Voigt had continued with his probing reports on Germany throughout 1936. Among British foreign correspondents of the era, few were regarded more highly. 'He had been a Berlin correspondent, understood and hated all its works, and was determined to see that others understood it too and took steps to bring about its downfall,' wrote Shiela Grant Duff, his apprentice in the Saar.[366] 'The *Manchester Guardian* was consistently better informed about German realities than any other newspaper,' the BBC's John Simpson wrote in his later history.[367] This was largely because of Voigt. He was never expelled from Germany – his swift withdrawal from Berlin in 1933 deprived the Nazis of the chance – yet he had continued to rile them since his departure from Paris to London amid rumours of a Gestapo plot. He emerges as one of the heroes of British journalism in this period, railing at the approach to Germany taken by the newspaper he reported for. Despite some constraints he offered some of the best reports on what life behind the Nazi curtain was actually like.

The year ended with a grim development for the foreign press contingent in Berlin. Karl Robson, the *Morning Post*'s reporter, was suddenly given three days to leave Germany by Nazi authorities. He was told that if he defied the order he would be expelled, along with his pregnant wife and child. He had already been warned that the authorities considered his reports unfriendly to Germany. But the official justification they gave for his expulsion appeared relatively minor: his report that the German Foreign Office had not been convinced of the innocence of a German engineer arrested in Russia. It was a flimsy excuse for an expulsion and suggests it had been a long time coming. They would have used any excuse to expel Robson after he attacked Goebbels as 'the biggest organiser of deception the world has ever seen'. But doing so at the time, nine months earlier, would have proven controversial given the heightened tensions over the Rhineland. So the Nazis chose a quieter moment, once the crisis had passed and the Olympics were finished, when the world was distracted by the emerging story of the abdication crisis in Britain. The plan was calculated, and largely worked in terms of minimising the impact of the expulsion. A small report in the *Chicago Tribune* reported that 'Robson, who spent three years in Berlin, is the sixteenth member of the Association of the Foreign Press to be ordered to leave Germany since the Nazis assumed power.'[368] The crackdown on criticism was accelerating.

-CHAPTER XII-

'THE BEST CORRESPONDENT HERE LEFT THIS EVENING'

By the fourth anniversary of Hitler's rise to power in Germany, his Reichstag speech at the end of January had become a closely watched annual tradition. He would stand, back straight and eyes wild, to boast of German might while assailing other European countries on grounds that shifted every year. The foreign correspondents in Berlin had learned by now that Hitler's words were not a reliable indicator of how he would act in future weeks and months. Too many promises had been broken for that.

His speech to the Reichstag at the start of 1937 announced that Germany's territorial ambitions were satisfied and the 'period of surprises' was over. Ebbutt of *The Times* had correctly predicted the speech would 'be in general of a soothing nature calculated to keep public opinion abroad, especially in Great Britain, occupied for some weeks or even months arguing about its merits and meaning'.[369] The accuracy of his foresight was a product of his long years of experience in Berlin. In 1937, he marked the tenth anniversary of his appointment as the main Germany correspondent of

The Times. He was still relatively young, having celebrated his forty-third birthday four days before Hitler's speech. Ebbutt's dark view of Hitler meant he expected the coming years to be the most important of his time as a reporter in Germany.

Nazi flags hang from a building overlooking a square in the German capital, 1937. (PA-1456 Thomas Neumann, The National Archives of Norway)

Hitler's speech was greeted by a mixed reception from newspapers in Britain. A combination of optimism and caution prevailed, typified by a *Guardian* editorial asserting that since Hitler 'says he is for cooperation, he should be taken at his word'.[370] Voigt was more cautious in his diplomatic correspondence column the next day, which reported an emerging view within the British Foreign Office. 'Second thoughts only confirm the view taken here that Herr Hitler's speech is entirely negative as far as relations between Germany and the rest of the world are concerned.'[371] By this time Voigt had established strong links with senior figures at the Foreign Office, from Foreign Secretary Anthony Eden downwards.

His closest link was Lord Vansittart, who continued his efforts behind closed doors to convince British diplomats and politicians to share his anti-Nazi views. Eden and Vansittart had a useful disciple at the Foreign Office in Rex Leeper, the department's head of news, who briefed journalists and forged close links with the small but influential band of diplomatic correspondents in London.

On 3 February, the *News Chronicle*'s Vernon Bartlett wrote a front-page story after returning from his first visit to Berlin for six months. He did not share the cautious optimism of others in the newspaper industry. 'There is a virtual inevitability of war,' he wrote, and Germans as a whole now saw war 'as one of the few certain events of an uncertain future.'[372] This was a candid assessment based on Bartlett's reporting on the ground, rather than simple coverage of Hitler's pacifying words to the Reichstag. The report helped cement the *News Chronicle*'s position as one of the two newspapers, alongside the *Guardian*, that most infuriated the Nazis.

It was the turn of *The Times* to aggravate the Nazis in April, when the newspaper was the first to report on Luftwaffe involvement in the bombing of the defenceless Basque town of Guernica. The Spanish Civil War had started the previous year, with socialists challenging the iron rule of General Franco's nationalists. Mussolini and Hitler allied themselves to Franco and their air forces were deployed in the controversial Guernica bombing. The Nazis reacted furiously to the initial (accurate) *Times* report, sending a wave of anti-British sentiment through the state-controlled German media. There was concern within the newspaper's headquarters at Printing House Square that it had been over-hasty with its first report, but other newspapers in Britain soon corroborated it. The German overreaction, wrote Ebbutt, 'suggests that the path to an understanding will be remote indeed while Germany remains under the influence of her present political prejudices'.[373]

In a stirring editorial, headlined '*The Times* Bombs Guernica', the news-paper hit back against German claims. 'What is the destiny of the world in which no responsible organ of the press can tell the simple truth without incurring charges of Machiavellian villainy?' *The Times* asked.[374] This strong public response was quite an answer to the newspaper's growing band of critics accusing them of going soft on Germany. These attacks on *The Times* were related to its editorial stance, rather than the strong on-the-ground reports from Ebbutt. But he was himself unhappy.

Since returning to Germany after a bout of sickness in 1933, Ebbutt had reported valiantly on Nazi excesses despite fears for his safety, which were first relayed to him at that time. He continued to socialise with other foreign correspondents at the Taverne restaurant in Berlin, and William Shirer noted in his diary that Ebbutt was usually the central member of the party:

> Normally Norman Ebbutt presides, sucking at an old pipe the night long, talking and arguing in a weak, high-pitched voice, imparting wisdom, for he has been here a long time, has contacts throughout the government, party, churches and army, and has a keen intelli-gence. Of late he has complained to me in private that *The Times* does not print all he sends, that it does not want to hear too much of the dark side of Nazi Germany and apparently has been captured by the pro-Nazis in London. He is discouraged and talks of quitting.[375]

Ebbutt's fears centred on Geoffrey Dawson, the newspaper's editor. A proud Yorkshireman, Dawson had edited *The Times* throughout the 1930s. He had enjoyed a long career in newspapers, rising to prominence in the trade as a young man with his appointment as editor of the *Johannesburg Star*. His love for the British Empire was sustained by an overriding belief in its power to civilise and improve the lives of those in other parts of the world. To Dawson, being born British was a greater cause for pride even than his Yorkshire roots. 'The British Empire is the most powerful bulwark in the world today against the spread of international discord,' he wrote in a *Times* leading article in May 1934. Maintaining the strength of the empire 'is by far the greatest and most practical contribution which British states-manship can make to the welfare of mankind'.[376] Such comments were far from atypical.

This ruggedly built countryman had already edited *The Times* between 1912 and 1919 when he agreed, after the death of its proprietor Lord North-cliffe in 1922, to take up the role for a second time. During his first spell in charge he had been unhappy with interventions made by Northcliffe, who had great power in government circles during the First World War – but the press baron's death offered a clean break. Dawson's independence under the newspaper's new owners established, he began a nineteen-year editorship that would prove one of the most controversial in the newspa-per's long history.

Dawson enjoyed being close to those in power. In the late 1930s he spoke regularly to Prime Minister Stanley Baldwin, and to Neville Chamberlain, who rose to the premiership in May 1937. Dawson was a regular lunch com-panion of Lord Halifax, with whom he shared a background of Yorkshire, Eton and Oxford. The men shared similar outlooks on all manner of things – from the supremacy of the British Empire and Conservative principles to most foreign policy issues. Dawson viewed these relationships as an important part of his job, as the intelligence gleaned from his network of powerful contacts helped form the positions taken by his newspaper.

To critics, however, these contacts exposed the newspaper's lack of inde-pendence. They thought the independence from proprietorial influence that Dawson had fought for was fatally undermined by his closeness to the ruling elite. The reputation of *The Times* for being the newspaper in Britain most likely to echo the government's viewpoint was well-established by the 1930s. But Dawson's approach only reinforced this reputation, much to the irritation of staff. In government circles, Dawson's fawning relationship with Halifax was ridiculed. 'Dawson eats out of his hand,' Oliver Harvey, private secretary to Lord Halifax in the Foreign Office, noted in his diary towards the end of the decade.[377]

For the influence it carried with regimes abroad and within government circles at home, *The Times* is widely judged to have been the most important British newspaper of the 1930s. Its circulation rose steadily throughout the decade, from 187,000 in 1930 to 204,000 in 1939. The *Daily Mail* may have been read by several times that number, but in terms of power and influence, the 'quality' *Times* was several leagues removed from the 'popular' *Mail*. *Times* dispatches on Germany and other major areas of foreign policy were read with interest around the globe.

Ebbutt had long thought his articles were meddled with and suspected, rightly, that the paper's leadership in London was keen to appease Germany. A letter written by Dawson soon after the Guernica affair to H. G. Daniels, a senior journalist who served as *The Times*'s man in Berlin before Ebbutt, revealed his keenness to have a smooth relationship with Germany. This desire impacted the newspaper's content. 'It would interest me to know precisely what it is in *The Times* that has produced this antagonism in Germany,' Dawson wrote. 'I did my utmost, night after night, to keep out of the paper anything that might hurt their sensibilities.'[378]

Coote, the *Times* leader-writer who had been dismayed by his paper's response to Hitler's Rhineland action, was increasingly alarmed by events in the newsroom. He later remarked that Dawson's letter to Daniels was a macabre example of the blind eye appeasers were willing to turn to bloodshed and suffering in the pursuit of Hitler's friendship. 'Not only is the tone plaintive – almost whining – but also it would not be gathered from the wording that the bombing of Guernica was a revolting horror,' Coote wrote. 'It was carried out by German airmen lent to Franco in the Spanish Civil War, against an undefended town; there was much damage and great loss of life. This was a scandalous butchery.'[379]

Coote remarked on a second letter sent by Dawson, this time to Lord Lothian, where he comments on inserting words and lines to soothe the Germans. 'Geoffrey Dawson spent much time in keeping out of the paper anything that might offend the Germans,' Coote observed.[380] He felt that Dawson's adulation of the British Empire and friendships with senior politicians blinkered his perspective.

> Feelings and friendships caused Geoffrey Dawson to disregard and indeed to distort the dispatches which he received from Norman Ebbutt, *The Times* correspondent in Berlin; in addition to disregarding the minor screams of people like myself. He really ought to have known better.[381]

By the middle of 1937, Coote was only being asked to write leading articles that dealt with British rearmament – the subject of relations with Germany was entrusted to other writers. Rearmament was strongly favoured by Dawson. He had a similar attitude to Rothermere at the *Daily Mail* – pursue a friendship with Germany, but be sure to be well-armed just in case. Coote called British rearmament 'Dawson's insurance against disaster arising from his pro-German policy'.[382]

In Berlin, Ebbutt heard rumours of these newsroom splits. He had other, more pressing matters to immediately deal with, however. Goebbels was a particularly vehement opponent of Ebbutt's reporting – a dangerous foe to have in the wilds of Nazi Germany. His disdain for *The Times* and its well-connected reporter had taken a further downward turn during the Guernica affair. The Nazis took special exception to *Times* reports, no doubt largely because of the newspaper's unique global influence. In the wake of the Guernica reports, anti-*Times* sentiment reached fevered levels in the German press. The country's media embarked on a savage campaign against the newspaper, pointing out, in all seriousness, that 'Times' spelt backwards is 'Semit' and alleging that the newspaper was secretly pursuing a pro-Jewish crusade. Such desperation in Germany to cast aspersions on the motives of *Times* journalists vindicated the newspaper's reporting. However, the self-incriminating letters of Dawson and the conflict with some staff members were damaging.

Ebbutt remained in Berlin. Though Goebbels was sorely tempted to remove him after the Guernica affair, the expulsion of a reporter from as eminent a publication as *The Times* would have made international news and drawn more attention to the bloodshed. He was therefore one of the thousand or so British citizens invited to the Berlin Embassy in June as the new British ambassador, Sir Nevile Henderson, threw a party marking King George VI's birthday. About two-thirds of the British expatriates living in Germany turned up at the embassy, which was situated on the Wilhelmstrasse – described as 'Downing Street on a larger scale' by Henderson.[383] The high turnout of British citizens was partly the result of curiosity; few of them had met the new ambassador and they wanted to get his measure. The opportunity to sip champagne and gossip in the grand reception rooms on the ground floor was too good to miss. For Henderson, too, the chance to meet British subjects in Berlin and glean their views on events in Germany was a great one. He enjoyed himself. 'The British colony in Berlin was an extremely poor one, and I do not think that any party which I ever gave provided me with greater pleasure than that one,' he wrote.[384]

Henderson was a 54-year-old veteran of the diplomatic service. Tall and lean, with a long face and thick moustache, he was a debonair individ-ual, rarely seen without a dark red carnation in his buttonhole. He had joined the service in 1905 and his first junior posting was to the embassy in St Petersburg, where he would have known Reynolds. But there is no evi-dence that the pair got on – and Henderson had a distinctly different view about the Nazis from Reynolds in the late 1930s.

Henderson had limited knowledge of his new brief but sought quickly to master it. He chose to travel back from Argentina on a German passenger ship in order to learn the language. He used the time to read *Mein Kampf* for the first time. It struck him as 'a remarkable production,' he said, 'on the part of a man whose education and political experience appeared to have been as slight, on this showing, as Herr Hitler's'.[385] It was a somewhat ambiguous comment to make about a book in which Hitler laid his anti-Semitism bare. Rumbold, Henderson's predecessor-but-one as ambassador, had condemned it as evidence of Hitler's bad character as early as 1933.

Henderson arrived in Berlin on 30 April 1937. Within a few days he had heard Hitler speak for the first time. 'His speech contained a scathing ref-erence or so to the effete democracies, particularly Britain, against whom there was, as usual, a press campaign raging at the time,' wrote Henderson, who was impressed. Though he found Hitler's voice to be 'harsh and unsympathetic', he thought Germany's leader had the 'gift of rhetorical exhortation'.[386] Henderson was impressed, too, by Hitler's achievements in office. 'He had restored to Germany her self-respect, and recreated orderliness out of the chaos and distress which had followed her defeat in 1918.'[387] As his offhand attitude to *Mein Kampf* made clear, Henderson found Hitler's achievements far more worthy of comment than his faults.

A short time after his arrival in Berlin, Henderson gave a speech to assorted members of the Nazi leadership, including Himmler. 'In England,' he said:

far too many people have an erroneous conception of what the National-Socialist regime really stands for. Otherwise they would lay less stress on the Nazi leadership and much more emphasis on the great social experiment which is being tried out in this country. Not only would they criticise less, but they might learn useful lessons.[388]

This may have been acceptable to say when Hitler took power in 1933, but by the time Henderson assumed his role in Berlin four years later, many observers saw the Nazi reality clearly enough. To speak of an 'erroneous conception' at this stage may have been a clumsy attempt by Henderson to ingratiate himself with his hosts. More likely it reveals where his own sympathies lay. Perhaps unsurprisingly, Henderson did not mention this particular speech in his memoirs.

———

By the summer of 1937, Ebbutt was exhausted. After a decade leading the *Times*'s reporting in Berlin, he was mentally and physically spent. Daniels had rejoined him by this time to lend a hand. Ebbutt continued to pay close attention to the fate of the church in Germany throughout the year as conditions for worshippers and the clergy worsened. His church reporting during the 1930s won him the admiration of Reynolds, whose job at the *Daily Mail*, with its focus on sensational news, precluded him from focusing on an issue close to his heart. He was impressed by his rival. Ebbutt was a 'careful writer, against whom a charge of reporting events in Germany inaccurately could not be brought,' wrote Reynolds. 'The tone of his dispatches was disliked and objection was taken to the copious information he gave of the persecution of the clergy, who were resisting the attempt to Nazify the Protestant Church.'[389]

In July 1937 Martin Niemöller, a protestant clergyman who had initially welcomed the rise of the Third Reich, was arrested. His support for Hitler had quickly evaporated once the grim reality of life in Nazi Germany became clear. He became an outspoken critic as the Nazis tried to tighten their grip on the Christian church. He felt it personally: his phone was tapped by the Gestapo and he was arrested several times for speaking out. 'The faith is in danger!' Reynolds heard Niemöller declare at one of the pastor's public meetings in Berlin that so annoyed the Nazis. 'The words rang through the hall and thrilled the great audience,' Reynolds wrote.[390]

The latest arrest was greeted with uproar by British newspapers, including *The Times*. The *News Chronicle* and *Guardian* were also persistently vocal on the church issue in Germany. Later that month, Britain expelled three Nazi reporters from London on the grounds of espionage. It was the opportunity Goebbels had been waiting for. Nazi authorities swiftly requested Ebbutt's withdrawal from Berlin in retaliation. *The Times* held firm at first but had no choice but to extract their reporter when Goebbels issued a formal expulsion order. For a newspaper as prestigious as *The Times* to have their reporter expelled was a momentous event and it made international news. 'Norman Ebbutt of the London *Times*, by far the best correspondent here, left this evening,' wrote Shirer in his diary on the evening of 16 August 1937. He continued:

> He was expelled, following British action in kicking out two or three
> Nazi correspondents in London, the Nazis seizing the opportu-
> nity to get rid of a man they've hated and feared for years because
> of his exhaustive knowledge of this country and of what was going
> on behind the scenes. *The Times*, which has played along with the
> pro-Nazi Cliveden set, never gave him much support and published

only half of what he wrote, and indeed is leaving Ebbutt's assistant, Jimmy Holburn, to continue with the office here.[391]

Shirer and around fifty other foreign correspondents in Berlin gathered at Charlottenburg station to see Ebbutt off. They were warned not to – word had filtered through from the Nazi authorities that their presence would be considered an unfriendly act towards Germany. Shirer noted with amusement that some correspondents were too frightened to come, 'including two well-known Americans'. It is not known whether Reynolds attended. The platform swarmed not only with foreign correspondents but also Gestapo agents. They took details of who had turned up and photographed them. But the reporters still managed to give the long-suffering Ebbutt a warm sendoff. Shirer said the *Times* man was 'terribly highly-strung, but moved by our sincere, if boisterous, demonstration of farewell'.[392]

Soon after Ebbutt's return to Britain, his health failed. Though only in his mid-forties he suffered a severe stroke that paralysed him and left him a shadow of his former self for the rest of his life. It was a sad, abrupt end to an illustrious career, no doubt brought on by the stress of his life in Berlin. 'He was a man in the prime of his life; but the strain was too much for him. After his return to England, his health suddenly broke down and he has since lived in retirement,' Reynolds wrote a couple of years afterwards.[393]

The extent to which *The Times* interfered with his dispatches to soften their tone towards Germany remains an unanswered question. There is widespread agreement that Ebbutt frequently filed stories that were too long and required significant lopping by sub-editors. Two things seem indisputable. First, Dawson periodically tried to make what went into *The Times* more appealing to German eyes. He himself admitted this. Second, Ebbutt had issues with how some German issues were presented in the newspaper.

Written shortly after the war, the fourth volume of the official *History of the Times* was unsparing in its criticism of Dawson and the manner in which he handled the reporting of German affairs. His decision not to appoint a new foreign editor in 1929 when the vacancy arose was criticised as 'the most important decision of Dawson's second innings and most deliberately reached'.[394] Dawson thought the role was obsolete and the function could be better performed by a new team structure, but it undoubtedly gave him more control over coverage of foreign affairs. The fifth volume of the *History of the Times*, published in 1985, was much more sympathetic to Dawson. 'Objective testimony gives little support to the common charge that Dawson and (deputy editor) Barrington-Ward stopped any news that they did not like from going into the paper.' Yet it admits that Dawson's letter, in which he admits doing his utmost to keep content that might hurt German sensibilities out of the paper, 'defies a wholly convincing explanation'. The fact that Ebbutt was expelled for his reports in *The Times* is held up as proof that his work was not altered. It is a persuasive point, but not supported by other evidence.[395]

Staff at *The Times* were split over who had been behind Ebbutt's expulsion. Dawson's deputy, Robert Barrington-Ward, thought Goebbels was responsible. His successor in Berlin, James Holburn, saw the hand of Ribbentrop, the ambassador in London. The ambassador spent a lot of time reassuring anxious British politicians that Hitler's intentions were honourable. Ebbutt's firm and incisive reporting on Nazi foreign policy and the regime's treatment of the church in Germany was widely read in London and made Ribbentrop's job more difficult. If Ebbutt was not in Berlin, Ribbentrop's life would be a great deal easier.

Ebbutt returned to Britain less than a year after his friend Robson of the *Morning Post* had been expelled. Robson had not spent much time in London in the intervening months. Instead he had continued to report on how the Nazis were stoking disquiet beyond the borders of Germany, travelling to Austria, Danzig in Poland, the Memel region, Latvia, Czechoslovakia and even as far afield as Turkey. He met Lord Vansittart at the Foreign Office and the two men found they shared a similar perspective on events in Nazi Germany.[396] But the *Morning Post* would not exist for much longer to print his dispatches. Its owner was looking for a buyer and in October Lord Camrose stepped forward. Instead of running the newspaper alongside the *Daily Telegraph*, he merged it with his flagship title, ending the *Morning Post*'s 165-year history as an independent publication. Representations were made to Prime Minister Chamberlain that this storied paper should be kept in business. He apparently answered by saying he had no time for Conservative newspapers that criticised his government, particularly on the sensitive issue of finding an accommodation with Germany. The *Morning Post*'s criticism of both the Nazi regime and the British response to it had been an acute source of annoyance to Chamberlain in his first five months in office. The newspaper would not be saved.[397]

In Berlin, Holburn faced the daunting challenge of maintaining the standard of dispatches set by Ebbutt. He was helped by Iverach McDonald, a young *Times* reporter sent with his wife from London to assist the Berlin bureau after Ebbutt's expulsion. McDonald was shocked when he arrived in Berlin – it was a more sinister and oppressive environment than he had realised. 'Anyone who lived in Berlin during the last year or two before the war must recall the time with disgust and anguish,' he later wrote. 'One knew beforehand that Hitler had set out to de-civilise the German nation, but it was dreadful to see the process in action as Goebbels and the newspapers harped day by day on the lowest passions of greed, fear, blood-lust, and greed.'[398]

McDonald noticed how the lives of correspondents in Berlin differed from those working in other cities. The threat of expulsion hung like a cloud over all the foreign reporters in the city. It was not a fun place to be a journalist in the final years of the decade. But the grim reality of Nazi Germany merely prompted Reynolds and the other reporters to live their lives as fully as possible in those years. McDonald likened the feeling to a 'traditional eve-of-Waterloo release from care among westerners' in Berlin. 'British, French and American diplomats and journalists and their wives met in the happiest of dinners and dances that were deliberate withdrawals from the reality outside.'[399]

McDonald and his wife were told by Jewish acquaintances about the frequent pogroms and arrests, many of them secret, which targeted Jews in the country. 'The sheer magnitude of the evil was at times hard to grasp.'[400] He was also surprised by the intimidating reception he received from Henderson, the British ambassador. 'He more than once warned me, with his eye on the latest issue of *The Times* on his desk, about the dangers of picking out German events which did not fit in with the picture of the amenable Reich which he saw and which he commended to London.'[401] The British government's message was clear, even in Berlin – friendship with Germany was the most important objective.

-CHAPTER XIII-
APPEASEMENT BUILDS

Nazi flags flutter above crowds lined up for a central Berlin parade.
(PA-1456 Thomas Neumann, The National Archives of Norway)

I n November 1937, Britain's leading politicians joined King George VI on Whitehall for the first Service of Remembrance of his reign. Heads bowed, they stood in neat lines around the Cenotaph, the imposing monument of Portland stone built seventeen years earlier, to lead tributes to the country's war dead. The occasion was crowded with members of the public, most of whom had vivid memories of the First World War. The sombre ceremony was interrupted halfway through when a man ran forward from the crowd to shout at the assembled politicians and dignitaries: 'Cease this hypocrisy. You are conniving in a new war.' He was quickly bustled away by police. Home Secretary Sir Samuel Hoare later told the House of Commons the man was suffering from delusions.[402]

The heckler was dismissed as a madman but the incident reflected a growing tension in Britain about how to deal with German aggression. Chamberlain's ascent to the premiership in May had brought new urgency to efforts begun by the last government to find common ground with Hitler's regime. The Prime Minister and his most important lieutenants, including figures such as Lord Halifax and Sir Horace Wilson, were convinced that Hitler could be tamed and better relations were possible. The more hawkish attitude of Foreign Secretary Anthony Eden and his leading civil servant Lord Vansittart, both of whom continued in the positions they had held under Baldwin, were regarded as unhelpful by the new leadership.

While Neville Chamberlain was irritated by the attitudes of his men at the Foreign Office, his opinion of journalists bordered on contempt. As he became more comfortable in power he started to refuse to answer off-the-cuff questions and declared that he would only answer enquiries submitted at least four hours in advance. The only contact in the press he liked was the *Sunday Times* editor W. W. Hadley – and that was largely because Hadley could be relied upon to support his decisions.[403]

Chamberlain's right-hand man Sir Horace Wilson was his adviser on foreign affairs and the man he sent to speak to proprietors and editors when necessary. The Prime Minister himself despised contact with members of the press pack. Another useful associate was Sir Joseph Ball, who had emerged from a shadowy background in the intelligence world at MI5 to assist with Chamberlain's attempts to control the press. Ball was tasked with briefing lobby journalists at Westminster, who eagerly relayed the government's thoughts to readers without challenge. It was lazy, but the London-based reporters knew stories based on these briefings would guarantee them column inches in the paper. They became unwitting accomplices in spreading the government's emerging appeasement agenda. This was the perfect outcome for Ball, a skilled operator whose talents extended to the underhand – in 1939 he tapped the phones of supporters of Anthony Eden to monitor the status of a man who had become a potential threat to his master.[404]

Nothing was off limits for Ball. In 1935 he had suggested to Prime Minister Baldwin that the government try to buy a small newspaper and turn it into a publication that would happily toe their line. He felt that *The Times* and *Daily Telegraph* were admirable newspapers and welcomed their support, but was frustrated by their small circulations. He wanted to control a publication with a greater readership and influence over the masses. *Truth*, an organ with a history of radical thought, was thus bought in 1936 by a friend of Ball's, Lord Luke of Pavenham, and supported the government for the rest of the 1930s. Its role as a propaganda organ was exposed by the ever-watchful Lord Vansittart during the Second World War.[405]

The Foreign Office had a more sophisticated approach to interacting with newspapers. Rex Leeper had served Eden and Vansittart as the head of the Foreign Office News Department since 1935. He treated journalists with caution rather than disdain and built up a network of trusted diplomatic correspondents, including Voigt of the *Guardian*, Victor Gordon-Lennox of the *Daily Telegraph*, William Ewer of the *Daily Herald*, Charles Tower of the *Yorkshire Post* and Vernon Bartlett of the *News Chronicle*.[406] Leeper had fed news to reporters, which helped Vansittart drive forward his campaign to reveal the reality of German intentions. For instance, in March 1935 Leeper had leaked documents relating to German claims of air parity to the *Telegraph*'s Gordon-Lennox.[407] The publication of these documents, which the government had been keen to keep out of the public domain, renewed the debate about rearmament.

In this way, news became a battleground at the heart of the growing tension between the Foreign Office of Eden and Vansittart and Prime Ministers Baldwin and Chamberlain. The tight relationship between the diplomatic correspondents and the Foreign Office attracted some criticism from other journalists. Robert Dell, the *Guardian's* Geneva-based correspondent, thought Voigt had become too close to Leeper and Vansittart. He criticised Leeper for attempting to persuade all British diplomatic correspondents to say the same thing.[408]

In November 1937, Leeper's news operation faced an unprecedented challenge. Chamberlain had instructed Halifax to fly to Germany for secret talks with Hitler at his mountain retreat in Berchtesgaden. Halifax had the official role of Leader of the House of Lords, but his influence with Chamberlain meant he had more power than anyone in government except the Prime Minister himself. Chamberlain hoped that Halifax might be able to deal with Hitler as he had dealt with Mahatma Gandhi in India at the start of the 1930s. While Halifax was Viceroy of India, he was seen as having tamed the leader of the Indian independence movement. 'Were not both of these "mad mullahs", wrote Arnold Toynbee, a commentator in Britain, in reference to Hitler and Gandhi. He thought the pair – both 'non-smokers, non-drinkers of alcohol, non-eaters of meat, non-riders on horseback, and non-practisers of blood-sports in their cranky private lives' – were faintly similar.[409] Maybe Halifax could repeat with Hitler the success he had enjoyed with Gandhi, another 'mad' foreign individual.

Halifax's visit to Germany clearly undermined the authority of Foreign Secretary Eden. Anti-appeasement figures in Whitehall viewed the talks as an improper way of conducting foreign policy and feared they would lead to more demands by Hitler. He had been speaking in increasingly angry terms about the possible return to Germany of some African colonies taken away from the country after the war, leading some to think that colonies were his next objective. Leeper leaked news to the *Evening Standard* that a potential deal between Britain and Germany could see Hitler granted a free hand in central Europe in return for a ten-year truce on the colonies issue.

Chamberlain and Halifax were furious. They viewed the leak as a sabotage attempt and blamed the Foreign Office. Eden's department denied responsibility and briefed that the Italian Embassy had been responsible (Voigt, who was close to Vansittart, was sure this was not the case).[410] Chamberlain need not have worried. The press reaction to the leak was mostly favourable, with many papers, particularly on the right of politics, holding the view that some accommodation with Hitler should be found. As early as 1935, Lord Rothermere had used the *Daily Mail* to argue for the return of some German colonies. 'We cannot expect a nation of he-men like the Germans to sit forever with folded arms under the provocations and stupidities of the Treaty of Versailles,' he wrote in typically bellicose fashion. 'To deny this mighty nation, conspicuous for its organising ability and scientific achievements, a share in the work of developing backward regions of the world is preposterous.'[411]

Chamberlain twisted the leak to his advantage by briefing that the trip had a greater scope than the Foreign Office wished, and was therefore sending Halifax. He met Hitler on 19 November and received a long harangue about the unfair reporting of the British press, which Hitler viewed as immensely hostile to Germany. Halifax was stunned by Hitler's sensitivity to adverse newspaper opinion. Rather than disregarding Hitler's apparent upset, which was a tactical ploy to leverage further concessions, Halifax took him at his word. He concluded that a firm future understanding with Hitler may not be possible unless he could get control of the press in Britain.[412]

Halifax spoke to the British correspondents in Germany and told them there was a 'need for the press to create the right atmosphere if any real advance were to be made towards a better understanding'.[413] He also met Goebbels, who underlined Hitler's message about the press. Ever thin-skinned, Goebbels mentioned Norman Ebbutt as an example of someone he viewed as a rogue reporter and criticised 'the spiteful taint given to him in reports' by the *Times* man.[414]

Halifax spent time with Henderson, the British ambassador. The two men were well acquainted, having socialised together at the Cliveden home of the Astor family in Buckinghamshire. The phrase 'Cliveden Set' was coined around this time after Claud Cockburn, the editor of *The Week*, had written about a group of eminent and influential figures within British society who discussed their pro-appeasement views during meetings at the grand country home. Halifax and Henderson were supposed members, as well as Garvin and Dawson, the editors of *The Observer* and *The Times*, and government members Lord Lothian and Sir Samuel Hoare.

In Berlin, Halifax told Henderson that he planned to meet the owners of the *News Chronicle* and *Daily Herald*, and persuade them to tone down their dispatches about Germany. He was also thinking about how to get to David Low of the *Evening Standard* – Halifax said his cartoons had proved 'the most troublesome' to Goebbels.[415] Low was the cartoonist who made the greatest impact with his sketches lampooning the appeasement set. His most famous cartoon of the era was published on 28 November 1937, soon after Halifax's return from Berlin. It showed Dawson and Garvin with Lord Lothian and Nancy Astor, their legs aloft, in a dance being conducted by Goebbels. The message was clear: all were mere puppets of Nazism. So strong was Low's position at the newspaper that he was permitted on occasion to parody even its owner, Lord Beaverbrook. But he too came under pressure to soften his message in the weeks that followed.

Halifax tracked down Lord Southwood of the *Daily Herald* and Sir Walter Layton of the *News Chronicle*. They were told in no uncertain terms that some of the reports in their newspapers were unhelpful to government efforts to strike a new understanding with Germany. Rather than stand up for the British press and politely but firmly tell Goebbels that newspapers were free to do as they pleased, Halifax was all too happy to pass on his complaints. Will Dyson, a cartoonist with the *Daily Herald*, came in for particular criticism. On 1 December one of his cartoons caused Halifax to complain that it was an 'unjustly cruel cartoon' that undermined attempts to solve 'international problems'. Fittingly, such a complaint almost caricatures British government ineptitude when it came to Nazi Germany – Halifax's grand strategy appeared to consist of little more than going after individual cartoonists.[416]

In 1937, seemingly in response to German complaints about British newspapers, Halifax had meetings with about eighty press outlets to stress that stories could affect foreign policy and weaken Britain's position during negotiations. He later boasted that pressure on the BBC led to restricted coverage of the German colonies issue. Though supposedly independent, the BBC was considered a fair target for attack. Lord Reith, its director-general, was summoned twice in one week for a ticking-off delivered by Chamberlain's faithful colleague Horace Wilson. On the first occasion Chamberlain had taken umbrage at a news report carrying, in his opinion, excessive coverage of speeches in the Commons attacking him. In the second case he was upset by coverage of criticism of the Air Ministry, a story covered only by the BBC and *News Chronicle*.[417]

Henderson did not stand up for the British correspondents working in Berlin. Instead he wholeheartedly supported Halifax's efforts to control the press. 'I have the greatest respect for the power and freedom of that "chartered libertine", the British Press,' he remarked, before adding: 'I must, however, reluctantly, but in all honestly, record that it handicapped my attempts in 1937 and 1938 to contribute to the improvement of Anglo-German relations, and thereby to the preservation of peace.' Hitler's feelings were, as ever, of the utmost concern. 'However justifiable the majority of press criticisms undoubtedly were at this time, they were also sometimes biased and unfair. It would not have mattered so much had Hitler been a normal individual, but he was unreasonably sensitive to newspaper, and especially British newspaper, criticism.'[418]

Henderson was a recurring source of deep annoyance to anti-appeasement figures. During discussions over German colonies, Eden became infuriated by Henderson's propensity to over-enthusiastically yield concessions and signal Britain's openness to German desires. 'I wish he would not go on like this to everybody he meets,' the Foreign Secretary snapped.[419]

Voigt watched from London as British politicians kept their lines of communication open with Hitler. Following the furore over Halifax's visit caused by the *Evening Standard*'s article, he wrote a perceptive letter to Crozier, his editor, about the state of the press in Britain:

> The incident is over – but the forces that are trying to change our foreign policy remain. They are sure to renew their attempts. I wish the Labour Party were more on the alert in the House [of Commons]. But it never seems to have any inkling of what goes on anywhere. It is a calamity that there are only two free papers left in the country – the *Manchester Guardian* and the *Yorkshire Post*. *The Times* and *The Observer* are in with Lothian and the Astors. The *Daily Telegraph* is stodgy and accepts dictation from the Government. The others don't count except for stunts.[420]

Other figures were also watching in dismay as some of the most influential names in the press supported the government's shift to wholehearted appeasement. After reading the day's newspapers, the Labour politician Hugh Dalton noted in diaries on 28 November: 'There is a great barrage in favour of concessions to Germany... [*The Observer*] carries the usual Garvin slobber, including proposals for a wholesale return of colonies.'[421]

The momentum was building in favour of those who wanted to take a softer line towards Germany. At the start of 1938, the pro-appeasement faction claimed its biggest scalp to date. On the first day of the year, Lord Vansittart was replaced as Permanent Under-Secretary at the Foreign Office by Alexander Cadogan. Vansittart was handed the role of Chief Diplomatic Adviser to the Government. It sounds a grand title, but in reality he was sidelined. The Foreign Office had lost its most ardent critic of British policy towards Germany, the man who had taken up the early warnings sounded by Sir Horace Rumbold in Berlin. It was a crushing blow for Eden.

Friends of Vansittart thought he should have spoken out publicly. But that was not how loyal civil servants were trained. 'He ought to have resigned with the greatest noise and fury possible, instead of allowing himself to be kicked upstairs,' recorded Colin Coote of *The Times* later. 'We often discussed this in later years, and I think he did regret his observances of the traditional code of the civil servant.'[422]

Later in January came the fifth anniversary of Hitler's rise to power. In a leader on 29 January the *Guardian* focused on the Nazi regime's brutal persecution of the Jews. Many other newspapers overlooked this and instead focused on the Nazis' economic achievements, particularly in unemployment. Persecution 'has not abated for one moment,' the *Guardian* said. It attacked Hitler for a range of other reasons:

> Constant maladministration of justice, the secret and terroristic
> trials, the torture of prisoners, the concentration camps, the low-
> ering of ethical and aesthetic standards, the habits of servility that

have grown up amongst the ruled under the arrogance of the rulers, the incessant propaganda that is killing truthfulness in the German people, who used to be, above all, truth-seekers, the militarisation of old and young, and the new educational ideals that threaten to produce a new generation animated by a barbarous and militant nationalism.[423]

As February progressed, Anthony Eden's position as Foreign Secretary became less and less secure. On one of the main foreign policy issues of the day, relations with Germany, his great office of state was being left behind as Chamberlain and his supporters in the press pursued their own policy. As his departure became inevitable, the Prime Minister moved to protect his own position by ensuring Eden's resignation was not reported to be the result of a great fracture in foreign affairs policy.

Eden resigned in February 1938. The scale of his disagreement with Chamberlain and Halifax over the Government's stance on Germany had widened from a crevice to a canyon. His resignation speech was pointed. 'I do not believe we can make progress in European appeasement ... if we allow the impression to gain currency abroad that we yield to constant pressure.'[424] But newspapers were briefed and even the *Daily Telegraph*, whose reporting of foreign policy had put other papers to shame, was persuaded by Chamberlain's efforts. Victor Gordon-Lennox, its diplomatic correspondent and a friend of Eden, cried when he read his paper's criticism of the outgoing Foreign Secretary.[425]

Eden was replaced by Lord Halifax. Though he had already been serving as Chamberlain's Foreign Secretary in all but name, his formal appointment greatly encouraged the appeasement lobby. Vansittart and Eden joined Churchill on the sidelines. There was no formal government policy describing it as such, but appeasement of Germany was now the key element within British foreign policy. Hitler would be trusted and German claims given a hearing.

An emboldened Halifax continued to make his case to the press. Early in 1938 he met Esmond Harmsworth, who was now firmly in control at the *Daily Mail*, to try and influence the newspaper's line.[426] Several of his attempts at influencing the press proved successful. Later in the year Hugh Dalton took Douglas Jay, the city editor of the *Daily Herald*, to lunch. Jay told him that Halifax's attempts to persuade Lord Southwood to bring the newspaper's position into line had met with success. There had 'been some reflection of this pressure to prevent too critical a line on foreign policy' in the newspaper. Halifax's entreaties to Southwood obviously made an impact.[427]

Jay had the sense that the *Daily Herald* ownership regarded journalists 'as political extremists who were endangering the circulation and worse still the advertising revenue of the paper'.[428] He despaired at the uncritical attitude some British newspapers took towards Hitler in the final years of the 1930s. 'Almost the entire press poured forth news articles and twisted news stories designed to prove that Hitler meant little harm, and that warnings of danger were bad for business anyway.'[429]

-CHAPTER XIV-
ANSCHLUSS

On 12 February 1938 the Austrian Chancellor Kurt Schuschnigg left Vienna, ostensibly for a weekend of skiing. Instead he headed across the border to Germany, where Hitler had invited him to a secret meeting to discuss Austro-German relations at his Berchtesgaden home in the mountains. The two countries had endured fraught relations for much of the thirties, especially since the assassination of Chancellor Engelbert Dollfuss by Austrian Nazis in 1934. Dollfuss had drawn Nazi wrath by banning the party in Austria, but Schuschnigg had pursued a more amicable approach, despite continued agitation by Hitler's supporters. Some felt Schuschnigg was himself running something akin to a fascist regime. But it was not enough for the Nazis who longed for Austria to one day become part of the German Reich. An Austrian by birth, Hitler felt this desire more keenly than any of his followers.

The secret meeting was a scarring experience for the Austrian Chancellor. Hitler bullied and hectored his guest, demanding that Nazis be given important posts in the Austrian Cabinet. News of the meeting was slow to emerge, but in the following days mixed reports started appearing in British newspapers. 'From the very start of the interview Chancellor Schuschnigg found himself subjected to great pressure,' the *News Chronicle* reported four days later.[430] The *Daily Telegraph's* correspondent in Vienna, Eric Gedye, was the British correspondent closest to the unfolding events. 'The Führer went so far – and I can assert this positively, in the face of any subsequent denials – as to threaten that in the case of disorders in Austria, he would "march", Gedye reported.[431] It was clear – Austria was Hitler's next target. In an editorial, the next day's *Telegraph* likened any talk of a settlement with Germany to 'the twittering of sparrows in a thunderstorm'.[432]

The *Daily Express* and *Daily Mail* were more sanguine about the meeting. The *Express* adhered to its isolationist line and pressed the case for non-interference, while the *Mail* said Hitler's attitude towards Schuschnigg at Berchtesgaden had been perfectly reasonable. But they were blinding themselves to the near-inevitability of events to come. Hitler had moved onto Austria and would not be content until he had achieved the joining of the two countries, or 'Anschluss', that he had craved since taking power.

Spectators take their seats in grandstands erected in front of the Stadtschloss, the City Palace of Berlin, ahead of a party rally. (PA-1456 Thomas Neumann, The National Archives of Norway)

In Berlin, the hapless ambassador Henderson continued to be ineffective in his dealings with Hitler. On 3 March he had an audience with the Führer in which he aimed to renew the British government's attempt to reach an accommodation with Germany. 'Nothing, [Hitler] said, could be done until the press campaign against him in England ceased,' Henderson recorded. 'He never failed to harp on this subject in every conversation I had with him.'[433] In a singularly weak gesture at the end of the meeting he produced a drawing of Hitler, sent to him by an artist in New Zealand who had asked for it to be signed, and requested the Nazi leader's autograph. British diplomacy did not leave Hitler quailing.

It was almost as if Henderson viewed politics and negotiations as distasteful – he was more comfortable discussing the latest fashions or his sporting prowess. On one occasion he participated in a stag-shooting weekend at Göring's estate in the country. 'When I got there the stag was kindly standing broadside on, and I shot it through the heart. From that moment my reputation as a sportsman was secure,' he wrote.[434] Henderson's priorities were skewed. Though he may have thought otherwise, skill with a shotgun did not equate to talent as a diplomat.

The pressure on Austria increased. Schuschnigg relented by installing some Nazis in his government but simultaneously made plans for a referendum that would offer Austrians a choice on whether the country became part of Germany. There was a real possibility Austria's electorate would vote against the proposal. He announced the referendum on Wednesday 9 March. Hitler reacted with predictable rage and his response was swift. Three days later, purportedly at the request of Nazis in Schuschnigg's Cabinet, Hitler ordered the German army into Austria. The Anschluss had begun. Again, Price of the *Daily Mail* had a ringside seat for the action. In the following days he tracked Hitler down in Linz, a large north Austrian city on the Danube. He was on his way to Vienna. Price talked his way onto the balcony from which Hitler was addressing a large crowd gathered in the town square. The Nazis received a generally favourable response from the invaded country's population. Price recounted how crowds looking towards Hitler chanted the slogan of the Nazi Party: 'Ein Reich! Ein Volk! Ein Führer! (One State! One Nation! One Leader!)'

'Hitler's face took on a look of ecstasy as he heard this manifestation of devotion to himself and his regime,' Price wrote. 'His mood was certainly one of triumph when I had a conversation with him in the small hotel where he spent the night.' Price asked him how he expected to be received in Vienna the next day. 'I will show you tomorrow,' Hitler replied. 'You can join the motor-cavalcade that will bring me to Vienna, and you will be able to see for yourself what the people of Austria feel about me.'

Price travelled the 150 miles to Vienna in the third car of a convoy transporting the Nazi leadership. He wrote that it produced 'the most excited demonstration of enthusiasm that I have ever witnessed. All the way crowds of Austrians were waiting to greet Hitler with what was obviously genuine joy.'[435] Price saw Hitler being 'bombarded' with flowers in every town they passed through.

The reaction in Britain to Hitler's latest act of aggression was less breathless. *The Times* called it the 'Rape of Austria' in an editorial. 'Never, indeed, has the mailed fist been wielded with such dramatic effect as by Germany,' asserted the *Telegraph*.[436] 'Remember that what has happened in Austria over the weekend is largely our own fault,' opined the *News Chronicle*. 'Our hesitation has encouraged cumulative acts of aggression and treaty breaking across the world. Manchuria, Abyssinia, the Rhineland, Spain, China, Austria. Who next?'[437] It added that the western democracies should pledge to fight for Czechoslovakia if Hitler moved against her next. Part of the country was now virtually encircled by German-controlled territory after the Anschluss.

The *Daily Mail* maintained its strong message of rearmament. 'Arm, arm, arm! That has been the lesson of the past few years. That is the lesson which is underlined and emphasised by Austria today,' Rothermere's paper said, while emphasising a message of isolationism. 'Today the resolve of the British people will be to have nothing to do with the situation in Europe. Not one British soldier, not one penny of British money must be involved in this quarrel which is no concern of ours.'[438]

There was no question of western democracies stepping in to save Austria. Hitler's latest move had started on a Saturday but been less of a surprise than his other weekend strikes. Many saw the Anschluss as a natural and by no means undesirable development. The two countries shared much in terms of language, history and culture. The aggressive manner in which Hitler had acted, rather than the act itself, was the chief source of anger abroad. Hitler brushed off the criticism, though he had taken notice of it. In Austria he stood before the crowds and turned to Price. 'Is that a rape?' he asked, gesturing to the cheering crowds below, in reference to the recent *Times* headline.[439]

Monitoring events from *The Times* headquarters in London, Geoffrey Dawson was left in no doubt about the speed and power of the Nazi invasion by a letter from his correspondent in Vienna, Douglas Reed. 'In my wildest nightmares, I had not foreseen anything so perfectly organised, so brutal, so ruthless, so strong. When this machine goes into action, it will blight everything it encounters like a swarm of locusts,' Reed wrote to Dawson four days after the commencement of the Anschluss.

Reed thought the scale of the destruction of a new world war would make the Great War look like the Boer War. He added that Britain was unprepared and did not realise that Hitler's ultimate aim was Britain's destruction. 'This is a thing which nobody can understand, apparently, who has not lived with the Germans. Their real hatred is for England.'[440]

Ugly scenes followed in Austria in the weeks after Anschluss. Jews in the country were visciously targeted in a wave of anti-Semitism far more brutal and organised than anything seen in Germany so far. The *Telegraph's* Gedye led reporting on the surge of violence against Austria's Jews. The German authorities brought their existing press tactics to bear in Austria and expelled him. Gedye was ordered to be 'over the frontiers of Germany, including Austria,' by noon on 28 March.[441]

John Segrue, a long-serving correspondent in Europe for the *News Chronicle* and Catholic friend to Reynolds, was working in Vienna when the Nazis marched in. A small Liverpudlian who adored his pair of pet Dachshunds, Segrue was a distinguished foreign correspondent who had been the first British journalist in Germany after the First World War. The Nazis had hated the candid manner in which he reported their treatment of Jews in Germany. He offered financial assistance to many repressed people and employed in his office a Jewish girl who would have struggled to find a job elsewhere.

Segrue was one of the many correspondents expelled from Berlin by the Nazis during the 1930s. He had then moved to Austria, predicting that Hitler would soon turn his eye towards his homeland. Segrue maintained his defiant attitude towards the Nazis after Anschluss. One story in particular was remembered proudly by his *News Chronicle* colleagues. Wandering around Vienna in the days after the German invasion, he came across a crowd in the Jewish quarter. Himmler's SS were aggressively forcing a large group of Jews of all ages to wash their cars. An unsympathetic mob watched the crowd of Jews as they were bullied and manhandled by the uniformed officers.

Suddenly a member of the SS stepped forward and ordered Segrue to help. 'There, you damned Jew; get to work and help your fellow swine,' he yelled. Segrue obeyed and helped an elderly woman with the car she had been assigned. Afterwards he walked back to the SS officer, presented his passport and declared: 'I am not a Jew, but a subject of His Majesty the King of England.' He then turned to an SS commander. 'I could not believe that the stories about your brutality were true. I wanted to see for myself. I have seen. Good day.'[442] Segrue's fearless attitude meant he did not last long in Austria. The Nazis soon expelled him for a second time.

It did not take long after Anschluss for the focus to shift to Czechoslovakia, and in particular its Sudeten region peopled by German speakers. It was the obvious next target for Hitler. The British government's response to Anschluss was defensive and offered scant support to other countries bordering Germany. Chamberlain's view of Czechoslovakia chimed with many on the right-wing of politics in Britain – that it was a recently formed country, created hastily in the wake of the First World War, and not worth going to war over.

But Czechoslovakia had been a beacon for democracy in the post-war years, in contrast to countries such as Poland and indeed Austria, where fascist elements had risen to power. It was France that pushed the most positive and supportive case for Czechoslovakia. The two countries were bound by a military alliance struck in 1925, but also by a conviction that Czechoslovakia had been a success in its pursuit of democracy since its formation after the war. The country 'had done more for the minorities than any other European state' in the opinion of French Prime Minister Édouard Daladier.[443]

In Britain resolve was less strong about the status of Czechoslovakia. Kingsley Martin, the editor of the *New Statesman*, 'felt that things had gone so far that to plan armed resistance to the dictators was now useless. If there was a war we should lose it. We should, therefore, seek the most peaceful way of letting them gradually get all they wanted.'[444]

The major newspapers were divided. While the *Guardian* remained opposed to rearmament, *The Times* continued to encourage it, but was opposed to a British pledge of protection to Czechoslovakia. James Garvin, the *Observer*'s editor, thought that Germany had a right to interfere in central and eastern Europe, and that it was of no concern to Britain. The *Sunday Times* agreed. 'We have no alliance with Czechoslovakia, no interest of our own to serve except the remote contingency that later if Germany won and turned to invade France we might be fighting along on her side without Eastern allies,' declared the newspaper's *Scrutator* column.[445]

For the *Daily Mail*, Price was telling peers from other newspapers in private that Czechoslovakia was 'about to plunge civilisation into war because she was so obstinate about the Sudetenland'. He said this to Leo Kennedy of *The Times*, who dismissed him as a 'Nazi heart and soul'.[446] Kennedy's lacerating view of Price and the *Daily Mail* was shared by an increasing number of observers as Hitler continued to reveal his true colours. In May 1938 the *Daily Express* took a swipe at its rival, saying Rothermere's paper 'has spent the last five years assuring us that 'Dolfie Hitler is a wonderfully good fellow and is very fond of Britain'.[447]

In Berlin, Reynolds despaired. Levels of Nazi brutality were rising by the week, yet the newspaper he worked for maintained its placatory attitude to the Nazis. 'Czechoslovakia is not of the remotest concern to us,' Rothermere wrote in the *Daily Mail* on 6 May. 'If France likes to burn her fingers there, that is a matter for France.' A. L. Cranfield, the editor of the *Daily Mail*, passed proof versions of the article to the German ambassador in London before its publication.[448] Rothermere's words and Cranfield's actions sum up the complete control of the paper's leadership over its reporting on Germany.

Reynolds, together with Izzard, his assistant, and a correspondent named Paul Bretherton who came to help, continued running the *Daily Mail*'s Berlin bureau. But for all the big stories on their patch it was Price who did the reporting. Just a handful of articles carrying Reynolds's byline were printed in the paper in 1938. Increasingly frustrated, he took to saying the Holy Rosary prayer aloud in the streets. This drew the attention of bemused Nazi officials who could not decide if it was meant as a subtle demonstration. For the ageing Reynolds, who turned sixty-six in 1938, it was precisely that. The sight of a pious old Englishman muttering as he worked the beads through his fingers stood out amid the bland and colourless conformity of life under the Nazis. It was one small way in which Reynolds could resist their dominance, but it made him a potential target. Rothermere's sympathetic approach to German issues, however, meant there was little chance of his correspondents being expelled from Germany.

The journalists in the Berlin bureau became a magnet for Germans seeking foreign currency. 'A lot of the journalists went to Berlin to change their money there,' Izzard recalled. 'Whenever they could, they passed their straight currency on to individual Jews to help them get out of the country. This went on the whole time. These currency exchanges were local gathering points.'[449] The situation for Jews became increasingly desperate as it became more and more difficult for them to leave Germany.

The Nazis sought to extract high penalties from anyone wishing to leave, particularly Jews. Though sympathetic to their plight, other countries were growing intolerant of the wave of Jewish immigration. This was most particularly the case in Palestine, which was ruled by the British under a League of Nations mandate. There was increasing displeasure among Palestinians at the number of Jews coming to the country and buying land. Resentment in the region was rising and there was Arab support for Hitler, despite the fact that his oppressive treatment of Jews in Germany had caused so many to seek an exit to Palestine.

Reynolds was the close friend of a man doing his best to keep the route between Germany and Palestine open for Jews. Captain Frank Foley's official title was passport control officer attached to the British Embassy; but in reality he ran MI6 operations in Germany. A short and bespectacled man, Foley was not an obvious spy. Delmer of the *Daily Express* met him in 1933 and dismissed him as 'a rather commonplace little ex-captain'. But Foley had enjoyed an unusually successful career in espionage since being recruited after the First World War. He had helped recruit Jonny X, the Bolshevik agent Johann de Graff, who informed Britain about Soviet intelligence operations in the West during the 1930s.

Foley's cover role as passport control officer was far from trivial. It meant he was in charge of who had permission to leave Germany and move to the British Empire, a function that transformed in significance after Hitler's rise to power in 1933. Jews in Germany saw Palestine, Britain and America as destinations to which they could escape and leave the Nazi oppression behind. As the requests increased in the 1930s, the number of staff attached to the British Embassy's passport office rose from three to twenty-three. Foley arrived at his desk at 8 a.m. sharp every morning to handle the rising workload. 'No man in the service had harder or more heart-breaking work,' wrote Reynolds.[450] Foley had the utmost sympathy for the plight of Jews in Germany and disregarded official rules on how many visas could be granted, saving thousands of lives in the process.

Foley mixed with journalists including Reynolds and Ian Colvin of the *Morning Post* and later *News Chronicle*. In the course of 1938 alone, the Foleys met Reynolds for dinner on six occasions, according to the diary of Foley's wife, Kay. The MI6 man tried to recruit journalists to help with his work by passing on intelligence about Nazi activity. In 1933 he took Delmer to lunch and told him about the real nature of his work.

'Probably you know this already, Tom,' he said. 'But I must ask you to keep it secret all the same. I represent [MI6] here. We would like you to help us. You know all the Nazi bosses. If ever you get anything from them which you think might interest us, pass it on to me. I'll see that it goes straight to the Foreign Secretary himself.'[451]

Delmer was not interested in such work. 'Only very foolish newspaper men allow themselves to get mixed up with intelligence in peacetime,' he remarked in his memoirs.[452] Reynolds was more discreet than Delmer about his dealings with Foley, but he certainly had a closer relationship with MI6's man in Berlin. Whether he helped in an official or merely informal way is unknown. He had experience of the intelligence services from his wartime work for MI7. He may even have been active in St Petersburg – Arthur Ransome, who succeeded him in Russia for the *Daily News*, worked as a spy during the Bolshevik Revolution.

There is evidence that Frederick Voigt, a peer of Reynolds in 1930s Berlin, worked in intelligence. The assistant chief of MI6, Sir Claude Dansey, ran a shadowy 'Z' organisation to monitor Europe with the help of Lord Vansittart and other Whitehall hawks who viewed Germany as a threat. Voigt was recruited to help provide intelligence.[453] The truth about Reynolds is likely hidden forever. But he was certainly sympathetic to the Jews and other oppressed minorities in Germany. Like Foley, he did his best to help. 'Hundreds of victims of Nazi persecution and terror received from him material and moral support in an uneven fight with an evil system,' Reynolds's colleagues in the press pack later said.[454]

———

Tension over Czechoslovakia continued to simmer. On Thursday 19 May reports emerged from the country that Hitler was massing his army on the border. It seemed to be evidence of preparation for one of his weekend strikes. Britain and France had been nervously monitoring the volatile situation but did not expect Hitler, who had instructed his agents to spread unrest in the Sudeten region, to act so soon. A frantic sequence of diplomatic back-and-forth ensued before the two countries informed Hitler that they would not stand by if Germany invaded Czechoslovakia. For once, he stood back from the brink.

There was jubilation in the British press, which celebrated the passing of the crisis as a triumph of diplomacy. 'By refusing to be hurried into irremediable action or promises, by maintaining steadiness and calm, Mr Chamberlain has again revealed himself, to quote a foreign commentator, as an "exceptional statesman", proclaimed a leader in the *Mail*.[455] Voigt's column in the *Guardian* attributed the avoidance of war to the 'skilful precautionary measures of the Czechoslovak Government, thanks to the energetic diplomatic effort made by Great Britain, and thanks to the far-reaching collaboration between Great Britain and France'.[456]

Voigt's article in the aftermath of the May Crisis was the source of more tension between the reporter and his editor: 'I am afraid you will think I have omitted rather a lot of your article tonight, but it's a matter of tactics,' Crozier wrote to him. 'What you write about the German plans for the conquest of Czechoslovakia is vivid, and, I have no doubt at all, accurate.' However, Crozier did not want Voigt to publish details of likely German aggression for fear that it may rile the Nazis. 'On the other hand, I don't think that tonight, when we are hoping that we have just escaped, even if only for the time being, from the imminent outbreak of war, is the right time to describe the German plans for making war.'[457]

The passing of the May Crisis did not herald the end of Hitler's focus on Czechoslovakia. Incensed at the press reaction in the West, he redoubled his efforts. Ever sensitive to German feelings, Henderson in Berlin cautioned that jubilation would only make Hitler more determined. Rather than signal the beginning of a strong and united front against Germany, Britain and France again shrank back. There was a growing feeling that

Hitler, despite all his aggression, may have a case for some sort of say over the Sudeten lands. Even as critical an observer as Winston Churchill felt relaxed enough in June 1938 to assert in the pages of the *Daily Telegraph* that 'without the championship of armed Germany, Sudeten wrongs might never have been redressed'.[458]

Labour demands for an enquiry into Britain's air defences were rebuffed. As Hitler's pressure on Czechoslovakia remounted in the summer, the British government continued to baulk at the prospect of taking firm action. Defence spending was reviewed but not increased significantly. Churchill suggested to Halifax that 'a joint note to Berlin from a number of powers' might demonstrate to Germany that Britain objected to its aggression. He demurred. Suggestions that the British Navy assemble a fleet at Scapa Flow were rejected.[459]

Hitler was emboldened. 'See Germany for yourself. You will find truth in personal contacts. A hearty welcome awaits you,' read German tourism adverts in *The Times* in July 1938.[460] Talk grew of how Britain could somehow give way to Germany over Czechoslovakia, which would potentially be the last of her grievances. Some thought, in effect, that if war could be avoided over the issue, Europe would be home and dry. 'I don't myself object, and I have never objected, to the British government advising the Czechs to give way to the utmost degree that they can without endangering their existence,' Crozier wrote to Voigt on 26 July. 'But the British government should not push Czechoslovakia to a point where the Germans can get all they want by shaking Czechoslovakia to pieces from within.'[461]

Those on the right wing of politics and the newspaper trade were less cautious. An increasing number argued for some sort of accommodation with Hitler over Czechoslovakia. Many felt that the stance adopted by Britain and France during the May Crisis had been too firm. But they continued to press the case for rearmament, unlike papers on the left.

'You do not seem to know that today Great Britain, instead of being largely invulnerable as she was in 1914, is, owing to the development of aircraft, the most vulnerable country in Europe,' Rothermere wrote in an open letter to former *Times* editor Wickham Steed. 'If you and your friends had your way, you might provoke a war infinitely more disastrous that the Great War of 1914.'[462]

For the reporters in Berlin, getting to the truth of events was harder than ever. 'I listened to the barrage of abuse falling on Czechoslovakia,' wrote Reynolds. 'Goebbels' technique was the same as that which he had employed in the attack on Austria. To disentangle truth and falsehood in the columns of the newspapers, which it was my business to read, was impossible.' Reynolds suspected that the picture presented by Goebbels of the Sudetenland was not a true one. The Ministry of Propaganda described for the correspondents in Berlin a picture of 'ruthless oppression of German brothers across the frontier'. It was, noted Reynolds, 'in glaring contrast to the accounts given of peaceful towns and quiet countryside by travellers who passed through Sudetenland'.[463]

Reynolds was sure of one thing in the summer of 1938: that if Germany did wage war with Czechoslovakia, 'war would not be with Czechoslovakia alone'. He was convinced that Britain and France would maintain the solid stance established during the May Crisis. Like the rest of the world, he tensely looked on as politicians in Europe scrambled to bring the situation to some kind of conclusion.

By the summer of 1938, Iverach McDonald's short assignment for *The Times* in Berlin was over. In Germany, he had surveyed, with his foreign correspondent colleagues, the British government's growing drive for friendship with Germany. 'The parliamentary reports and the political speeches which we read from home left us floundering. There was nothing on which the mind could grip. Chamberlain was obviously dealing with a

Hitler of his own imagination, not the homicidal madman whom we heard screaming in the Reichstag,' he wrote. 'Worse still, for us who worked on *The Times* the confusion and sense of unreality were far the greater because the leading articles were descending steadily, step by step with Neville Chamberlain, to the paper's nadir of appeasement.'[464]

-CHAPTER XV-
'QUARREL IN A FAR-AWAY COUNTRY'

Towards the end of July 1938 came a scoop for *The Times*. Dawson's continued fraternisation with Chamberlain, Halifax and other government ministers bore fruit when his paper was the first to report on a new government attempt to calm the growing crisis in central Europe. Lord Runciman, a former Cabinet member, was to be sent to Czechoslovakia to mediate between the government of Edvard Beneš and Sudeten German Party politicians. Though the 'Runciman Mission', which took place over a few days at the start of September, did not produce a resolution to the Sudeten dispute, the British press warmly welcomed the initiative.

Ahead of the talks came an incident that permanently broke Chamberlain's faith in Rex Leeper's Foreign Office News Department. The section leaked news to the *Daily Herald*'s diplomatic correspondent that Hitler's friend, Captain Wiedemann, had met with Halifax at the Foreign Office. This report was considered to be grossly unhelpful, as was all news relating to the government's discussions with Germany. Leeper was informed that his department should say nothing about upcoming discussions led by

Lord Runciman.[465] It was the beginning of the end. Leeper was removed from his post later in the year.

Great columns topped by Nazi and German symbols in front of the Brandenburg Gate, pictured by eighteen-year-old Anthony Hewson in August 1938.

A second picture of central Berlin taken by Hewson in August 1938 during a visit to Reynolds.

Runciman was in Czechoslovakia when *The Times* was preparing an article that would transform the debate around central Europe. Dawson's attitude to Czechoslovakia had been criticised in the summer of 1938 by John Walter, a co-owner of *The Times*, whose forebears had founded the newspaper. He was a figure of some authority but was very much the junior partner to the Astor family. He criticised *Times* policy in the summer of 1938 in a letter to Dawson, suggesting it was favouring the wolf of Germany over the lamb of Czechoslovakia. Dawson replied saying he did not think Germany wanted a revision of borders.

But Dawson was not prepared to rule it out altogether. On Tuesday 6 September he returned to the office after almost a month away to find some draft leading articles awaiting his attention. One of them focused on Czechoslovakia. He worked on it until after midnight, rewriting and tweaking, and published it the next day. The leader raised the possibility of Sudeten secession, saying Czechoslovakia could be 'a more homogenous state by the secession of that fringe of alien populations who are contiguous to the nation with which they are united by race'.[466]

The article caused a global sensation. For *The Times* to be putting forward the suggestion that Czechoslovakian borders may need to be adjusted was a landmark moment. The paper's reputation as a mirror for government thinking meant many thought this was Chamberlain's way of slipping his preferred solution into the open. Other even more cynical critics thought it bore the fingerprints of the German Embassy. Under pressure from Czechoslovakia the Foreign Office issued a statement saying the *Times* leader did not reflect its own views. Even Runciman admitted that the final paragraph appeared to recommend an Anschluss. Behind the scenes, diplomats contacted the British Embassy in Prague and asked it to underline to the Czech government that it was not representative of official thinking in Britain.

The uproar sparked by the editorial conspired with the ongoing summer tension to offer Hitler an opening. He planned to capitalise on the tumult. The annual Nuremberg rally was scheduled for the following days. The 1938 edition was named the 'Rally of Greater Germany' to celebrate the country's Anschluss with Austria six months earlier. Hitler used his speech to attack Beneš and make aggressive noises about the treatment of Sudeten Germans in Czechoslovakia.

The press barons moved to make their presence felt. In the Manchester office of the *Daily Sketch*, a popular newspaper owned by *Sunday Times* proprietor Lord Kemsley, sub-editors were busily laying out the paper's coverage when the phone rang. The London office, after speaking to the proprietor, had a very specific instruction. They wanted the Nuremberg report to be accompanied by a favourable photograph of Hitler alongside the word 'peace'. The message was passed onto the chief sub-editor, who responded: 'Well, that's not my reading of Hitler's speech.' But the order had been made. 'It was another instance of journalistic knowledge, experience and sense of responsibility to the public being overridden by the fiat [decree] of a press lord,' a staff member told the Royal Commission on the Press after the war.[467] It was an early example of the increasing interference by British press proprietors over how their papers covered relations with Germany, which reached a peak during negotiations in September and October 1938.

Runciman returned to London with the message that Czechoslovakia could not continue in its current form indefinitely. Chamberlain asked him to go and speak to Hitler but Runciman refused – he had been unwell in the summer heat and wanted to play no further part. In an unexpected development, Chamberlain himself decided to go and meet Hitler in Berchtesgaden. The press barons remained onside. Lord Beaverbook assured Chamberlain that it had the backing of his newspapers as he negotiated with central European countries.[468]

Neville Chamberlain flew to Germany on 15 September. It was his first ever flight in an aeroplane. He travelled in a silver twin-engine Lockheed

Electra and landed at Munich airport at 12.30 p.m. He was greeted by Henderson, who remarked that 'Mr Chamberlain stepped out of the machine looking remarkably fresh and quite unperturbed.'[469] Also present was Price of the *Daily Mail*, who had a unique ability to be present for the most important moments in European foreign affairs. He later produced a colourful description of Chamberlain. 'A stiff wing-collar and grey silk tie completed the English character of his appearance, and in his hand was grasped the umbrella which was soon to become famous.'[470]

Hitler had organised a special train to take the party of thirty, which included Chamberlain, Ribbentrop, Henderson and Horace Wilson, to Berchtesgaden. The passengers made their way through a five-course meal of turtle soup, trout, roast beef and Yorkshire pudding, cheesecakes and fruit during the journey, which lasted several hours. At Berchtesgaden Chamberlain was cordially greeted by Hitler. The two men agreed the outline of a deal whereby Hitler would have control of areas in the Sudetenland where more than half of the population was German. But Chamberlain still needed the approval of the French – and would have to inform the Czechoslovakian government, which was sidelined from the process altogether.

Around this time Henderson's view of Göring dimmed. The ambassador had previously got on well with Hitler's senior lieutenant and his wife. The trio had shared a light-hearted relationship. On one occasion, when Emmy Göring declined to eat a desert, Henderson asked if it was a 'question of her excellent figure', to which she replied: 'Oh no. Hermann likes women who are fat.'[471] But Göring joined Hitler in making threats about Czechoslovakia. 'If England means to make war on Germany, no one knows what the ultimate end will be. But one thing is quite certain. Before the war is over there will be very few Czechs left alive and little of London left standing,' Göring warned.[472]

Chamberlain spoke to the French and got approval for the proposed settlement. The proposals were then sent to Prague. 'We have chosen a shameful peace and shall have a terrible war,' a despairing Voigt wrote in his diary. 'If only we would learn the lesson and pull ourselves together, put our industries on a war-basis and [conscript] men and money. All would not be lost then. But we won't do it, we won't! Disaster is coming, hastened on by ourselves.'[473] Churchill wrote a bullish dispatch from inside Czechoslovakia for the *Telegraph*, saying there was 'an absolute determination to fight for life and freedom'.[474]

A week after the Berchtesgaden meeting, Chamberlain returned to Germany to inform Hitler that their outlined deal had been approved. They met in the western German city of Bad Godesberg, where Hitler had an unpleasant surprise for his guest. He was no longer happy with their previously proposed settlement and wanted all of the Sudetenland. Chamberlain refused. The failure of the second meeting meant that war looked likely. Price, who was reporting on the meeting, received a blunt message from the London office:

> From every part of Germany we are getting news of troops marching, and ordinary trains held up to make way for military transport. The Czech army is being mobilised. It looks as though war may start at once. When are you getting out of Germany yourself? It won't be a good place for an Englishman after the Prime Minister has left.[475]

It was a similar situation in Berlin. On 26 September, three days after Chamberlain's departure, Reynolds was sitting in a coffee-house listening to Hitler speak on the radio. It was a live transmission of a speech he was making in the *Sportpalast*, a huge indoor sports arena in Berlin. He attacked Czechoslovakia in the harshest terms and demanded freedom for its Sudeten population. Reynolds thought the game was up. The faces of the men and women around him were 'grave, like masks,' he wrote. 'Once a woman clapped her hands feebly, but nobody followed her example.'[476]

Believing war to be inevitable, Reynolds left Berlin. He did not have the time to organise his belongings or say goodbye to his many acquaintances. Other members of the British press pack in Berlin did the same. 'Some went one way and some another,' wrote Reynolds. 'The train taking several of us westwards went through the night across the German plain. It was a relief to wake early in the morning and find oneself in Belgium, in freedom and in safety.'[477]

Reynolds spent his first night outside Germany in Amsterdam, where he had been instructed to open an office. Taking breakfast the next morning, he read in his newspaper the news that the governments of Britain, France, Germany and Italy were to meet in Munich to discuss the situation. 'There was to be no war,' Reynolds later wrote. 'I ordered a place in an aeroplane and returned to Berlin.'[478]

Chamberlain had taken events at Bad Godesberg terribly. 'How horrible, fantastic, incredible it is that we should be digging trenches and trying on gas masks here because of a quarrel in a far-away country between people of whom we know nothing,' he said in a public address on 27 September. But talks at Munich offered a small window of hope. He was desperate and felt no option but to reach again for a settlement, despite Hitler's dishonourable actions. The House of Commons greeted the announcement of more talks with fevered cheers.

'The whole place was on its feet. A huge prolonged cheer and a tempest of waving order papers,' wrote Robert Barrington-Ward, deputy editor of *The Times*, who was watching from the public gallery. 'It was electrifying.' He returned to the office and penned an editorial titled: 'On to Munich'.[479]

On Thursday 29 September, Chamberlain rose at 6.30 a.m. He shaved and dressed before joining his wife for an early breakfast. At 7.50 a.m., he walked to a waiting car that took him to Heston Airport, to the west of London. He arrived forty minutes later and was surprised to find that most of his Cabinet had gathered to see him off. 'If at first you don't succeed, try, try again,' he said in a short, light-hearted speech.[480] The mood was positive.

Price lingered on the sidelines. Lord Halifax beckoned him over, holding up one of the day's newspapers, which had 'Hitler Sees the Red Light' splashed across its front page. 'If you hear any reference to that in Germany today,' said Halifax, 'tell them that it does not at all represent the point of view of the British public.'[481] The instruction gave away the mood of the British government ahead of the Munich talks – its priority was to keep Germany happy. The best way of doing this was by appeasing Hitler.

Some of the press had been sceptical of a third round of talks. 'The nation cannot prudently afford to purchase present ease at the expense of future trouble,' the *Telegraph* wrote in a leading article in the days beforehand. 'With the will to peace it is possible to make accommodation. It is vain to ignore the fact that throughout this crisis all the concessions have come from one side.'[482] But most were supportive of the attempt to find a solution at Munich. The alternative to success appeared to be war.

Chamberlain met with Hitler, Mussolini and Daladier at Munich. The deal that emerged gave Hitler exactly what he wanted: the Sudetenland. Vernon Bartlett, reporting for the *News Chronicle*, was among the first to learn of the proposed settlement, which required Hitler to sign a commitment to future peace. He rang the office in London to pass on the news. He said it was as bad as could be – that Chamberlain had sold out the Czechs. The editor Gerald Barry wanted to do a strongly critical leader, but his chief, Walter Layton, refused. 'If that's the news, it's too yellow to print,' he said.[483]

There were rumours in the press that Chamberlain despised Hitler at the time of agreement but felt he had no option but to negotiate. On his return from Munich, the Prime Minister apparently said Hitler was the 'most dreadful man' he had ever met. He also knew Hitler may well break his vow of peace, but felt that securing it was important so that the American government would subsequently realise the extent of his bad faith.[484] Whatever the truth, Chamberlain returned to London a hero. He was able to wave Hitler's commitment to peace in the air as evidence that he had secured 'peace for our time'. Henderson wrote him a glowing letter of praise. 'Millions of mothers will be blessing your name tonight for having saved their sons from the horrors of war. Oceans of ink will flow hereafter in criticism of your action.'[485] Both statements proved accurate. But in the immediate aftermath of the Munich Agreement, criticism was drowned out by praise.

The *Sunday Times*, edited by Chamberlain supporter W. W. Hadley, was the most uncritical. Even the *Telegraph* and *Daily Herald*, papers that had criticised government policy over relations with Germany, were initially applauding. 'Journals were all but unanimous in their expression of the warmest gratitude to the government, and especially to the Prime Minister, for the maintenance of peace,' Hadley later wrote. 'In not one of them was it suggested that in the discussion with Germany about Czechoslovakia any issues were raised which justified war.'[486]

Pressure was brought to bear on the *News Chronicle*, the paper that, along with the *Guardian*, infuriated the Nazis most. The Home Secretary Sir Samuel Hoare had made a special effort with the newspaper, owned by the conservative Cadbury brothers and managed by Layton. The *News Chronicle* had criticised Britain's approach to the question of Germany and Czechoslovakia right up until 27 September. Hoare had then made a series of direct interventions to try and persuade it to tone down its coverage. These interventions made an impact on Layton, blunting the paper's coverage around the time of the Munich Agreement.

Shortly after the talks began, a *News Chronicle* correspondent had brought back a leaflet bearing a purported timetable of Hitler's planned conquest of Europe. Layton blocked publication that night, but promised the paper could print it within twenty-four hours. He then changed his mind and sent it to Chamberlain, who asked for it to be withheld. The document was not reported until March 1939. After the Munich Agreement, Bartlett described it as 'an almost complete capitulation to Hitler'. Layton's intervention ensured this message, too, was not printed.[487]

On another occasion, the *Chronicle*'s Berlin correspondent H. D. Harrison, who had worked in Germany since his expulsion from Yugoslavia in 1937, received information about plans in the Brown House in Prague for a Nazi takeover of Czechoslovakia and other territories. Layton asked Chamberlain, just as he returned from Munich, whether to publish. He was advised not to and obeyed.[488]

A poll after Munich revealed that 86 per cent of the British public did not believe Hitler when he said he had no further territorial ambitions – but Layton, the *News Chronicle* editor, refused to publish it. Instead, he wrote to Chamberlain to explain the reasons behind his decision. 'I fear that so blunt an advertisement of the state of British public opinion on this matter would exacerbate feelings in Germany.'[489] Again, German feelings took precedence over the freedom of the press.

The *Daily Mail* remained unwavering in its support of the government's efforts at Munich, though Rothermere's attitude to the discussions veered. He was stunned by German demands at Bad Godesberg for the complete secession of all the Sudetenland on 26 September, but his faith in the process was quickly restored. The Munich Agreement 'brings to Europe the blessed prospect of peace', was the *Mail*'s verdict on the day the agreement was struck.

Rothermere and other newspaper proprietors fell over themselves in attempts to praise Chamberlain following the Munich Agreement to such an extent that the Prime Minister started to consider himself untouchable. On a visit to Paris later in the year, he was booed as he walked the streets with the French Prime Minister Édouard Daladier. The press in Britain reported on this, much to his annoyance. That a Prime Minister should take umbrage at perfectly legitimate reporting of booing perhaps demonstrates just how thin his skin had become in office.

The Times welcomed the Munich Agreement, to the great upset of several staff members. Some junior staff resigned, seeing it as the outcome of a process started by *The Times* editorial on 7 September, which mooted the possibility of border changes.[490] *Times* coverage of German relations and the Munich Conference led to the resignation of its parliamentary correspondent, Anthony Winn, in October 1938. He had worked for the *Yorkshire Post* before joining *The Times* at a young age, where he was highly regarded. Soon after assuming day-to-day control at the *Daily Mail* in 1937, Lord Rothermere's son Esmond Harmsworth tried to recruit him.

Winn's dismay about Chamberlain's efforts to negotiate with Hitler was shared by his friend Alfred Duff Cooper, who served in the government as the First Lord of the Admiralty. Several senior members of the Cabinet considered resigning in the wake of the Munich Agreement, but only Cooper took the step. Informing Chamberlain of his desire to leave the government, Cooper said he would have accepted 'war with honour or peace with dishonour', but not a situation that he felt would lead to war with dishonour. After his speech in Parliament, Churchill leaned forward with a note. 'Your speech was one of the finest parliamentary performances I have ever heard.'[491] In the same House of Commons debate, Churchill expressed his sorrow at the deal made in Munich. 'Silent, mournful, abandoned, broken, Czechoslovakia recedes into the darkness,' he intoned. 'We have sustained a total and unmitigated defeat.'[492]

Winn submitted his account of Cooper's speech to be published in his lobby correspondence column the next day. The *Times* editor overseeing the piece altered it and described the speech as a 'damp squib'. When the piece appeared the next day, this damning verdict appeared as Winn's own opinion.[493] He resigned from the paper, telling Dawson that he could no longer work for a newspaper that had advocated Sudeten secession and supported the Munich Agreement. Dawson, who had been something of a father figure to the young journalist, took it personally. The paper closed ranks after that. Dawson sought solace by writing to Lady Astor, the beating heart of the 'Cliveden Set', informing her that he had discovered Winn had been offered a job at the *Daily Telegraph* before quitting *The Times*. His meaning was clear – though Winn supposedly left over Munich, he was only ever focused on his own career.

Another man who resigned in the wake of the Munich Agreement was Douglas Reed, who had worked for *The Times* in Vienna. He joined the *News Chronicle* in December. The newspaper's leadership took their staff's resistance personally. 'Most of the office is against Dawson and me!' wrote Barrington-Ward after discussions with staff in October had revealed the extent of the unhappiness.[494]

The government continued its efforts to influence what newspapers wrote about British foreign policy. It was not just politicians such as Chamberlain and Halifax who pondered how this could be achieved. In October 1938, just days after Munich, Rothermere cabled Halifax to highlight German fears that newspapers in London, 'with their cartoons and comments will provoke war between Britain and Germany'. His worry was palpable. 'Can nothing be done?' For a newspaper owner to lobby a government minister about taking steps to censor the press was surely a unique moment in history.[495]

Some newspapers would not be swayed. Less than a fortnight after its initially warm response to Munich, the *Telegraph* had reverted to a critical position. In a leader the newspaper pointed out that Hitler had 'obtained, through the machinery of Munich, a still larger slice of Czechoslovakia than he had sought by the method of the ultimatum at Godesburg'.[496] Its more independent mindset compared to other newspapers on the right of politics in this period stemmed in part from the independence of its owner. Of all the press barons in the 1930s, the *Daily Telegraph*'s owner Lord Camrose had the least contact with the governments of the day. This was curious, since the Conservatives had held power for much of the decade and the paper was regarded as a respected defender of conservative values in the press (more so than *The Times*, which had a tendency to ally itself with the current government, whatever its colour). But Camrose ensured his newspaper's independence. It is perhaps telling that he was one of the proprietors to have enjoyed a close relationship with the ever-hawkish Churchill.

The *Guardian* finally started arguing for more rearmament after Munich. 'No government can discharge its duty or protect its interests unless it has behind it material strength and confidence,' it said in a leader on 29 October. At this point the *News Chronicle*, despite its criticisms, was still not arguing for rearmament. Bartlett, who had become a star reporter for the newspaper, responded to the Munich Agreement by standing as an independent candidate at a by-election in the Somerset seat of Bridgwater later in 1938. Campaigning solely on the basis of opposition to the deal with Germany, he won the hitherto safe Conservative seat and held onto it for a further twelve years.

Another journalist facing a battle who showed commendable independence of spirit in the days after Munich was Arthur Mann, the editor of the influential Conservative-leaning *Yorkshire Post* newspaper. He was a man ahead of his time. He had quietly rejected two offers of a knight-hood from Stanley Baldwin in 1923 and 1929, believing that they would undermine his independence as a newspaperman. Owners and editors of other Conservative newspapers had no such qualms. He showed a similarly independent attitude in criticising the government's policy of appeasement in the 1930s despite objections from the newspaper's owner, Rupert Beckett.[497]

The tension between Mann and Beckett, who expected his editor to sup-port the government of the day, especially if it was Conservative, hit a fresh peak after Munich. Mann persistently tried to voice opposition, drawing the ire of Chamberlain and other government figures in London. 'I believe that most editors follow a golden rule not to be in close social relationships with ministers of the crown,' Mann later said during a BBC radio broadcast. 'For as journalists they may be called upon to criticise them.'[498] At the time of the Munich Agreement he put these words into practice.

In Berlin, the days after the Munich Agreement were fraught. Reynolds could not believe that Chamberlain had struck a deal so injurious to Czechoslovakia without inviting them to join the discussions. He con-sidered resigning, but hesitated. His job required him to remain in Berlin and report on the unfolding drama. Hitler wasted no time in ordering his army across the border into the Sudetenland.

Reynolds accompanied the first detachment of German troops to cross the Czech border and reported on 3 October that 'German troops are tonight still taking peaceful possession of the territory ceded to Germany by Czechoslovakia.'[499] Appeasement critics in London mourned the news. 'Today they march in. Poor Czechoslovakia! I wouldn't mind so much if I thought we would learn the lesson – and arm, arm, arm!' Voigt wrote in his diary.[500]

The next day Reynolds was in the Bohemian region of Egerland to report on Hitler's speech. 'Never again shall this land be torn away from the Reich,' Hitler told a large crowd.[501] These reports were the last series of dispatches Reynolds sent from Germany. He knew in his heart he could not go on reporting on the events for a newspaper that remained so uncritical. He started to plan his departure from Berlin.

-CHAPTER XVI-
BROKEN GLASS

Take the number 41 bus from the centre of Bedford and you will soon find yourself in the picturesque village of Turvey. It is surrounded by pretty English countryside, and the thirteenth-century church of All Saints stands proudly at its heart. Less visible is the Monastery of Christ Our Saviour, tucked away just off the main road into the village. It is home to a small order of Benedictine monks who worship five times a day, quietly and peacefully preserving an ancient way of living at odds with the noise and tumult of modern life.

The eldest monk there is Herbert Kaden, an extraordinary man born a German Jew in Dresden in 1921. He had fled to Britain in 1938 with his mother and joined relatives, while they were still able to escape. He subsequently became a Catholic and, years later, a monk. I met him for the first time in February 2015, one month after his ninety-fourth birthday. 'We don't normally celebrate birthdays here, but made an exception on this occasion,' he reflected with a grin.[502] Tracking Kaden down had not been easy, but he was the first person I was able to interview who had personally known Reynolds.

On moving to Britain, Kaden and his mother had lived at 3 Belvoir Terrace in Cambridge, next door to the house that Reynolds later lived in when he returned from Germany. The pair had spoken several times and Reynolds's sisters, Kathleen and Marjorie, took Kaden to his first Catholic church service in December 1939. It was the first Midnight Mass of the war. Seventy-six years on, his memory pencil-sharp, Kaden vividly recalled stories from his youth before giving me a tour of the monastery. Bald, slightly built and with a bushy white beard, Kaden walked spryly through the grounds, using his wooden staff more as a propulsion device than for support. It was a struggle to keep up.

His observations and recollections proved useful in the writing of this book, not just when it came to the Reynolds family. His memories of growing up a Jew in Nazi Germany provided a haunting picture of the harsh circumstances facing the Jewish community under Hitler. One of many low moments came when Kaden and his mother were evicted from their flat. 'The landlord said, "I am sorry but I have to give you notice, as you are Jewish." We tried to find other lodgings in the town, very naively. When my mother told them we were Jewish, they wouldn't take us,' he recalled.[503] His uncle eventually persuaded them to leave Germany – in the nick of time, as it transpired.

Others were not so lucky. Life for the Jewish population the Kaden family left behind in Germany was already difficult, but conditions plunged to a new low in November 1938 with the events of *Kristallnacht*. It was the most serious outbreak of violence against the country's Jewish population yet. Persecution of the Jews had caused almost 150,000 to emigrate from Germany between 1933 and 1938,[504] but the majority of the country's Jews had stayed – some were unable to leave, while many remained in the belief their oppression would not worsen. On *Kristallnacht* their worst fears were realised.

The violence that began on the night of 9 November was precipitated by an attack on a member of the German Embassy in Paris by a seventeen-year-old Polish Jew, Herschel Grynszpan. The diplomat died of gunshot wounds and the result was a pogrom quietly encouraged by the German authorities. Its impact was brutal. The glass fronts of Jewish shops were destroyed, leading to the brutality being given a name – 'the Night of Broken Glass' – which almost trivialises the violence of events. One hundred Jews died as homes and temples were razed to the ground. About 20,000 Jews were arrested and sent to concentration camps.

Goebbels ordered the rioters to cease but it had little impact, with the violence continuing for a second night. Reynolds witnessed the brutality and the unwillingness of police and firefighters to stem the disorder and destruction. In the days that followed, he heard several Berliners joke that Jews were re-opening their shops so that rioters could swap the plundered goods they had stolen. Reynolds found it difficult to get an accurate picture of the level of violence. 'News of such crimes is not published by the German papers, and it was only little by little that one formed a picture of the horror of those November nights.'[505]

He spoke to one woman whose house had been broken into by three men, two wearing Nazi uniforms, in the middle of the night. 'They threw over the wardrobe and smashed everything within their reach,' she said. 'And then they took my husband away.'[506] The man was taken to a concentration camp before returning ten days later, feeling too threatened and intimidated to speak about what had happened. In another instance, Reynolds heard about brave German parents who had been harangued by their children for sheltering a Jewish couple from the violence. Only narrowly had they convinced their offspring – who were 'ardent Nazis and Storm Troopers' – not to denounce them to the authorities.[507]

For Reynolds, the events were proof of the depravity of Hitler's regime. 'The murder [in Paris] gave the German government the long-desired occasion for carrying out its plan for totally crippling the Jewish minority,' he wrote, 'completing the process of cutting them off from the rest of the nation and of depriving them of the means of gaining a livelihood.'[508] After years of observing steadily rising levels of state oppression towards Germany's Jews, Reynolds knew exactly how calculating Hitler had been to achieve his latest and most effective victory against them. Tens of thousands of young men were 'primed with tales of a conspiracy of the Jews of the world against the German people' and then 'sent into the streets of the towns of Germany to ravish, destroy and terrify'. After this, 'laws, as cruel as the laws by which Elizabeth condemned the Catholics of England to a life of fear and seclusion, could be published and made known to the world'.[509]

The assassination in Paris and subsequent anti-Jewish rioting gave the Nazis the pretext they needed to act. This much was clear from the menacing statement of intent that accompanied Goebbels's call for the rioting to end. 'Jewry fired on the German people in Paris. The German Government will reply to this in a legal but in a hard way. Laws and decrees which settle the question are to be expected.'[510]

'Hard' was an understatement. The subsequent decrees issued by Göring made it almost impossible to exist as a Jew in Germany. The first decree barred Jews from selling their goods and services in markets and other public arenas. 'Thus, thousands were doomed to beggary in a morning,' Reynolds wrote.[511] Even his dentist was barred from practising, due to his Jewish grandparents of which he became aware only when attempting to prove his Aryan descent. That dentist had himself replaced Reynolds's previous dentist, also a Jew, who had wisely chosen to move to America at the start of the Nazi reign of persecution.

Other decrees forced Jews to pay punishing fines and banned them from making insurance claims after the damage they had suffered during *Kristallnacht*. They were stopped from visiting certain areas of Berlin. Reynolds was damning about how the wider German population had reacted to the oppression. 'The German people has not displayed the heroic qualities required to resist a policy that is condemned as unjust by a large majority of the population.'[512] He felt judges, employers and police were all to blame for acceding too easily, or even enthusiastically, to the Nazi will. During these bleak days, Reynolds made the final decision to leave Berlin. 'To look on, helpless, at the suffering inflicted on innocent people, was to lose all joy in life.'[513]

Rothay (far left) with friends in Berlin in 1938, pictured by Anthony Hewson. His time in Germany was nearing an end.

After striking a bullish and supportive tone towards Hitler and the Nazis for most of the 1930s, the *Daily Mail*'s reporting on *Kristallnacht* marked a new departure for the paper. The brutality was too flagrant to turn a blind eye. The paper's news pages described the events in a straight fashion, with a special late edition reporting 'Anti-Jew riots in Germany' the day after the first night of violence. In the days that followed, headlines included:

'Jew-baiters defy Goebbels' order'

'Jewish shops' stock hurled into street'

'Nazis threaten to ration Jews' food'

'1,000 Jews sent to gaol camp'

'German Jews to pay £250 each'

On Sunday 14 November, five days after the start of *Kristallnacht*, came a strident editorial, 'The World Protests', which struck a different tone from previous columns.[514] The contrast with the newspaper's support for the Munich Agreement and prior lack of criticism towards Germany and Hitler is striking.

'The world is appalled by the crushing nature of the new penalties imposed on the Jews in Germany,' the leader said. 'Their disabilities were already so heavy that it seemed impossible that their condition could be worsened. Now they are to be denied not only freedom of movement and opportunities for advancement but almost the right to live.' It sounded like something Reynolds would have written himself, so closely did the sentiment reflect his own feelings. 'To punish a helpless minority of 600,000 people for the act of an unbalanced youth is to outrage the name of justice … Christendom cannot shut its eyes to this wholesale oppression.' It ends by imploring the Nazi leadership to exercise restraint and control the rioters responsible for the violence. 'Even now, hopes were expressed last night that Germany might yet heed the call of humanity and show moderation – and mercy.'[515]

The stinging editorial echoed the united response of the British press in general, which was uniformly critical of the events of *Kristallnacht*. The American ambassador returned to Washington in protest. But the *Daily Mail*'s change of tone came too late to convince Reynolds to stay. His relationship with the newspaper had deteriorated too substantially. Ageing and tired of life in Germany, by the end of 1938 he was ready to come home. As his disapproval of the Munich Agreement had shown, Reynolds knew that Hitler's near-total dominance in the country and increasing confidence on the world stage made war inevitable. He continued to lament Britain's policy of appeasement.

Depressed, Reynolds battled to keep warm through yet another harsh German winter. His palatial Tiergarten flat was ideal for parties but hard to heat. He was tired of Berlin. By 1939 he had spent seventeen years in the city, for which he had initially felt no particular fondness. To him it could not compete with the cuisine of France or the Catholic splendour of Warsaw, and their contrast with the German capital grew in his mind as the storm clouds continued to darken. 'I felt an ever-increasing weight of oppression,' he wrote. 'The gaiety that nature had given me was being quenched in the gloom around me.'[516]

Bitterness and regret consumed his final months there. At sixty-six, his years were advancing, and it saddened him to think he was leaving and his career ending at such a dismal time. He later gave the following account of everyday life at the time:

> Bread was grey and disagreeable, giving people indigestion. Last Christmas [1938], the German people had no oranges, no coffee, and the less one investigated eggs the better. Butter was rationed – and that was in a time of peace. But they must not grumble in Germany: an overheard grumble meant a hand on the shoulder and a concentration camp. At that time every penny was being diverted to the war machine. One could not get a yard of decent cloth in the whole of Berlin.[517]

Reynolds was desperate for the home comforts of England. 'Who is contented in Germany after six years of Hitler's rule?' he asked. 'The number, judging from conversations I have had with people of every class, is small.'[518] He left in February 1939. Mystery surrounds the exact circumstances of his departure. He was not expelled by the Nazis – the *Daily Mail* was one of the few foreign newspapers whose correspondents could rest easy on that front.

But he certainly left under a cloud. There were suggestions in a history of the *Daily Mail* written in 1998 that he was dismissed by the newspaper. Homosexuality was given as the likely reason.[519] It is possible that a journalist would be fired on such grounds in light of the attitudes and laws of the era. The truth of the claim in respect to Reynolds, who remained a bachelor his whole life, is unknown. He referenced girlfriends on occasion, but it is impossible to know the full truth. Had he been gay he would have had to be immensely discreet, as he was in all things. Perhaps more important is that, by the start of 1939, Reynolds and the newspaper were more than happy to part ways. It is possible that after the Munich Agreement his hostility to the newspaper's favourable attitude to Hitler spilled into open argument with the office in London. With homosexuality a crime, could such a rumour have provided a convenient excuse for him to be pressured out of the newspaper? No evidence remains to suggest this was the case, and at sixty-six he was past retirement age. Yet his decision to later resume work as a foreign correspondent for another newspaper suggests he was not ready to stop.

Reynolds packed his belongings and prepared to depart. It was not an easy task to get permission to send his many books and household goods to Britain. Receiving permission to even leave the country was no easy business, though Reynolds had a much easier time than Germany's remaining Jewish population, who had to retrieve the passports they had been forced to give up. In some instances, Reynolds wrote, 'emigrants are not infrequently stripped at the frontier on the pretext that they may be concealing money or jewels'.[520] A customs official came to Reynolds's flat to watch his belongings being packed away. 'So many people are leaving Germany,' he said, 'that we cannot cope with the work.'[521]

Reynolds, who was replaced by his assistant Izzard, was about to take on a fresh challenge. On his departure from Berlin he had already begun planning a book about his time in Germany. He wanted to reveal the full truth as he saw it, without the restraints imposed by working for the *Daily Mail*. It was his chance to reveal his true views about Hitler and the Nazis. After nearly two decades abroad, it was with some relief and indeed enthusiasm that he returned to Britain.

———

'It is pleasant to be in England again,' Reynolds wrote, continuing:

> Here men do not turn their heads to see whether anybody is within earshot before daring to criticise a decision made by the government. No nervous visitor throws his coat over the telephone on my desk before beginning to talk. Fear of the denunciator does not poison life. No victim of persecution comes to me to unfold a tale of undeserved misery and to implore my help to get to some friendlier land. I am not filled with anxiety by news of the arrest of a colleague or friend.[522]

The first signs of spring greeted Reynolds on his arrival in Britain, further boosting his mood at being home and out of Germany. He knew war was coming, but at least in Britain he could relax with family and friends he had been separated from for so long. Soon after his arrival he was invited to speak to students at Oxford University. He told them in his speech that he firmly believed that they would soon be fighting against Hitler.[523]

Reynolds considered settling in Canterbury, but ended up returning to his university roots at Cambridge. He lived on the edge of the town with his three surviving siblings, Kathleen, Ronald and Marjorie. 'This house is like a London house with a drawing-room upstairs,' he said in a letter to a relative. 'We have quite a big garden, with flowers, vegetables and fruit, which is a great pleasure. There one might be in the country, while actually we are close to my old college, Pembroke.'[524]

Reynolds's first months back in Britain were a soothing contrast to life in Berlin. For the first time in years he could relax, though he remained pained by memories of his time abroad. 'The things seen and heard in the years in Germany cannot be banished from the mind.'[525] His new quieter surroundings, and their contrast with the bustling urban pace of Berlin, were essential for the task he now set himself: writing a full and uncensored account of the Nazi rise to power. This was therapeutic in one way – at last he could give a true account of life in Berlin, with editors far less likely to interfere than at the *Daily Mail*. He started the task of finding a publisher for his book.

———

Events in Europe continued to accelerate. Chamberlain had resisted calls for a quicker pace of rearmament for fear of undermining the Munich Agreement. He did not want to rile Germany in any way. Warnings from the Secretary of State for Air, Sir Kingsley Wood, that the air force was 'seriously deficient as compared with Germany' were overruled.[526] Not only did British ministers believe the agreement to be worth safeguarding, they were prepared to tolerate German air superiority as the price of its protection. Yet in the early months of 1939, Hitler was planning a move that would blow apart the Munich Agreement.

The *News Chronicle*, whose strong reporting and sharp criticism in the run-up to Munich had been blunted at the eleventh hour by the intervention of Walter Layton, its editor-in-chief, found its teeth again as the new year got underway. The author H. G. Wells wrote an article in which he described Hitler as a 'certifiable lunatic'. This piece was the cause of considerable angst within Chamberlain's government, which continued to be keenly sensitive on Germany's behalf.[527]

They would have reacted with horror to the book that the *Daily Telegraph*'s Eric Gedye was in the final stages of writing at the start of 1939. Since his expulsion from Austria in March, he had been working on his anti-appeasement tome *Fallen Bastions*, which fiercely criticised the foreign policy of Neville Chamberlain. He had continued working for the *Telegraph* in Prague while writing the book, which was being published by Hodder & Stoughton in London. In the publisher's 1939 spring list, the book was advertised as telling 'the uncensored truth'. This did not go down well in the *Telegraph*'s London headquarters. At the start of 1939, the editor Arthur Watson recalled him at short notice to the office. An argument ensued, with Gedye accused of breaching his status as an impartial correspondent by writing the book. He was given six months' pay and removed from the newspaper.[528]

Given that the *Telegraph* was one of the most fervent critics of appeasement, this attitude seems surprising. What may have drawn the wrath of the paper was the accusation, implicit in the 'uncensored truth' advert, that his dispatches were somehow meddled with and that the *Telegraph* prevented him telling the whole truth. It is ironic that his time with the paper ended in this way, for he was one of the few foreign correspondents whose reporting was *not* interfered with in some way when it came to Hitler and the Nazis. Gedye's response to the affair was acerbic. The *Telegraph* editor had announced that his resignation had been agreed by mutual consent. 'That,' said Gedye, 'is correct. It is equally correct that Herr Hitler invaded Czechoslovakia by "mutual arrangement" with President Hácha.'[529]

He returned to Prague and continued working there for the *New York Times*. He was at the eye of the storm when, in the middle of March, Hitler ordered his tanks over the Sudeten border and instructed his army to occupy the rest of Czechoslovakia. It was his most blatant and aggressive act to date, leaving the Munich Agreement in tatters. Chamberlain and Joseph Ball were playing golf when news came of the German invasion of Czechoslovakia.[530]

It was widely seen as the end of appeasement. Vernon Bartlett was hundreds of miles away from Prague, convalescing on the remote Scilly Isles off the coast of Cornwall, when Hitler acted. 'The only real consolation about all this miserable business,' he wrote, 'is that the Prime Minister must be finding it very difficult to continue, under the attractive title of "appeasement", a policy which is destroying all those freedoms which his and our ancestors fought to win.'[531]

This was the moment when the *Daily Mail* finally changed its attitude to Hitler. Until the Nazis moved against the rest of Czechoslovakia, Lord Rothermere's paper had been arguing that British foreign policy in relation to Germany was working. 'War was avoided last September by Mr Chamberlain. Nobody disputes that,' it wrote in an editorial on 13 March, shortly before Hitler sent his army over the border towards Prague. 'Today even his opponents have been forced to recognise that his policy of peace and security is working out along the right lines.'[532]

Just three days later the *Mail* was reporting on Chamberlain's anger as he addressed the House of Commons. 'The hushed and shaking words of the Prime Minister amounted to a bitter accusation that Herr Hitler, his fellow signatory at Munich, had broken at any rate the spirit of that agreement.'[533] A day after this report the *Mail* declared in an editorial that 'Hitler has killed Munich'. The paper's support for the dictator was finally broken. 'His historic aim of restoring German minorities to the Fatherland was understandable, though his methods may have been deplored,' it continued. 'But he has no sanction either in law or morality for this subjugation of a free and sovereign people.'[534]

The rest of the British press followed suit. To the newspapers which had previously felt able to offer him the benefit of the doubt, Hitler had revealed his true nature. The *Observer* editor James Garvin is the best example of this reversal in attitudes. He had been one of the biggest supporters of appeasement and argued that events in Czechoslovakia were of no concern to Britain. He had welcomed the Munich Agreement. But the Nazi entry into Prague finally disabused Garvin of the notion that Hitler could be negotiated with. He was thereafter transformed into one of Hitler's foremost critics.

The Nazi capture of the rest of Czechoslovakia was swift. 'The whole crisis had only lasted five days. Hitler had staged another of his lightening [*sic*] coups, and once more the world was left breathless,' wrote Ambassador Henderson, with something approaching admiration.[535] When the Germans arrived in Prague, Eric Gedye took shelter with two press colleagues in the British Embassy. They avoided arrest by the Gestapo and were permitted to leave Czechoslovakia a week later. He went on to work as Moscow correspondent for the *New York Times.*

Towards the end of March, Ian Colvin of the *News Chronicle* returned to London and met with Neville Chamberlain, Lord Halifax and other senior members of the government. He pressed on them the danger that Poland was now in. He believed a German strike against that country may be imminent. On the last day of March, in part as a result of these warnings, Chamberlain announced to the House of Commons that Britain would defend Poland if it was invaded by Germany. The chances of war, already high, became close to a racing certainty.

Price was present for the *Daily Mail* in Memel when the Nazis turned their attention to Lithuania. Standing alongside the Nazis leadership, Himmler turned to him and said: 'With regard to the Jews, you English have had no experience of the danger that they constitute as a political and economic factor. It is a race against which we must defend ourselves.'[536] The Nazis were already planning to extend their menacing regime over Jews to eastern Europe. New and even more sinister plans were being hatched.

The dangerous situation facing foreign correspondents in Berlin became almost impossible. Hugh Carleton Greene (the future director-general of the BBC and brother of the novelist Graham Greene), who had led the *Telegraph*'s reporting in Berlin since 1938, was expelled in May 1939. Later that month, Germany and Italy signed their Pact of Steel. Henderson continued his efforts in Berlin. Many newspapers in Britain thought the diplomat should not have returned to Germany after *Kristallnacht*, but he continued with his ill-starred attempts to tame the Nazi leadership.

During one meeting with Göring in the summer of 1939, he was distracted when the leading Nazi showed him a set of tapestries he proposed to hang in his country retreat at Karinhall. In an official dispatch, which was inadvertently made public, Henderson described them as 'naked ladies'. Almost laughably, Henderson was subsequently distracted from his task by worries over the publication of this coarse word. He later wrote: 'Had I anticipated that my despatch would ever be published, I should certainly have written "nude figures" in place of the cruder expression which I actually used.'[537] Priorities, again, were skewed.

In June of 1939 Henderson held his annual party to mark the king's birthday and just three or four hundred attended, less than a third of the number present two years earlier. Britons were leaving Berlin in advance of a likely war. 'The whole general atmosphere in Berlin was one of utter gloom and depression,' Henderson wrote.[538] In July he tried to see Hitler, who was at Bayreuth attending a Wagner musical. 'It was a complete failure. I had car trouble on the way down,' wrote Henderson. Hitler had left by the time he arrived. 'The sole satisfaction that I derived from Bayreuth was to hear a marvellous performance of *The Valkyrie*.'[539]

Criticism of Dawson and *The Times* policy on Germany persisted until virtually the outbreak of war, with other newspapers not missing an opportunity to attack their esteemed rival for its attachment to appeasement. Following the infamous *Times* editorial of 7 September 1938, *The Week* newsletter claimed it had been sent to the German Embassy for prior approval, prompting a rare legal threat from Dawson.[540] Author and playwright J. B. Priestley did not let the Yorkshire background he shared with Dawson stop him writing this pointed attack in July 1939. 'Nearly every day in *The Times* there are persuasive letters, from good addresses, telling us that it is all a slight misunderstanding, and that if we knew the Gestapo better (as we may do soon) we should discover that they are fine stout fellows.'[541] The article so riled Dawson that Priestley was forced to make a 'frank apology' and the *News Chronicle* explained the article away, slightly unconvincingly, as 'exuberant hyperbole'.

Even after the events of March 1939, Chamberlain continued to think Hitler was a man whose demands he could – and should – try to meet. 'If dictators would have a modicum of patience,' he wrote to his sister in July, 'I can imagine that a way could be found of meeting German claims while safeguarding Poland's independence and economic security.'[542] A week later he told his sister that he thought 'Hitler has concluded that we mean business and that the time is not ripe' to go to war. 'The longer the war is put off the less likely it is to come at all as we go on perfecting our defences and building up the defences of our allies. That is what Winston and Co. never seem to realise.'[543] In the British press, one man hung on to the belief that a deal with Hitler could be done. Lord Kemsley was meeting Hitler in Berlin as late as August 1939 to try and strike an agreement and prevent war.

-CHAPTER XVII-
WHEN FREEDOM SHRIEKED

R eynolds was in Britain for almost all of 1939. It was his longest time
in the country since the First World War. He appreciated the change
of pace. It was relaxing to have respite from the pressure of following and
breaking news after so many years. After six weeks sorting his affairs and
finalising matters with the book's publisher, Victor Gollancz, Reynolds
began writing in April 1939, the month after Nazi tanks rolled into Prague.
Anger at Hitler's power-grab in Germany and the ensuing years of totali-
tarian rule was raw in his mind as he wrote.

Sir Victor Gollancz's publishing house in London had released many
books by foreign correspondents in the 1930s, including Vernon Bartlett's
Nazi Germany Explained in 1933, as well as works by promising up-and-
coming writers such as George Orwell. As a Jew, Gollancz was especially
interested in exposing the truth about the reality of life for Germany's
Jewish population. He relished the opportunity to publish a first-hand
account of life in Weimar and Nazi Germany by a journalist such as
Reynolds, whose politics were more liberal than the newspaper he had
worked for. Reynolds could now write with freedom and did not have to

worry about his book causing problems with an employer in the manner of Eric Gedye.

The process of collecting his thoughts each day as he wrote *When Freedom Shrieked* was therapeutic on one hand, but did not help ease the pain. Reynolds may have felt at home in Britain, but he was hardly at peace. Memories of his time in Germany haunted his sleep. As Cambridge sweated in the summer heat, Reynolds worked day and night to complete his 318-page book. He was too busy to write to some of his relatives until after he finished, informing one:

> I have been tied to my desk since April writing this book, a horrid
> task. I had far too much material – to write easily about a foreign
> country one should visit for a month and come back with clear ideas,
> undisturbed by questioning and doubts.[544]

His work was interrupted at the start of September by the news that Hitler had ordered his army into Poland. Britain was at war. Germany's invasion of Poland was no surprise to Reynolds. It added even more urgency to his task and allowed him to write in the book's foreword, penned on 29 September:

> The title of this book, suggested by a line of Thomas Campbell's
> *Pleasures of Hope*, has proved to be more terribly appropriate than
> I could have foreseen when I chose it. Filled with distress at the fail-
> ure of the heroic attempt of the Poles to loose themselves from the
> grasp of their oppressors, the poet wrote:
> > Hope for a season bade the world farewell,
> > And Freedom shriek'd – as Kosciusko fell.
> > As I wrote, I had in my ears the shriek of freedom across the plains

of Germany. My work was almost at an end, when the tyrant who drove freedom out of Germany invaded his neighbours' land. Again Polish heroes fought and fell; and again the shriek of freedom resounded through the world.

Champions of freedom have arisen: and we are at war with the enemy of the rights of man. I have not, however, found it necessary to alter or modify in a time of war what I have written in a time of peace.[545]

With Poland occupied, Reynolds's tone against Germany hardened still further. 'Germany must not merely be defeated, but punished for her atrocious cruelty. I am constantly thinking about the Poles who are being turned out of their homes,' he wrote to a relative. Reynolds backed up his strong words with good deeds – over the course of 1939, he would host two refugees at his home in Cambridge, one Polish and one Russian.

For the handful of British correspondents remaining in Berlin, the coming of war marked the beginning of a desperate bid for safety. If they remained in Germany after war started they would be behind enemy lines and arrested if found. The *Daily Mail*'s Izzard and four of his colleagues from the press fled thirty-six hours before hostilities commenced. An already precarious existence was becoming a battle for survival.

Izzard, Selkirk Panton of the *Express*, Ewan Butler of *The Times*, Anthony Mann of *The Telegraph* and Ian Colvin of the *News Chronicle* boarded a train to Denmark. They would have preferred to head to Holland but the train journey was longer and they wanted to cross the German border as soon as possible. They stayed in the Hotel D'Angleterre in Copenhagen.

'It was built around a courtyard. I was staying in a corner room and I could hear all the telephoning going on throughout the hotel,' Izzard recalled. 'I heard an American and he said, "Well, the war's on," and that's how I found out the war had started.'[546]

From there he went to Amsterdam. Panton and Mann stayed on in Copenhagen and were arrested by the Germans when they invaded in April 1940. They were interned for the rest of the war on a cold island in the Baltic. A month later the Nazis invaded Holland. Izzard was on the last British ship out of the country when the German paratroopers started dropping. It was one of the most terrifying moments of his life.

Sefton Delmer was in Warsaw when the Nazis first bombed Poland at the start of September 1939. He was with Richard Mowrer of the *Chicago Daily News* (the nephew of Edgar Ansel Mowrer) and Jerzsy Bau, a Polish journalist. They came under poison gas attack and then drove south into Romania in an unofficial press convoy, behind a car containing Carleton Greene of the *Telegraph*, Willie Forrest of the *News Chronicle* and Patrick Maitland of *The Times*. Warsaw held out for another fortnight against the German army. Delmer felt shame for leaving too early and not reporting over the radio on their brave resistance, but he made amends by remaining in Paris the following June until the morning of the day the Germans marched in.

———

Reynolds monitored events from Cambridge. The city was transformed in the midst of war. Living next door to the Reynolds siblings at this time was Herbert Kaden, then a young German Jew still adjusting to a new life in Britain. Here he describes how Cambridge changed in just a few days:

All the young people were asked to fill sandbags and put them round the walls of the colleges. Women had to sew blackout curtains and we helped to put them up at Newnham College. There was a curfew and blackout at night. If anyone forgot to draw their thick curtains after dark, people from the street were heard to shout: 'Put those lights out!' Then soldiers' gas masks were given out. Thank God they never had to be used in earnest, as I believe they were in the First World War. At the beginning of this Second World War, there was great hope that it would only last a short time. Soon the first air raid warnings were sounded.[547]

The change was noted by Reynolds on a rare trip to the capital. 'London is frightening at night,' he wrote to a relative in November.[548] He eagerly anticipated the publication of his book that month. Just as his work as a translator in the First World War had allowed him to help the national effort, he viewed *When Freedom Shrieked* as 'the best contribution I could make to our cause'. However, he was nervous about how the book would be received. 'I hope it will be widely read,' Reynolds wrote.[549] He need not have worried. The book went into a second edition in less than two weeks and received positive newspaper reviews, including from his former employer.

'Extensive experience joined with the habit of trained observation gives the book a background lacking in many other works written about the Nazi regime,' asserted the *Mail's* reviewer. Any previous clash of opinion with bosses at the newspaper was conveniently forgotten.

It is a quiet, careful account of the deterioration of a whole people illuminated by many small episodes which together make up the life of a nation. There is not striving after horror – though the horror naturally is there – and the story gains enormously because it makes no effort to be sensational.[550]

A reviewer in the *Melbourne Argus*, then one of Australia's most prominent newspapers, got closer than any other to understanding the conditions Reynolds had faced writing for the *Daily Mail* in Berlin:

> Now that the war they predicted has broken out, the foreign correspondents have not packed away their manuscripts or abandoned the hope of seeing their day-to-day observations preserved between stiff board covers. Fired, perhaps by Gunther's example, they are still producing their eye-witness accounts of Europe's progress towards war.
>
> To a public which is still trying to find out for certain why the war is being fought and how it is likely to end, such accounts need no apology. Sometimes, as in the case of Rothay Reynolds's *When Freedom Shrieked*, they are more valuable than the same writer's daily dispatches.
>
> Reynolds was *Daily Mail* correspondent in Berlin from 1921 to the outbreak of the war and in those eighteen years he was able to gather impressions, information and 'inside stuff' which could hardly have been published in peacetime, and certainly not in the *Daily Mail*, which for a long time regarded Hitler as the saviour of Europe.
>
> This record of his stewardship is a sweeping indictment of German fascism which shows step by step how freedom, democracy and human decency were trodden underfoot by the forces of reaction. Reynolds writes vividly and forcefully, making it clear that the whole German nation was being deliberately prepared for war even at a time when Whitehall persisted in regarding its intentions as peaceful.[551]

The Observer described *When Freedom Shrieked* as 'a heart-breaking book, but a good book, written by one who knew and loved Germany'. It 'achieves the unusual feat of combining easy and abundant reading for relaxation (for "stiff" is the last word that could be applied to him) with an excellent and connected explanation of Germany's evolution in the present century'.[552]

The *Manchester Guardian* was similarly praiseful. 'Its first-hand impressions of world-shaking events are woven into a narrative that has the liveliness of contemporary journalism and the accuracy of historical research.' The reviewer lauded Reynolds as 'one of the most experienced of foreign correspondents'.[553] The book won praise on the right of politics, too. *The Spectator*'s reviewer said it should 'bring home to the Englishman who has no experience of the kind what it means to live in a police state dominated by Himmler', continuing:

> It has long tormented those who knew Germany well that they were unable to induce the British people to look National Socialism in the face. Now that tragic events have dissipated the lazy tolerance of England, an outburst of publications about Germany has naturally occurred. Mr Reynolds has written a simple and straightforward account of what it felt like to live in Germany between the two wars. His book is valuable in a number of ways.[554]

There would be no review in the *Yorkshire Post*, however. The newspaper was in effect closed down in November 1939 when it was combined with the *Leeds Mercury* to form a single paper sold at a lower price. The editor Arthur Mann, whose crusade against appeasement had stood out like a beacon, resigned. In a letter two years later he blamed 'wire-pulling politicians' and a 'very short-sighted sort of commercialism' for the loss of editorial responsibility and integrity he judged within most parts of the British press. He thought newspapers had lost the confidence of readers by failing to question the Munich Agreement and other key government decisions.[555]

His book published, Reynolds turned his attention to how he could further help the war effort. In December he took the train north to Halifax and spoke to a crowd of 2,000 about his time in Germany. 'I enjoyed it as soon as I found my voice was carrying,' Reynolds wrote to a relative. He began with an account of his meeting with Hitler in 1923 before describing conditions in the country after six years of Nazi rule. He said Germany had become enormously powerful and dangerous, and that the future of the British Empire and her allies was at risk.

ROTHAY REYNOLDS, M.A.

Topical Lectures of Extraordinary Interest.

As correspondent of the DAILY MAIL in Berlin for eighteen years Mr. Reynolds has watched day-by-day the gradual restoration of the military power of Germany. He has seen the people among whom he lived pass from freedom under democratic rule to serfdom under Nazi despotism.

Mr Reynolds is personally acquainted with the men in whose hands the fate of Germany lies. He has travelled with Hitler, talked with Goering, Ribbentrop, Rosenberg and the other Nazi leaders. He knew Rathenow and Stresemann, and has been in close touch with Germans of every class—he is therefore able to throw a vivid light on the country which is the cause of all unrest and tension throughout Europe to-day.

Formerly Mr. Reynolds was correspondent of the DAILY NEWS in St. Petersburg. During the years in Russia, and while in Germany, he frequently visited Poland and is thus able to speak from personal experience of the Poland partitioned by three powerful Emperors, and of the independent Poland of modern Europe.

The Lecture League strongly recommends these lectures.

A leaflet promoting Reynolds's lectures on Nazi Germany.
He delivered one to a crowd of 2,000 in Halifax.

Religion remained a central pillar in Reynolds's life to the end. Faith was one of many things put at risk by the Nazis, he told the crowd.

> It is a struggle to preserve the great traditions of Christendom and of Christian civilisation. I am an ageing man, but my experience has taught me that unless we get back to the principles embodied in the Ten Commandments and the sermon on the mount, our civilisation will disappear.[556]

Reynolds spent the Christmas of 1939 corresponding with relatives and mulling his options. He had been back in Britain for ten months – a relaxing yet restless period, in which he had worked hard to complete *When Freedom Shrieked*. At sixty-seven he had earned his retirement, but had no interest in slowing down – his work ethic seems to have been ferocious throughout his life – and with Europe at war he felt a particularly acute need to contribute. He considered his next step.

-CHAPTER XVIII-
A FINAL ASSIGNMENT

Reynolds was in Cambridge at the start of 1940. He had spent many long winter nights considering what he wanted to do and early in the new year, he finally decided. He wished to go abroad once more. In some ways, his family and friends were surprised by his desire to travel again, at his age and during a war. In other ways, they were not surprised at all. They knew Reynolds was a restless spirit who enjoyed life most when away from home. He consulted his contacts, including Eustace Wareing of the *Daily Telegraph*, who had left Berlin in 1938. This led to an agreement with the newspaper that he would travel to Italy and work as its correspondent in Rome. Italy had maintained a neutral position in the war but the world was waiting to see whether Mussolini would join his fascist ally Hitler in arms.

Reynolds's appointment was quite a coup for the *Telegraph*. After reporting for years in Berlin and recently writing a well-received book, his stock as a journalist was high. His ability with languages, including Italian, enhanced his credentials for the role, as did his knowledge – from personal dealings – of Hitler and other Nazi leaders. His age was not seen as an impediment. Reynolds, for his part, was enthused by the prospect of living in the fourth country of his life and the spiritual home of his Catholic faith.

He moved quickly to organise his affairs in Britain and, conscious that this trip could be his last, amended his will. While his family feared for their brother's journey across wartime Europe, friends in the press pack were jealous. They told him they envied his opportunity to swap ice and rain in Britain for Italian sunshine. Reynolds was not so confident and started the journey wearing the thick fur coat that had served him during many harsh Berlin winters.

He departed Britain halfway through February and was surprised by the smoothness of his journey, which 'turned out to be as simple as in times of peace'.[557] He crossed the Channel in an hour and a half before making his way to Paris, one of his favourite cities. Snow was melting when he arrived and he thought the city looked less 'warlike' than London. The only change he noticed was the lack of tourists. He travelled south and crossed the border from France to Italy without difficulty before taking a train to Florence, where he stayed for two weeks with a family he knew to sharpen his Italian. The skies were leaden and a cold wind was blowing on his arrival – a far cry from the warm conditions his friends at home had anticipated.

He then continued to Venice, where he filed his first article for the *Daily Telegraph* on 1 March. The piece was printed the next day with the headline, 'Italy's Heart is Not With Those Who Force War on the World'.[558] Reynolds was billed as a 'Foreign Politics Expert' by the newspaper in a short introduction to their new correspondent. 'Few British journalists have a longer and wider experience of European politics,' it said. 'He starts with the advantage of a formidable army of languages. Besides French and Italian he also knows Russian and German. He has also the somewhat rare accomplishment of talking Polish.'

The piece focused on how Italians were feeling about the war and their country's potential involvement. Interested to see how the situation would develop, *Il Duce* stayed his hand, maintaining an independent approach in the opening months of the Second World War. But his defensive alliance with Germany, the Pact of Steel, meant it was highly likely that full hostilities with the allies would come – it was only a matter of time. Reynolds relayed details of a number of conversations, with the overriding sentiment being that Italians, by and large, were in no mood to fight. They did not feel any special loyalty to Hitler and also feared that their country would quickly struggle to feed itself in a war. 'This war is so terrible, and nobody knows what it is about,' Reynolds heard from one lady on a train. He encountered no animosity on account of his own nationality, something he had been slightly worried about.

For Reynolds, despite the anxious circumstances, it was a joy to be abroad again. Life in Britain had at first provided a respite from the stresses of life in Nazi Germany, but he had longed to travel once more. Wartime had reinforced this desire: foreign correspondents could serve a useful function and he was keen to do his bit. Rome was the ideal posting, with the world waiting for Mussolini to reveal his hand. But there was more than that. For Reynolds, a deeply religious Catholic convert, it was a pleasure to live in the capital city of his faith. His religion had only intensified in Nazi Germany; it was a useful source of comfort in dark times. He relied on it to sustain him if Italy, too, became a difficult posting.

Reynolds had sent his first dispatch from Venice, where, after arriving during a thunderstorm, the skies soon cleared. In a positive mood he described how Venetians, untouched by war, were sitting around on sunlit piazzas drinking vermouth. He then made his way to Rome, where he made quite an impression on Bernard and Barbara Wall, British journalists based in the city, who shared his Catholic faith and made him feel welcome. Bernard wrote a glowing account of Reynolds's refreshing attitude to journalism. 'Amongst journalists Reynolds was considered rather a surprising figure, and it was often said of him that he seemed more or less uninterested in what was considered the day's "scoop," but would wander off to find some unique angle of his own.' This angle would invariably have a religious or historical element; Reynolds was keen to maximise cultural opportunities while living in Rome. 'When printed,' Wall continued, the angle he had discovered 'would bring belated telegrams from London and New York to the agencies, asking them to go into Reynolds's story.'[559]

Two weeks after his arrival, Reynolds reported on his biggest story since arriving in Italy. Hitler had travelled south to Brenner, a mountain pass in the Alps between Austria and Italy, to meet Mussolini in a hastily arranged meeting. There was international interest in what the two dictators were discussing. Some felt this meeting could precipitate Italy's entry into the war. They spoke in a bulletproof train carriage for two and a half hours before parting. Reynolds's report on the meeting made the front page of the *Telegraph* the following day. Its headline, 'Divergent Reports on Brenner Talks', reflected the confusion in Rome and other European capitals about what had been discussed.[560] There were some hopes, desperate but real, that the talks may lead to peace. In the following days these hopes ebbed away as it became clear that there had been no break between Hitler and Mussolini. Italy's entry into the war remained likely.

Reynolds spent time in Rome with Douglas Woodruff, the editor of the Catholic newspaper *The Tablet*, who was on an assignment in the city. 'I saw a lot of him in Rome this April, when things were becoming difficult for English correspondents, and held him in high regard,' Woodruff wrote. He admired Reynolds's endurance and tenacity for wanting to continue, at his age, sending dispatches from abroad. 'Modern journalism is considered a young man's game, but Reynolds, at a sixty-seven he did not look or feel, was up to all its exigencies,' he wrote. 'What he sent from Rome till Italy entered the war ranked with the best for its exposition of a quickly changing and carefully obscured situation.'[561]

Things were becoming difficult because the Italian entry into the war was looking increasingly likely. Italian officials were well aware of this and treated foreign residents, especially journalists, with suspicion. But Reynolds maintained his composure and calm disposition despite the increasing nerves afflicting all foreign correspondents in the city. To remain in Italy a day too long could mean internment if the country suddenly entered the war. It was an anxious existence, but Reynolds coped well. The situation was not dissimilar to the fraught summer of 1938 in Berlin.

Bernard Wall was impressed not just with the unflappability of his new friend, but also the ease with which he mixed with different sections of society. Reynolds was comfortable in situations ranging from 'a Vatican concert to an eats kitchen near the Trevi fountain, a very unusual thing in a man of sixty-seven,' Wall wrote. Reynolds spent most evenings together with the Walls from April onwards, 'a time when we were never sure that we would not waken up the following morning in an enemy country'.[562]

Mussolini had hesitated about entering the war because of worries about shortcomings in the Italian military and whether the country had the resources to survive a long war. He did not want to get drawn into a stalemate conflict. Hitler did not wait for his fascist ally and instead took the initiative in May 1940 by marching his army into the low countries of France, Belgium, Luxembourg and the Netherlands. By the start of June the success of the operation was seen as inevitable. Mussolini was being pushed towards action. Reynolds and other foreign correspondents in Rome, as well as the diplomatic community, knew Italy's entry into the war was only a matter of time.

On 10 June, with Paris vulnerable before the Nazis after the French government fled to Bordeaux, Mussolini finally acted. Italy would join the war. He thought a German victory was all but inevitable and calculated that it would be preferable to have fought on the winning side. In America,

President Roosevelt accused Italy of sticking a knife into the back of France. Reynolds and other foreign correspondents had been advised to stay inside and not head to any of Rome's main piazzas when Mussolini made his announcement. He quickly packed his bags and planned his departure.

The only question was where to go next. Reynolds had a visa to cross France but that was no longer safe, with Nazi tanks sweeping across the country. The German army would march into Paris on 14 June, completing an embarrassing capitulation for the French. Reynolds was instructed by his office to head for any safe location, where, if possible, he could continue sending dispatches. He obtained a special visa from the Italian Foreign Office to leave the country for Yugoslavia, which had not been subjected to aggression in the war so far. Despite now being in an enemy country, Reynolds was still treated warmly by Italians as he left Rome on 11 June. Staff at his hotel seemed sheepish at Mussolini's decision; others said Reynolds should stay because the war was unlikely to last long.

His departure from Rome was a painful moment for Reynolds. His devout Catholicism had contributed to his decision to leave a comfortable English retirement and work in the Sacred City, but it was over all too soon. After crossing the Adriatic he continued overland to Belgrade, the Yugoslavian capital, from where he filed a dispatch that appeared on 21 June. 'Mussolini declared war against the will of the majority of the Italian people. That is the conviction with which I left Rome on Tuesday,' he wrote. 'Never has a more reluctant nation been sent to war.' He provided the views of everyday Italians on their decision to fight alongside Germany. 'We are behaving like brigands,' a friend had said to him. 'If the allies are not victorious our civilisation is ended,' another had said.[563]

His next report six days later focused on Yugoslavia and its attitude to the war. The country had a neutral stance but felt threatened by Germany and Italy, a country with which it had endured volatile relations. Reynolds reported on a widespread desire to remain out of the war and the strong general contempt felt towards Germany. He mentioned that the French premier Philippe Pétain's move towards peace with the Nazis had been greeted with despair in Yugoslavia, though a speech by Churchill, the recently appointed British Prime Minister, had boosted spirits. Reynolds found space in the article to relay impressions of his new surroundings. 'I find Belgrade assuming quite an American air. Yesterday I was shot up in a lift to the sixteenth storey of the splendid Post Office.'[564]

Reynolds did not plan to stay. He was soon on the move again, and his family were shocked when they heard about where he had agreed to travel: Jerusalem. His decision to head to Palestine was greeted warmly by the *Telegraph*. In a world war, the fate of the ancient city of Jerusalem was a topic of hot interest. Under a British mandate, more and more Jews had set up home there, spreading discontent among an Arab population that felt the lands they had held for centuries were being taken over. Under British control because of a League of Nations mandate, it was certainly safer than many other parts of central Europe and the Middle East. But the journey would be far from straightforward.

From Belgrade he boarded a train to the Romanian capital of Bucharest. He spent a couple of days in the country, which was concerned about Russian intentions and would eventually enter the war on Germany's side. It had long been under the sway of the Ottoman and Austro-Hungarian empires, but now Romanian leaders felt Russia could threaten its independence. Reynolds was in Bucharest at an important moment. Russia shocked Romania by delivering an ultimatum on 26 June, pledging that unless Romania yielded some northern territories, its army would invade. Romania agreed to yield and Reynolds promptly left the country, boarding a steamer that took him across the Black Sea to Istanbul. 'The Russian ultimatum was as great a surprise here as in Bucharest,' he reported from

Turkey in a *Telegraph* article on 2 July. 'The Turks, having for long realised that Soviet policy is the same as that of the Tsarist regime, are naturally apprehensive.'[565]

Reynolds had been travelling for more than three weeks. It was an exhausting trip, rushing from border to border during an uncertain wartime atmosphere. It was also blisteringly hot, with temperatures regularly in the mid-to-high thirties. Despite the composed tone of his newspaper reports, he suffered, relaying to relatives at home the hair-raising nature of the journey. Istanbul marked roughly the midway point from Rome to Jerusalem. The weather would only get hotter and the circumstances more fraught.

Reynolds journeyed south from Istanbul to Ankara, which had been the Turkish capital since the fall of the Ottoman Empire. There was much confusion about what was happening across Turkey's southern border in Syria, which had been ruled by the French under a League of Nations mandate since the First World War. With France now under German occupation, there were fears of a Syrian uprising against the ruling power, whose authority was at risk of collapse. Reynolds visited the French consulate in Ankara to check on the status of his visa to cross Syria and ask if it allowed him to spend time in Beirut, which was also under a French mandate. 'You will stay at your own risk and peril!' was the abrupt reply, which did not give Reynolds confidence in the French ruling powers.

Reynolds crossed the border and travelled to Aleppo in the north of Syria. 'The authority of the French is at present unimpaired, though their prestige, as was inevitable, has sadly suffered in the eyes of the native population,' he reported. 'All hopes for the future in both Syria, with its Muslim majority, and Lebanon, with its Christian, are based on a British victory.'[566]

He reported on French displeasure in Syria at the British Navy's decision at the start of July to destroy the French fleet based at Mers-el-Kébir,

west of the French Algerian port of Oran, to prevent it falling into possession of the enemy. More than a thousand French sailors were killed,
causing widespread French anger towards Winston Churchill, who had
ordered the operation. But among Christians and Muslims in the Middle
East, Reynolds reported, the action had been well-received and seen as
a sign of British strength. British naval dominance of the Mediterranean
was regarded as essential.

Though their authority remained intact – for now – the French spirit
was draining quickly throughout Reynolds's time in Syria. Frenchmen felt
that it was pointless for Britain to continue fighting, which made personal
relations 'difficult' for Reynolds. 'The attitude of French Syria is like that
of a boxer who has been knocked out and feels that the defeat of another
champion would excuse his own poor performance,' he wrote.[567]

From Aleppo Reynolds travelled to Tripoli in the north of Lebanon
(which would win independence from the French in 1943) and then to
Beirut. The city greatly impressed Reynolds. 'The beautiful city of Beirut,
rising from the sapphire waters of the bay and surrounded by mountains, might be a city on the French Riviera.'[568] He drove south through
the desert, crossing through three checkpoints recently installed by the
increasingly nervous French. Reynolds referred to 'countless underground
movements among the native population' in Lebanon, which were spreading fears of insurrection. There were other fears too. With confidence low,
'many men are anxious to return to their wives and children in France and
in the colonies,' Reynolds reported. The checkpoints had been installed
partly because of worries among French generals that officers may try to
escape into Palestine.

The coastal road south, with the Mediterranean on one side and desert
on the other, was breathtaking. Though Reynolds was exhausted, tired and
missing the comforts of home, it would have been one of the most exciting

episodes of his life. The sun on his back, the fevered atmosphere of war pushing him forward, he crossed the frontier into Palestine about a month after leaving Rome. He motored on to Jerusalem and crossed the threshold of the ancient city walls in the middle of July. His journey was complete.

———

Jerusalem had been a magnet for foreign correspondents in the couple of years before Reynolds made the decision to travel to the city. The *Daily Mail*'s G. Ward Price had been there early in 1939. He described how the British High Commission building was surrounded by barbed-wire defences. 'Sentries at the gates levelled their rifles at my car as it approached,' he wrote. It was a nervous atmosphere.

Before the commencement of war, the city was a hotbed of spies and diplomats as rival powers sought to influence the future of this sacred Middle Eastern city. 'Apart from the critical situation in Europe, the most troubled centre was Palestine, where the hostility between Arab and Jew amounted almost to a state of war,' Price wrote. 'In this campaign the British were defending Jewish immigrants against attacks from Arabs who feared and resented the economic consequences of the constant arrival of more Jewish settlers.'[569]

Another eminent foreign correspondent to report from the city was the *Daily Express*'s Delmer. He travelled there after reporting on the Munich Crisis, to offer his take on Arab fears that the rising tide of Jewish immigration was weakening their grip on Palestine. The country's existing population did not trust the British authorities. Though the wave of immigration had been caused by Hitler's persecution, they believed the German radio stories spreading fear and stoking anti-British sentiment.

'The British are betraying us,' said a spokesman of the Arab resistance movement to Delmer. 'They allow more and more Jews to enter our country. The Jews buy our people's land from the peasants with money. The peasants spend the money and become landless paupers. The Jews then settle the land with their people. If this is allowed to go on they will soon drive us out of our homeland and make it theirs.'[570]

On one occasion, a nervous Delmer was pleased to leave the rebel headquarters safely, and in his excitement he forgot to take off his head-dress as he passed a British checkpoint. 'Alt!' cried the guard. 'What d'yes think yer playin' at?' he asked in a thick Scouse accent, 'Lawrence of Arybia?'[571] The tension was broken for a moment, but Jerusalem was far from an easy or carefree assignment.

That remained the case when Reynolds arrived in the summer of 1940, though there had been a slight easing of tensions since the start of war. Some Arabs in Palestine had come round to the idea that a German defeat would stem the flow of Jews into the country and perhaps encourage some to return. Jews in Palestine fully supported the ruling British powers, not least those who had escaped the horrors of Nazi Germany. 'The French debacle came as a great shock to Palestine, but it has not shaken the confidence of the people in the ultimate result,' the *Telegraph*'s roving war correspondent Arthur Merton wrote on 15 July.[572]

Soon after arriving in Jerusalem, Reynolds met up with Merton, who had been reporting from Palestine. The city was heavily fortified, as it had been since before the war because of the religious and territorial tensions. There was a nightly blackout across Palestine, which was regarded as a more likely target for German bombs than French-controlled parts of the Middle East. Reynolds filed a handful of reports after arriving in Jerusalem. He loved the city's ancient history and religious significance, but tragically he was not to enjoy it for long. Weak from his long journey, he contracted malaria. There were no effective drugs available to handle the condition.

He was passed into the care of doctors at the British government hospital, and in his fragile state, he caught pneumonia. There was little they could do.

But his pilgrimage was complete. He had made it to Jerusalem, one of the spiritual centres of his faith, and that knowledge brought him solace in his final hours. Broken memories of his travels flashed through his mind: meetings with Hitler, Mass at St Catherine's in St Petersburg, tea with Rupert Brooke before the last war. He remembered his parents, his early years in the Church of England, and his colleagues in the press pack. He thought of the siblings he had left behind. On 20 August, he died.

EPILOGUE

News of Reynolds's death was received with desperate sadness by his siblings in Belvoir Terrace. The fact that he had died in a distant land, and not surrounded at home by those who loved him, was felt sorely. But given the nature of his long career it was not altogether a surprise that he had passed away overseas. They focused on his achievements and the joy he had brought to those around him in life.

The news left a household of four at the home in Cambridge. Reynolds's sisters Kathleen and Marjorie, brother Ronald and Olga Rennet, a refugee they had taken in, remained. Rennet was able to buy a flat after Reynolds's death thanks to money he left her in his will, which he had changed just days before leaving for Italy. Herbert Kaden and his mother soon left Cambridge but used to return to visit her, as well as the remaining Reynolds siblings, at intervals in the following years. 'The whole family was fascinating. They were all very lovely – and kind to us,' Kaden told me in 2015.[573]

In late August, just days after his brother's death, Ronald received a phone call. A reporter from the *Catholic Herald* wished to talk about Rothay for an article he planned to mark his passing. Ronald duly obliged, grateful for the opportunity to discuss his brother's many achievements, and talked without reservation. 'He was once described, and not without justification, as Europe's best-dressed correspondent,' he said in tribute to his brother's sartorial flair. Then, mindful of the publication he was talking to, Ronald turned to religion. 'But what journalist friends could not so easily seize upon, and what did not appear obviously in his work, though it informed it, was his intense and active Catholicism.'

Ronald made clear that his brother had not been able to write all he wanted about the Nazis until returning to England. 'All the *Daily Mail* readers missed of his acute and penetrating appraisal of the Nazi regime he put into his book *When Freedom Shrieked*,' he said.

> He knew all the Nazi leaders personally, and from the very beginning seemed to sense the evil in them, which at the time not everyone allowed. He referred to them all as gangsters, and was never impressed by Hitler's social and economic experiments to the extent of losing sight of his underlying evil philosophy.[574]

Ronald was glad to highlight that Reynolds had seen Hitler and his associates for what they were at an earlier stage than his *Daily Mail* articles may have suggested. In the ensuing article the reporter was keen to press home this point, going further than Ronald wished. The reporter described Reynolds as a 'man of the world of affairs whose Catholicism enabled him to appraise more accurately than his employers wanted, Europe's evils'. The work conducted by Reynolds, the reporter continued, was 'especially difficult in view of the difference in philosophy and outlook of the paper for which he worked and his very Catholic view of events taking place'.

When he saw these two sentences in print, so soon after his brother's death, Ronald was deeply alarmed. He did not wish to make an enemy of the *Daily Mail* and its powerful owner. He wrote to the *Catholic Herald* making clear that the opinion belonged to the author and not him. He added, however, that his quotes on the subject were accurate. A small clarification followed in a later issue.

Ronald was chastened by this experience and rarely talked of his brother in public again. He no doubt felt guilty for not maintaining the discretion that his brother had showed to the end. Aside from hints in *When Freedom Shrieked*, his brother had never made public his anger at Lord Rothermere's open support for Hitler. Publishing the book had been his riposte, the method by which he vented the views that he had been forced to withhold. Reynolds fully recognised the book may look like a belated attempt to save his reputation after years of seemingly toeing a pro-Nazi line. But he was content to publish and let readers decide without directly casting aspersions himself towards his former employer. Ronald felt as if he had slipped in allowing such sentiments to emerge in a conversation, and with a journalist at that.

And yet the sentiment was justified. His brother had been restricted in what he could write for the *Daily Mail*. His friends in the press, as wary as Ronald of falling foul of such a powerful newspaper, could only refer to the situation in cryptic terms. The habitually outspoken Douglas Reed merely observed that being Lord Rothermere's correspondent in Berlin was a 'difficult task'.

In later years, there were rumours that Reynolds's death was the result of something more sinister than pneumonia. There was a theory that the Gestapo, having read his critical account of Nazi Germany, had tracked him down in Jerusalem. But there is no evidence for this. After the war, a 'Black List' did emerge of targets in Britain that the Gestapo would aim to eliminate in the event of a German invasion, but Reynolds had not been on the list. Predictably, Norman Ebbutt was. More surprising is that Reynolds's colleague at the *Mail*, G. Ward Price, also featured. In his memoirs after the war, Price used this fact to defend himself against accusations that he had been too close to the Nazis.

In the years during and after the war, countless words were written about how the British press had reported the events of the 1930s. Had they been too trusting of Hitler, too ready to turn a blind eye to how the Nazis treated minorities? Had they been too ready to accept the government's appeasement policy without question? Had the political stripe of newspaper owners been too important a factor in how events were reported? The commentator Malcolm Muggeridge highlighted this latter point as early as 1939. 'Accounts of contemporary Germany,' he wrote, 'range between a gruesome picture of butterless woe and non-stop jamboree.'[575] How could different newspapers reporting on the same situation report such different findings?

The four major newspapers that emerged from this period with their reputations enhanced were the *Manchester Guardian, Daily Telegraph, News Chronicle* and *Morning Post.* The *Manchester Guardian* was the newspaper that most frequently and stridently highlighted the horror of life inside Nazi Germany. Its roving correspondent Frederick Voigt was fearless to continue reporting on the brutality despite the genuine danger to his life. His editor William Crozier was overall a supportive and encouraging presence, though he should have listened to Voigt earlier about rearmament.

The *Daily Telegraph* did not have a correspondent in Berlin who shone to Voigt's extent, but was nevertheless a strong and independent voice that made the right calls on rearmament and appeasement. While other right-wing newspapers took the easy route of vocally arguing for more arms while also encouraging appeasement, the *Telegraph* – together with its star columnist Winston Churchill – was on the correct side of both debates. Though it ceased to exist as an independent title in 1937, the *Morning Post* was an early voice campaigning for more rearmament and its correspondent in Berlin, Karl Robson, was one of the first British correspondents to be thrown out for his fearless reporting. It closed before having to make a judgement call on appeasement.

Intervention by senior figures at the *News Chronicle* at the time of the Munich Agreement was a stain on the newspaper's largely unblemished track record during the 1930s. Exceptional correspondents including Vernon Bartlett and Ian Colvin broke news about the reality of Nazi Germany. 'When I went out to Berlin I was told that I could safely report any kind of political news without fear,' its correspondent H. D. Harrison later wrote.[576]

The brave attitude of most *News Chronicle* reporters is exemplified by John Segrue, expelled by the Nazis from Germany and then Austria. He was in the Balkans when war commenced and was working in Belgrade in 1941 when the German army arrived. Other reporters had left on the last available British ship but Segrue had stayed. 'I must send my story first,' he told a messenger who was incredulous at his refusal to evacuate.[577] The Nazis captured him and he died a year later in a German concentration camp at the age of fifty-nine. Segrue stands out as one of the bravest reporters of the era and was not forgotten. In 1981 he was honoured by the Guild of Jewish Journalists for having 'alerted the world to the true evil of the Nazi philosophy'.[578]

The other major newspapers of the era have more mixed records when it comes to their coverage of Germany. The *Sunday Times* was too quick to support Chamberlain and its influential 'Scrutator' column on foreign affairs was too often on the wrong side of the debate. W. W. Hadley was too close to the Prime Minister. The other Sunday title, *The Observer*, provided some strong on-the-ground reporting, for instance, when it sent Shiela Grant Duff to report on events in the Saar in 1935. But as the decade wore on, the views of its domineering editor James Garvin steered the newspaper's approach. He was a staunch supporter of appeasement until Hitler's tanks were on their way to Prague in 1939. The *Daily Herald* also offered periods of strong reporting, but it should have done more, given its influential position with the Labour Party, to drive forward opposition to the Conservative government's policy of appeasement towards the end of the decade.

The Times boasted one of the finest foreign correspondents of the age in Norman Ebbutt, who was sceptical of Nazi claims and maintained a shrewd attitude in his reports. His work, however, was overshadowed by the support his editor Geoffrey Dawson and deputy editor Robert Barrington-Ward gave to Chamberlain and Halifax as they pursued an appeasement agenda. The evidence about the extent to which Ebbutt's reports were interfered with is inconclusive. While his editors certainly seemed keen to please Germany, his own reports were often long and needed cutting. There was certainly not a regimented campaign to suppress his work, but there were many occasions when there was subtle interference, and the period represents a blot on the paper's history.

Lord Beaverbrook's *Daily Express* was a curate's egg in respect to Hitler and Germany. The Canadian baron deserves credit for funding a network of foreign correspondents and the high volume of dispatches it yielded, but some of those reports were skewed. There was bias in the flamboyant Sefton Delmer's early reports, which was most likely a by-product of his inexperience rather than anything more sinister. As the decade wore on Beaverbrook interfered to introduce a pro-appeasement stance. Just as Delmer was too close to the Nazis in Berlin, so was Beaverbrook too close to the politicians in London.

The *Daily Mail*'s owner Lord Rothermere was too close to politicians in Berlin *and* London. The stance that resulted was a strident combination of support for Hitler and support for British rearmament. This gave

Rothermere cover – when he died in 1940, it was his early demands for more spending on the British air force, rather than his boosting of Hitler, that was most heavily featured in reports. But the contradiction was acute. Rothermere's newspaper 'blesses and encourages every swashbuckler who threatens the peace of Europe – not to mention direct British interests – and then clamours for more and more armaments with which to defend Britain, presumably against his lordship's pet foreign bully,' wrote A. J. Cummings in the *News Chronicle* in August 1937, after Norman Ebbutt of *The Times* had been evicted from Berlin.[579] It is hard to disagree with this piercing assessment.

The achievements of Northcliffe and Rothermere in revolutionising the British press through their stewardship of the *Daily Mail* should not be overlooked. 'Together the Harmsworth brothers found it an old-fashioned, ramshackle business and transformed it into a modern, stream-lined industry,' according to one recent history. 'They turned Grub Street into Fleet Street.'[580] But Lord Rothermere's support for the fascist movement and the dubious allegiances of his star reporter, G. Ward Price, form the basis of a regretful chapter in the paper's long history.

Reynolds's assistant Izzard went on to greater things. After serving in Naval Intelligence during the Second World War, he enjoyed decades of adventures with the *Daily Mail*. In 1953 he rose to fame after reaching the Himalayan Base Camp soon after the men on their way to the first successful Everest expedition – wearing casual shoes and without any specialist equipment, compass or map.

———

'All the papers have short, cold, and for the most deprecatory notices of my part in the international politics of the last few years,' Chamberlain glumly noted in his diary after leaving the political stage. 'Not one shows the slightest sign of sympathy.'[581]

Chamberlain was replaced as Prime Minister by Churchill in May 1940. Six months later, Chamberlain died. His ambassador in Berlin, Sir Nevile Henderson, died two years later. Lord Halifax, another of the arch-appeasers, lived until 1959. The 'Cliveden Set' had wanted Halifax to replace Chamberlain. It is quite possible that, if he had been named Prime Minister, Halifax would have agreed a deal with Hitler in the summer of 1940 that allowed Germany control of continental Europe.

———

Reynolds's friendship with Frank Foley, the MI6 station chief in Berlin, was a relatively late discovery during the research for this book. The two men were close and Foley made the effort to send a letter of condolence and a newspaper clipping of Reynolds's *Times* obituary (which Foley himself may have written) to his siblings in Cambridge after his death. It is unlikely Reynolds had been a spy. Like Foley, however, he certainly did his best to help the oppressed in Berlin.

Foley's efforts to help Jews escape Germany before the war were recognised decades later when he was named 'Righteous Among the Nations', an honour bestowed by Israel on non-Jews who risked their lives during the Holocaust to save Jews from extermination. In a quirk of history, a special burial took place on the dusty mountainside of Mount Zion in Jerusalem in 1974. It was thirty-four years after Reynolds had been laid to rest in the same location. The man being buried was a former Nazi Party member named Oskar Schindler, who had saved the lives of many Jews. Those efforts were later immortalised in *Schindler's List*, the award-winning film about the Holocaust released in 1993.

Reynolds's life spanned the Victorian and Edwardian ages, the entirety of one world war and the first year of a second. He lived in a diverse range of societies at different times. His time in St Petersburg was a defining period in his life and set him up for a career as a foreign correspondent. By the 1930s, this man, who had seriously considered becoming a monk, was one of the first passengers to fly across the Atlantic on an airship. He went through an enormous personal change to transform himself from one tempted by an ascetic life of solitude and prayer to a man at ease with all manner of modern technology, customs and fashions.

His convivial nature made him a perfect foreign correspondent. He had a wide network of friends and contacts. His commitment to the truth was utmost, despite being perfectly aware he was working for a newspaper that imposed a definite slant on reports. He berated any journalist who exaggerated or lied. Although his articles were sometimes prone to colour-ful language and superfluous details, he never inserted falsehoods. While reporting on the stone-faced locals during the British withdrawal from the Rhineland in 1929, he spoke to a young English reporter who planned to describe the opposite of this reality in his dispatch.

'I shall put in cheers, because in England they want to create a friendly atmosphere.'

Reynolds was not impressed. 'My dear boy, do you not realise that you are writing a paragraph of history?' he said.[582]

This summed up his attitude to reporting. But was Reynolds too close to the Nazis? Certainly not in 1923, when he wrote a critical report of his first meeting with Hitler and described Nazi headquarters as a madhouse. But in his reporting from 1930 onwards, the pro-Nazi slant imposed on all *Daily Mail* reports dealing with Germany marred his own. He was too discreet a man to complain publicly about this. If he was unhappy about the running of the *Mail* he could have left the newspaper in the 1930s, but that was not Reynolds's style. He knew his work gave him a unique vantage point on a crucial unfolding story. There would come a day when he could tell his side to it. Until his very final years in Berlin he had enjoyed life in Germany.

He died before he could pass on the full truth of his dealings with the *Mail*. After the incident with the *Catholic Herald*, his close family were not keen to touch the subject again. A couple of years after his death they moved out of the Belvoir Terrace home they had shared with Reynolds. The sadness they had felt at the circumstances of his death passed with time. They only had to read the final sentences of *When Freedom Shrieked* to realise that he had been happy in his heart when he died. 'The Christian paradox must never be forgotten, that peace comes through war,' he had written decades earlier. And now, following the weak capitulation at Munich, Britain had decided to fight.

'Never have I been so proud to be an Englishman as at this time,' he wrote, 'when all the men of my race, here and beyond the seas, have risen to restore freedom her rights.'[583]

ACKNOWLEDGEMENTS

Rothay Reynolds was an extraordinary man and piecing together the facts of his life, more than three-quarters of a century after his death, has been no ordinary challenge. I am therefore thankful to a large number of individuals and institutions for assisting me with this endeavour.

I should start with the handful of individuals who knew Reynolds personally and were happy to assist me. Anthony Hewson had just finished school when his mother, a first-cousin to Reynolds, organised his stay with him in Berlin in the summer of 1938. The young Englishman was riveted by the experience. He photographed Nazi swastikas displayed before the Brandenburg Gate, saw Hitler during a military procession and was present for parties with diplomats and reporters at Reynolds's flat. Seventy-seven years later, in 2015, I tracked Hewson down and spoke to him for the first time. He, his wife Jean and son Edmund have been unfailingly warm and helpful and kind enough to provide pictures of Reynolds. I extend the same thanks to Herbert Kaden, Reynolds's neighbour for a time in 1939, who has assisted with my research and welcomed me twice to his monastery in Turvey.

I am grateful to archivists at Bromley Local Studies and Archives; Douai Abbey; Dulwich College; Durham University; Guardian News & Media; Lewisham Local History and Archives Centre; London School of Economics; Malvern College; Marlborough College; News UK; Pembroke College, Cambridge; Peterhouse College, Cambridge; Reading University; and *The Tablet*, for their help. I would like to thank Aelred Baker of Prinknash Abbey in particular for his help in piecing together the early parts of Reynolds's career.

Much of the core research for this book was done at the British Library and London Library, and staff at both illustrious institutions have been immensely helpful. The Newsroom service at the British Library, in particular, has been an essential resource and provided access to many of the news reports featured in this book.

I was assisted on my travels by my good friend Vikas Hiremath, who provided a place for me to stay in Berlin, and I also thank Konstantin and Anna Kallas for a warm welcome on a cold night in St Petersburg.

I would like to thank in particular several former colleagues from my time working for *Bloomberg News* and *HFMWeek* magazine for their help and encouragement: Kirstie Brewer, Tony Griffiths, Gwyn Roberts, Neil Callanan and Richard Partington. I would also like to thank Dominic Bedford, Lizzy Shipton and Jerome Kirby for their help along the way.

I am grateful to Michael Smith at Biteback Publishing – the man who first brought Frank Foley's story to light – for taking such a strong interest in this project. Olivia Beattie and her team at Biteback have been unfailingly helpful, and in particular I thank Laurie De Decker for her thorough and skilful copy edit.

My family have been incredibly supportive throughout the endeavour. Thank you to my parents, Julia and Andrew, and siblings, Rebecca and Thomas. Mum is owed the biggest debt of thanks for her help with research into Reynolds's life and a close proofreading of the manuscript. I was also lucky to benefit from the love and encouragement of my grandparents,

John and Joan Reynolds, and my Aunt Catherine. I spent many enjoyable hours with them at Hatherley Road to discuss various aspects of the book as it progressed. Granpy, whose father, Cuthbert, had corresponded with Rothay, sadly passed away shortly before this book was published, but I will never forget his contributions and guidance.

Finally, thank you to Britannia for your support, and for putting up with more conversations about the Third Reich than any girlfriend should reasonably have to face.

A SHORT
NEWSPAPER GUIDE

Daily Express

Run by Canadian industrialist Maxwell Aitken, better known as Lord Beaverbook, the *Express* was the *Mail*'s main rival in the popular press. Readers were drawn from all levels of society, but most were working class. It became a powerful paper under Beaverbrook, with a circulation of more than two million – the biggest in the world in the late 1930s. The *Daily Express* supported appeasement but boasted fine foreign correspondents.

Daily Herald

Formed in 1912, the *Herald* was the Labour Party newspaper and had a readership drawn from the lower and middle classes. Its treatment of foreign affairs was bound to an extent by Labour policy, and staff were split on many key issues in the 1930s. The *Herald* did not support rearmament but had little love for Hitler. It was succeeded by *The Sun* in 1964.

Daily Mail

Launched by Alfred Harmsworth (the future Lord Northcliffe) in 1896, the *Mail* quickly became one of the biggest newspapers in the world. He pioneered a populist brand of journalism that drew readers from the middle and upper classes. Harold Harmsworth (Lord Rothermere), a fervent supporter of Hitler, controlled the newspaper between 1922 and 1937, when his son Esmond took over. Reynolds worked for the paper in Berlin between 1921 and 1938. In 1937, the paper had a readership of 1.6 million people.

Daily Telegraph
A conservative title that supported the National Government in the 1930s, the *Telegraph* had a middle- and upper-class readership. The paper supported British rearmament and opposed appeasement, unlike many of its rivals. The *Telegraph* reported with great clarity and verve on life in Nazi Germany, and was the last newspaper of Reynolds's career, sending him to Rome in 1940.

Manchester Guardian
Under the pioneering editorship of C. P. Scott, the *Guardian* had emerged as the leading liberal newspaper not just in Britain, but internationally. It carried great influence in liberal and intellectual circles. Coverage of Hitler and the Nazis was led by Frederick Voigt, who saw the regime for what it was from the start. Voigt did more than any other reporter to expose the truth about Nazi Germany.

Morning Post
Reynolds's friend H. H. Munro, famous for his short stories written under the pen-name Saki, was working for this conservative newspaper when the pair met in St Petersburg. It maintained a stridently right-wing line until merging with the *Telegraph* in 1937. Both papers were among

the most critical of Hitler in the 1930s, with the *Morning Post* being a strong early backer of rearmament.

News Chronicle

A leading liberal newspaper formed by the 1930 merger of the *Daily Chronicle* and *Daily News*, which had given Reynolds his first job in journalism in Russia, the *News Chronicle* reported bravely on Nazi excesses, but never backed rearmament. The author Michael Frayn described it as 'the poor old *News Chronicle*, the decent liberal paper that everyone liked but no one read'.[584] It became part of the *Daily Mail* in 1960.

The Observer

Owned by the well-connected Astor family, *The Observer* was founded in 1791, making it the oldest of the Sunday newspapers. James Garvin, its controversial editor in the 1930s, was an outspoken critic of the Treaty of Versailles and supported appeasement. When the Nazis marched into Prague in the spring of 1939, he reversed his position.

Sunday Times

Another influential Sunday newspaper, the *Sunday Times* overtook the *Observer*'s circulation in the 1930s. Lord Kemsley took control of the paper in 1937 and favoured negotiations with Germany. The *Sunday Times* published regular commentaries on foreign affairs under a column titled 'Scrutator', which repeatedly favoured appeasement. Its editor W. W. Hadley fervently supported Chamberlain.

The Times

The most important newspaper of the 1930s, *The Times*'s reports and editorials carried such influence that foreign governments read it for its insights into British policy. Its editor was Geoffrey Dawson, an old Etonian who enjoyed near-total control with little proprietorial interference. Norman Ebbutt in Berlin was one of the era's great foreign correspondents, but the paper's support for appeasement led to controversy.

LIST OF CITED WORKS

BY ROTHAY REYNOLDS

The Gondola, Mills & Boon, 1913

My Russian Year, Mills & Boon, 1915 (first published 1913)

The Story of Warsaw, Hutchinson & Co, 1915

My Slav Friends, Mills & Boon, 1916

When Freedom Shrieked, Victor Gollancz Ltd, 1939

BY OTHER AUTHORS

Bartlett, Vernon, *Nazi Germany Explained*, Victor Gollancz, 1933

Brendon, Piers, *The Life and Death of the Press Barons*, Secker & Warburg, 1982

Chambers, Roland, *The Last Englishman: The Double Life of Arthur Ransome*, Faber and Faber, 2010

Cockett, Richard, *Twilight of Truth: Chamberlain, Appeasement and the Manipulation of the Press*, Weidenfeld and Nicolson, 1989

Colvin, Ian, *Vansittart in Office*, Victor Gollancz Ltd, 1965

Cooper, Alfred Duff, *Old Men Forget: The Autobiography of Duff Cooper*, Rupert Hart Davis, 1954

Coote, Colin, *Editorial: The Memoirs of Colin R. Coote*, Eyre & Spottiswoode, 1965

Coulter, John, *Sydenham and Forest Hill Past*, Historical Publications, 1999

Dalton, Hugh, *The Fateful Years: Memoirs 1931–1945*, Frederick Muller Ltd, 1957

Delmer, Sefton, *Trail Sinister*, Secker & Warburg, 1961

Dodd, William, *Ambassador Dodd's Diary, 1933–1938*, Victor Gollancz, 1941

Dunn, Dennis J., *The Catholic Church and Russia*, Texas State University, 2004

Frayn, Michael, *Towards the End of the Morning*, Faber & Faber, 2000 (first published 1967)

Gannon, Frank, *The British Press and Germany, 1936–39*, Oxford University Press, 1971

Gilbert, Martin and Gott, Richard, *The Appeasers*, Phoenix Press, 2000

Glenton, George and Pattinson, William, *The Last Chronicle of Bouverie Street*, Allen & Unwin, 1963

Grant Duff, Shiela, *The Parting of Ways: A Personal Account of the Thirties*, Peter Owen, 1982

Griffiths, Richard, *Fellow Travellers of the Right: British Enthusiasts for Nazi Germany, 1933–1939*, Constable, 1980

Harvey, John (Ed.), *Diplomatic Diaries of Oliver Harvey*, Collins, 1970

Henderson, Sir Nevile, *Failure of a Mission*, Hodder & Stoughton, 1940

Jay, Douglas, *Change and Fortune, A Political Record*, Hutchinson, 1980

Kaden, Herbert, *Some Memories of my Life*, 2008

Kershaw, Ian, *Hitler*, Penguin, 1999

Kershaw, Ian, *Making Friends With Hitler: Lord Londonderry and Britain's Road to War*, Allen Lane, 2004

Langguth, A. J., *Saki: A Life of Hector Hugh Munro*, Hamish Hamilton Ltd, 1981

Larson, Erik, *In the Garden of Beasts*, Doubleday, 2011

Layton, Geoff, *From Bismarck to Hitler: Germany 1890–1933*, Hodder & Stoughton, 2004

Layton, Geoff, *Germany: The Third Reich 1933–45*, Hodder & Stoughton, 1998

Lonsdale, Sarah, *The Journalist in British Fiction & Film*, Bloomsbury, 2016

MacDonogh, Giles, *1938: Hitler's Gamble*, Constable, 2010

Martel, Gordon (Ed.), *The Times and Appeasement, The Journals of A. L. Kennedy, 1932–1939*, Cambridge, 2000

McDonald, Iverach, *The History of The Times: Struggles in War and Peace*, Times Books, 1984

Montefiore, Simon Sebag, *Jerusalem: The Biography*, Phoenix, 2011

Muggeridge, Malcolm, *The Thirties*, Hamish Hamilton, 1940

Neville, Peter, *Russia: A Complete History*, Windrush Press, 2003

Price, G. Ward, *Extra-special Correspondent*, Harrap, 1957

Read, Anthony and Fisher, David, *Colonel Z: The Life and Times of a Master Spy*, Hodder & Stoughton, 1984

Reed, Douglas, *A Prophet At Home*, Jonathan Cape, 1941

Reed, Douglas, *Insanity Fair*, Jonathan Cape, 1938

Shirer, William, *Berlin Diary: The Journal of a Foreign Correspondent, 1934–1941*, Penguin, 1979

Simpson, John, *Unreliable Sources: How the Twentieth Century Was Reported*, Macmillan, 2010

Smith, Michael, *Foley: The Spy Who Saved 10,000 Jews*, Biteback Publishing, 2016

Spurr, Barry, *'Anglo-Catholic in Religion': T. S. Eliot and Christianity*, Lutterworth Press, 2010

Taylor, S. J., *The Great Outsiders: Northcliffe, Rothermere and the Daily Mail*, Phoenix Giant, 1998

Taylor, S. J., *The Reluctant Press Lord: Esmond Rothermere and the Daily Mail*, Weidenfeld and Nicolson, 1998

The Office of The Times, *The History of The Times*, Volume IV, London, 1952

Tomalin, Claire, *Charles Dickens, A Life*, Viking, 2011

Waugh, Evelyn, *The Life of Ronald Knox*, Chapman & Hall, 1959

Wick, Steve, *The Long Night: William L. Shirer and the Rise and Fall of the Third Reich*, Palgrave Macmillan, 2011

Wright, William, *The Benedictine and Cistercian Monastic Yearbook 2015*

ENDNOTES

1. 'For providing information about events...' *The Thirties*, p. 267.

2. Details of funeral taken from notice in *Daily Telegraph*, 23 August 1940.

3. 'He is the sort of person...' Barbara Wall in the *Catholic Herald*, 30 August 1940.

4. 'A number of colleagues...' letter in *Daily Telegraph*, 23 August 1940.

5. 'He was one of the few...' *The Times*, 2 September 1940.

6. 'I am very sorry indeed...' letter from Frank Foley to Kathleen Reynolds, 23 August 1940.

7. 'Struggled hard to fulfil...' *A Prophet at Home*, p. 99.

8. 'Before Sydenham became...' *Sydenham and Forest Hill Past*, p. 57.

9. The UK's rule over India would outlast Reynolds by seven years, ending in 1947.

10. The modern street address of Blomfield House is 129 Widmore Road.

11. Author's interview with Anthony Hewson, who recalled being told the anecdote, 10 April 2015.

12. Details on London Electric Lighting Company taken from *Pall Mall Gazette*, 29 September 1892.

13. Governess anecdote in *The Gondola*, p. 45. The book's lead character is Richard Venning, whom Reynolds appears to have based on himself:

he was a Catholic journalist, multilingual, and spent several years working in Russia. It is a helpful source of autobiographical clues.

14. Details on tutors from interview with Ronald Reynolds in *Catholic Herald*, 23 August 1940.

15. Alumni details taken from Dulwich College website: http://bit.ly/1Ix9rts

16. Curriculum details provided by Dulwich College archivist.

17. Details of Ronald Reynolds provided by Malvern College archivist.

18. 'Departures from Kingstown per Royal Mail steamers' *Freeman's Journal*, 29 September 1894.

19. Details on Swete from his entry in *Oxford Dictionary of National Biography*, Oxford University Press, 2004.

20. Details on Ryle from his entry in *Oxford Dictionary of National Biography*, Oxford University Press, 2004.

21. 'Piously, soberly and honestly...' letter from Cambridge fellows to Lord Bishop of Durham, May 1896.

22. 'I entreat you...' letter from Reynolds to Cuthbert Reynolds, 23 December 1925.

23. Ordination reported in *Northern Echo*, 1 June 1896.

24. 'I hardly think...' letter from Reynolds to Green, 31 August 1897.

25. Details on church controversies from interview with Ronald Reynolds in *Catholic Herald*, 23 August 1940.

26. 'Popish leanings' author's interview with Anthony Hewson, 10 April 2015.

27. Details of Reynolds family conversions from Leslie Reynolds obituary in *The Tablet*, 17 May 1919.

28. Details on Carlyle's order from article by Rene Kollar: http://bit.ly/2d3E6YS

29. 'Forces itself on the attention' *My Russian Year*, p. 2.

30. 'God and His Mother...' *My Russian Year*, p. 3.

31. 'A magnificent city...' *My Russian Year*, p. 13.

32. 'Nobody ever loved a flat' *My Russian Year*, p. 15, p. 19.

33. 'Russian is soft...' *My Russian Year*, p. 140.

34. Details on conditions in Russia when Reynolds arrived from *Russia: A Complete History*, pp. 161–5.

35. 'Russification policies,' *The Catholic Church and Russia*, p. 62.

36. Details on *Daily News* taken from *Charles Dickens, A Life*, pp. 172–5.

37. 'The echoes of...' *My Russian Year*, p. 22.

38. 'What a chance...' *My Russian Year*, p. 33.

39. 'A bomb has just...' *My Russian Year*, p. 105.

40. Account of murder at restaurant in *My Russian Year*, p. 44.

41. 'It is going very badly...' *Daily News*, 6 September 1906.

42. Details on Munro influences from his entry in *Oxford Dictionary of National Biography*, Oxford University Press, 2004.

43. Account of Munro siblings' ordeal during Bloody Sunday, *Saki: A Life of Hector Hugh Munro*, pp. 133–4.

44. 'The Russian government...' *My Russian Year*, p. 110.

45. 'In Russian theory...' *My Russian Year*, p. 79.

46. 'When [Nicholas II] went to Poltava...' *My Russian Year*, p. 81.

47. 'When Nicholas II, on his own initiative...' *My Russian Year*, p. 138.

48. 'The elementary safeguards...' *My Russian Year*, p. 103.

49. 'I did not understand...' *My Russian Year*, p. 100.

50. 'Europe's best dressed correspondent' interview with Ronald Reynolds in *Catholic Herald*, 23 August 1940.

51. 'I have been to...' *My Russian Year*, p. 56.

52. 'It is a matter...' *My Russian Year*, p. 62.

53. 'When I left...' *My Russian Year*, p. 68.

54. 'Journalism was demoralising...' *The Gondola*, p. 27.

55. 'It is the devil!' *Saki: A Life of Hector Hugh Munro*, p. 181.

56. 'Exceedingly prosperous...' *When Freedom Shrieked*, p. 14.

57. 'Berlin in 1912...' *When Freedom Shrieked*, p. 15.

58. 'In summer, the innumerable trees...' *When Freedom Shrieked*, p. 17.

59. 'For the price of...' *When Freedom Shrieked*, p. 17.

60. 'A haunt of...' *When Freedom Shrieked*, p. 17.

61. 'With his mop...' *When Freedom Shrieked*, p. 18.

62. 'The astonishing thing is that Mr Reynolds,' wrote one reviewer in the *The Spectator*, '[spent his] years so happily that they went as quickly as one year, and he has been able to tell his story in Messrs. Mills and Boon's Library of Charming Years.'

63. 'Conversational, easy...' The *Times Literary Supplement*, 24 January 1913.

64. 'By far the most...' *Daily Telegraph*, 24 January 1913.

65. 'We have rarely...' *Manchester Guardian*, 10 February 1913.

66. 'The enchantment...' *The Gondola*, p. 11.

67. 'Exceedingly handsome...' *The Gondola*, p. 150.

68. 'Silly tricks' *The Gondola*, p. 200.

69. 'Were I not...' *The Gondola*, p. 258.

70. 'Unjust' *The Gondola*, p. 256.

71. 'In view of the...' *Devon and Exeter Daily Gazette*, 20 January 1914.

72. 'Found himself in a sweat' Reynolds tribute to Munro in *The Toys of Peace*, p. xxi.

73. 'He was determined...' Reynolds tribute to Munro in *The Toys of Peace*, p. xxi.

74. First World War statistics from *Pembroke College Chapel – A Walk-Around Guide*.

75. 'Our confidence in...' *Manchester Courier and Lancashire General Advertiser*, 16 March 1915.

76. 'If our friendship…' *Yorkshire Post and Leeds Intelligencer*, 24 September 1915.

77. 'Gave interesting particulars…' *Western Daily Press*, 23 March 1915.

78. 'It is impossible…' *Newcastle Journal,* 30 September 1915.

79. 'Swept by flame…' *Birmingham Gazette*, 27 July 1915.

80. 'A Menaced Polish City' *Birmingham Gazette*, 20 August 1915.

81. 'The unity of…' *My Russian Year,* p. vii.

82. 'Has any town…' *Story of Warsaw*, p. 20.

83. 'No Prussian occupation…' *Story of Warsaw*, p. 27.

84. *Spectator* review, 28 August 1915.

85. 'I have at the moment…' *My Slav Friends*, p. 118.

86. 'Essential unity…' *My Slav Friends*, p. 138.

87. 'Almost to propaganda' line from 'An Englishman's Sketch of Russia' article in *New York Times*, 5 November 1916.

88. 'AA Milne may not have liked MI7, but propaganda played a vital wartime role' Alan Judd article in *Telegraph*, 25 April 2013: http://bit.ly/2aYbWPD

89. *Armour Against Fate* provides a useful organisational chart.

90. 'Instructed to prepare…' History of M.I.7 (b), March 1916 – December 1918, Public Record Office.

91. 'I don't know…' *Armour Against Fate*, p. 303.

92. *The Green Book* is reproduced in *M.I.7b – the discovery of a lost propaganda archive from the Great War.*

93. 'The word propaganda…' *When Freedom Shrieked*, p. 36.

94. 'The material provided…' *When Freedom Shrieked*, p. 36.

95. 'War robbed England of him…' *When Freedom Shrieked*, p. 18.

96. 'They looked as if…' *When Freedom Shrieked*, p. 33.

97. 'As if they had been presented…' *When Freedom Shrieked*, p. 34.

98. 'She had not tasted…' *When Freedom Shrieked*, p. 33.

99. 'All the bells of…' *Daily Mail*, 13 April 1921.

100. Notice about Leslie Reynolds in *The Tablet*, 17 May 1919.

101. 'They may turn you out…' *When Freedom Shrieked*, p. 36.

102. 'What No Hun Can Understand' article in *Daily Mail*, 8 March 1921.

103. 'I found everywhere…' *When Freedom Shrieked*, p. 36.

104. 'We are regarded by…' *When Freedom Shrieked*, p. 40.

105. 'Of course you hate…' *When Freedom Shrieked*, p. 43.

106. Details from Augusta Victoria funeral taken from *When Freedom Shrieked*, p. 45.

107. 'The pleasing qualities of…' *When Freedom Shrieked*, p. 40.

108. 'It is a tragedy…' *Daily Mail*, 24 March 1921.

109. 'The Bells of Berlin' article in *Daily Mail*, 13 April 1921.

110. 'There are many people who…' *Daily Mail*, 11 June 1921.

111. 'We shall not rest…' *Daily Mail*, 13 Sept 1921.

112. 'There was not a better…' *When Freedom Shrieked*, p. 46.

113. 'Soldiers in fine uniform…' *When Freedom Shrieked*, p. 46.

114. 'They ought to give…' *When Freedom Shrieked*, p. 47.

115. 'Attain eminence, the church…' *When Freedom Shrieked*, p. 47.

116. 'An inflation of…' *When Freedom Shrieked*, p. 62.

117. 'An excellent luncheon…' *When Freedom Shrieked*, p. 64.

118. 'In 1923 I became a billionaire…' *When Freedom Shrieked*, p. 63.

119. 'An extra six and a half…' *When Freedom Shrieked*, p. 64.

120. 'Alice in Hunderland (Or, First Steps to German Finance)' article in *Daily Mail*, 7 December 1923.

121. 'Where there was enthusiasm…' *When Freedom Shrieked*, p. 47.

122. 'The National-Socialists…' *Unreliable Sources*, p. 196.

123. 'Here was a born natural orator…' Binchy's words quoted in *Guardian* online article, 6 May 2016: http://bit.ly/1WdCte5

124. 'He was holding the masses…' Ludecke quoted in Ian Kershaw's *Hitler*, p. 114.
125. 'Adolf Hitler has been described…' *The Times*, 22 May 1923.
126. 'Childish, childish' *When Freedom Shrieked*, p. 54.
127. 'Hothead of whom…' *When Freedom Shrieked*, p. 54.
128. 'International Jewish capitalists' *Daily Mail*, 23 October 1923.
129. 'He stared at me…' *Halifax Courier*, 16 December 1939.
130. 'It is not a question…' *Daily Mail*, 23 October 1923.
131. 'I went away thinking…' *When Freedom Shrieked*, p. 55.
132. 'I am afraid that the truth…' *Daily Mail*, 23 October 1923.
133. 'It was an extraordinary change…' *Halifax Courier*, 16 December 1939.
134. 'It is extremely difficult…' *Halifax Courier*, 16 December 1939.
135. Ian Kershaw's remarks on *Daily Mail* interview in *Hitler*, p. 112.
136. 'Unutterably painful to see…' *Unreliable Sources*, p. 203.
137. 'Whatever have policemen…' *Daily Mail*, 27 May 1924.
138. 'The masses of the people…' *When Freedom Shrieked*, p. 79.
139. 'There was new life…' *When Freedom Shrieked*, p. 81.
140. 'The great thing in life…' *When Freedom Shrieked*, p. 83.
141. 'We went to a great hall…' *Daily Mail*, 1 March 1924.
142. 'Tell me, do all…' *Daily Mail*, 27 November 1924.
143. 'In Berlin one big ball…' *When Freedom Shrieked*, p. 85.
144. 'Germany with increasing frequency…' *Daily Mail*, 26 March 1925.
145. 'For elegance, distinction, fashion…' *Daily Mail*, 17 January 1927.
146. 'It is remarkable…' *Daily Mail*, 12 March 1928.
147. 'Show a tendency to magnify…' *Daily Mail*, 16 April 1928.
148. 'Germany has been declared as…' *When Freedom Shrieked*, p. 80.
149. 'Certain to Command…' *Daily Mail*, 24 May 1928.
150. 'The restoration of the political…' *Daily Mail*, 2 Sept 1929.
151. 'Money was being poured…' *When Freedom Shrieked*, p. 80.

152. 'I had had the impression...' *When Freedom Shrieked*, p. 100.

153. 'They were faces...' *When Freedom Shrieked*, p. 99.

154. 'Within the building...' *When Freedom Shrieked*, p. 102.

155. 'If this cannot be done...' *Daily Mail*, 22 September 1930.

156. 'They represent the rebirth...' Rothermere article in *Daily Mail* quoted in *The Great Outsiders*, p. 291.

157. 'Hitler's Special Talk to the Daily Mail' article in *Daily Mail*, 27 September 1930.

158. 'Some became stupidly anti-French...' *The Appeasers*, p. 5.

159. 'No doubt that the Soviet...' *The Appeasers*, p. 8.

160. 'My Terms to the World' *Daily Express* article of 28 September 1930, quoted in *Unreliable Sources*, p. 209.

161. 'My Hitler Article and its Critics,' *Daily Mail*, 2 October 1930.

162. Sales figures from *The British Press and Germany, 1936–1939*, pp. 32, 56, 75.

163. 'Dr Brüning: Strongest Man Since Bismarck' *Daily Mail*, 4 June 1931.

164. 'There is not the slightest...' *When Freedom Shrieked*, p. 109.

165. 'It is very natural...' *When Freedom Shrieked*, p. 109.

166. 'The man who fought at...' *Daily Mail*, 9 March 1932.

167. 'Hindenburg is today the candidate...' *Daily Mail*, 9 March 1932.

168. 'Germany stands at...' *Daily Mail*, 9 March 1932.

169. 'The jovial little soldier...' *Trail Sinister*, p. 105.

170. 'I know the storm troops...' *Trail Sinister*, p. 105.

171. 'The very first impression...' *Trail Sinister*, p. 114.

172. 'Herr Hitler, your Stabschef...' *Trail Sinister*, p. 116.

173. 'Germany is marching with...' Delmer's *Daily Express* report on 3 May 1931, quoted on p. 117 of *Trail Sinister*.

174. 'He just sat there...' *Trail Sinister*, p. 148.

175. 'Ate only vegetable...' *Trail Sinister*, p. 153.

176. 'The truth was that...' *Trail Sinister*, p. 142.

177. 'I was up on...' *Trail Sinister*, p. 150.

178. 'His appeal to patriotism...' *Daily Mail*, 9 April 1932.

179. Simpson on Rothermere in *Unreliable Sources*, p. 206.

180. 'President von Hindenburg has accepted...' *Daily Mail*, 3 May 1932.

181. 'Once let loose...' *When Freedom Shrieked*, p. 112.

182. 'You have lived...' *When Freedom Shrieked*, p. 10.

183. 'The old man...' *Daily Mail*, 18 July 1932.

184. 'What have they done...' *When Freedom Shrieked*, p. 32.

185. 'Applauded without discrimination...' *When Freedom Shrieked*, p. 10.

186. 'The sobs and indignation...' *When Freedom Shrieked*, p. 33.

187. 'I did not hear...' *When Freedom Shrieked*, p. 34.

188. 'Hitler will go down...' *Daily Mail*, 18 July 1932.

189. 'Numbers of Germans...' *Daily Mail*, 3 November 1932.

190. 'One of the cleverest...' *Daily Mail*, 3 December 1932.

191. 'The clique around Hindenburg...' *When Freedom Shrieked*, p. 121.

192. Reference to Ian Colvin remark in his *Vansittart in Office*, p. 18.

193. 'Hitler has been well wrapped...' *When Freedom Shrieked*, p. 126.

194. 'We shall wait and see...' *When Freedom Shrieked*, p. 127.

195. 'I must confess that...' *Trail Sinister*, p. 178.

196. Schoolchildren crying *Verrecke*, *When Freedom Shrieked*, pp. 11–12.

197. 'There they were, standing in thousands...' *When Freedom Shrieked*, p. 140.

198. 'They were exhibiting themselves...' *When Freedom Shrieked*, p. 140.

199. 'In less than a month...' *When Freedom Shrieked*, pp. 175–76.

200. 'So they've done it...' *When Freedom Shrieked*, p. 144.

201. 'Beaten by that...' *Trail Sinister*, p. 185.

202. 'Without a doubt...' *Trail Sinister*, p. 187.

203. 'You see this building...' *Trail Sinister*, p. 189.

204. 'I could have that communist…' *Trail Sinister*, p. 193.

205. See *When Freedom Shrieked* p. 144 for account of fire.

206. 'The police are given…' *Daily Mail*, 1 March 1933.

207. 'In Germany the elections…' *Daily Mail*, 7 March 1933.

208. 'It was the most beautiful…' *When Freedom Shrieked*, p. 159.

209. 'When I arrived…' *When Freedom Shrieked,* pp. 160–61.

210. 'The orchestra stalls…' *Nazi Germany Explained*, p. 108.

211. 'The Centre Party had to…' *When Freedom Shrieked*, p. 164.

212. 'Ceased to exist' *When Freedom Shrieked* p. 165.

213. 'For the terror as a whole…' *Manchester Guardian*, 24 March 1933.

214. 'The Express has caught…' *Unreliable Sources*, p. 216.

215. 'What would England do?' *Daily Mail*, 27 March 1933.

216. 'There is not a man…' *Daily Mail*, 27 March 1933.

217. 'All the leading Jews…' The *Guardian,* 1 April 1933.

218. 'The statement appeared…' *When Freedom Shrieked*, p. 213.

219. 'I found myself…' *When Freedom Shrieked*, p. 211.

220. 'If its object was…' *Nazi Germany Explained*, p. 114.

221. 'My cowardice came back…' *Nazi Germany Explained*, p. 115.

222. 'The decision to discriminate…' telegram in *Mirror* cited in *Unreliable Sources*, p. 219.

223. 'If a few Jews and socialists…' line by Gedye from 'Impressions of Hitler's Germany' article in *Contemporary Review*, 10 June 1933.

224. 'Some are so impressed…' *Nazi Germany Explained*, p. 8.

225. 'This movement, which claims…' line by Gedye from 'Impressions of Hitler's Germany' article in *Contemporary Review*, 10 June 1933.

226. 'I did what was possible…' line by Gedye from 'Impressions of Hitler's Germany' article in *Contemporary Review*, 10 June 1933.

227. 'A mean spirit of revenge…' letter from Rumbold to Vansittart on 15 March 1933, quoted in *Appeasers*, p. 10.

228. Wheeler-Bennett's failure to read *Mein Kampf* mentioned in *Appeasers*, p. 13.

229. 'It would be a mistake…' *Vansittart in Office*, p. 25.

230. 'Notoriously pathological cases…' *Appeasers*, p. 16.

231. 'Every rule ought to have…' *Vansittart in Office*, p. 23.

232. 'Hitlerism *is* exceedingly dangerous…' *Vansittart in Office*, p. 27.

233. 'Is powerless before the French…' *Vansittart in Office*, p. 24.

234. 'You have a telephone…' *When Freedom Shrieked*, p. 147.

235. 'We shall give them a chance…' *When Freedom Shrieked*, p. 167.

236. 'Has become an institution…' *Berlin Diary: The Journal of a Foreign Correspondent*, p. 41.

237. Details on Ralph Izzard from *The Reluctant Press Lord*, p. 1.

238. 'Physically sick' letter from Voigt to Crozier, 14 July 1932, *Manchester Guardian* archives, quoted in *The British Press and Germany, 1936-39*, p. 81.

239. 'I must try to write…' *The Times and Appeasement: The Journals of A. L. Kennedy*, p. 87.

240. 'De Ropp said that…' *The Times and Appeasement: The Journals of A. L. Kennedy*, p. 87.

241. 'Dirty communist rag' line from Gedye's 'Impressions of Hitler's Germany' article in *Contemporary Review*, 10 June 1933.

242. Details on Voigt from *The British Press and Germany, 1936–39*, p. 81.

243. 'Tom, you are the best…' *Trail* Sinister, p. 200.

244. 'Quite amiable, but with…' *Nazi Germany Explained*, p. 65. Bartlett must have misremembered. In fact, Hitler's eyes were blue.

245. 'There are times, I think…' *When Freedom Shrieked*, p. 200.

246. 'I found it difficult…' *Nazi Germany Explained*, p. 162.

247. 'Soon one began to notice…' *When Freedom Shrieked*, p. 191.

248. 'Identical opinions were expressed…' *When Freedom Shrieked*, p. 191.

249. 'There is no...' line by Gedye from 'Impressions of Hitler's Germany' article in *Contemporary Review*, 10 June 1933.

250. 'I beg you...' *When Freedom Shrieked*, p. 195.

251. 'The house of...' *When Freedom Shrieked*, p. 195.

252. 'Our profession became dangerous...' *When Freedom Shrieked*, p. 195.

253. 'Dr Goebbels is a slender...' *Nazi Germany Explained*, p. 162.

254. 'Particularly disliked on account...' *When Freedom Shrieked*, p. 195.

255. 'When are you coming...' *In the Garden of Beasts*, p. 106.

256. 'Some tribute ought...' lines by Wilkinson quoted in *The Journalist in British Fiction & Film*, p. 106.

257. 'All very anti-Nazi' *The Fateful Years: Memoirs 1931–1945*, p. 39.

258. 'The after-dinner gossip...' Jameson's *Journey from the North* memoir (pp. 318–320) quoted in *The Journalist in British Fiction & Film*, p. 108.

259. Reference to Rothermere's backing for managers over journalists taken from *The Great Outsiders*, p. 284.

260. 'The day-to-day production...' *The Great Outsiders*, p. 286.

261. Rothermere's threat to Bonar Law mentioned in Harmsworth's entry in *Oxford Dictionary of National Biography*, Oxford University Press, 2004.

262. 'A more prosperous and insolent...' *BBC Online* article 'Clash of the Titans', 14 July 2011: http://bbc.in/2ctH9M7

263. 'Their newspapers are not newspapers...' *BBC Online* article 'Clash of the Titans', 14 July 2011: http://bbc.in/2ctH9M7

264. 'The only evil man...' *BBC Online* article 'A Point of View: Power, politicians and the press', 16 March 2012: http://bbc.in/2cCtCz7

265. 'Youth triumphant' article in *Daily Mail*, 10 July 1933.

266. 'A policy that we all hope...' *The Great Outsiders*, p. 294.

267. 'Papers which were most bitter...' *Nazi Germany Explained*, p. 10.

268. 'Shouting and exaggeration' *The Times*, 27 September 1933.

269. 'Look at these East Fulham…' *Vansittart in Office*, p. 31.

270. 'A faithful and admirably…' *News Chronicle*, 27 October 1933.

271. 'I can hardly hope…' *Daily Telegraph*, 4 November 1933.

272. 'Hitler assured me…' *Vansittart in Office*, p. 31.

273. 'Grey depression, grey as…' *The British Press and Germany, 1936–39*, p. 82.

274. 'No town has suffered more…' dispatch in *Daily Express* in May 1934, quoted in *Unreliable Sources*, p. 222.

275. 'New Hitler Blow at the Jews' dispatch in *Daily Express*, 25 May 1934.

276. 'Constant misrepresentation of the peaceful…' *Daily Express*, 1 June 1934.

277. 'I was locked up like…' *Daily Express*, 2 June 1934.

278. 'Was it because…' *Daily Express*, 4 June 1934.

279. 'The heroes of British journalism…' *Unreliable Sources*, p. 226.

280. Reference to role of *Manchester Guardian* reporter in Berlin in *The British Press and Germany, 1936–39*, p. 80.

281. Rothermere offer to Mosley referenced in *The Great Outsiders*, p. 280.

282. Cigarette business referenced in *The Great Outsiders*, p. 281.

283. 'To cope with the grim…' *Daily Mail*, 15 January 1934.

284. 'What made it so agreeable…' *Extra-special Correspondent*, p. 194.

285. 'For over an hour…' *Manchester Guardian*, 8 June 1934.

286. 'The blackshirts are in the wash…' *The Great Outsiders*, p. 283.

287. 'The fact that I…' *When Freedom Shrieked*, p. 193.

288. 'It would do us great harm…' *When Freedom Shrieked*, p. 194.

289. 'When freedom went…' *When Freedom Shrieked*, p. 190.

290. 'Swiftly and with inexorable severity…' *Daily Mail*, 2 July 1934.

291. '"Clean-up" Completed' *Daily Mail*, 3 July 1934.

292. 'Reading over…' *When Freedom Shrieked*, p. 221.

293. 'The butchery...' *When Freedom Shrieked*, p. 222.

294. 'As the measure...' *When Freedom Shrieked*, p. 222.

295. 'Was welcomed to interviews...' *Fellow Travellers of the Right: British Enthusiasts for Nazi Germany, 1933–1939*, p. 165.

296. Hitler's dinner party mentioned in *Fellow Travellers of the Right: British Enthusiasts for Nazi Germany, 1933–1939*, p. 164.

297. 'He was by far...' *Extra-special Correspondent*, p. 219.

298. 'This provided British newspaper...' *Extra-special Correspondent*, p. 211.

299. 'As Chancellor Hitler will not...' *Trail Sinister*, p. 237.

300. 'I see you've been...' *Extra-special Correspondent*, p. 197.

301. 'But that was two centuries...' *Vansittart in Office*, p. 34.

302. 'I consider that the greater...' *Vansittart in Office*, p. 35.

303. 'The foundation of Herr Hitler's' *Vansittart in Office*, p. 35.

304. 'Many of the Saarlanders...' *Nazi Germany Explained*, p. 210.

305. Press conflict referenced in *The Parting of Ways*, p. 78.

306. 'Political animosity is finding...' *Daily Mail*, 3 January 1935.

307. 'The German Front...' *Daily Mail*, 5 January 1935.

308. 'Jewish shopkeepers have been asked...' *Observer*, 13 January 1935.

309. 'Here what seems a nightmare...' *The Parting of Ways*, p. 64.

310. 'The best way to do that...' *The Parting of Ways*, p. 66.

311. 'To feel capable...' *The Parting of Ways*, p. 67.

312. 'You cannot hope...' *The Parting of Ways*, p. 72.

313. 'Keep your eyes open...' *The Parting of Ways*, p. 75.

314. 'It was my first...' *The Parting of Ways*, p. 78.

315. 'Patiently he talked...' *The Parting of Ways*, p. 79.

316. 'Innocent, friendly, happy' *The Parting of Ways*, p. 81.

317. 'Outside the polling...' *The Parting of Ways*, p. 81.

318. 'That day, the face...' *The Parting of Ways*, p. 82.

319. 'For all Germans …' *Daily Mail*, 1 March 1935.

320. 'Herr Hitler's arrival …' *Daily Mail*, 2 March 1935.

321. 'This day should …' *Daily Mail*, 2 March 1935.

322. 'Has said explicitly to me …' *History of The Times Volume IV*, p. 890.

323. 'Ebbutt keeps reminding me …' *Berlin Diary: The Journal of a Foreign Correspondent, 1934–1941*, p. 34.

324. Cutting of line from Ebbutt's report mentioned in *History of The Times Volume IV*, p. 891.

325. 'Many Jews come to us …' *Berlin Diary: The Journal of a Foreign Correspondent, 1934–1941*, p. 36.

326. Letter from Rothermere to Chamberlain on 5 October 1934, quoted in *The Great Outsiders*, p. 299. See 'Butter' chapter for more information on the warnings and examples of correspondence.

327. 'Aeroplanes at present …' letter from Neville Chamberlain to Lord Rothermere on 30 October 1934, quoted in *The Great Outsiders*, p. 305.

328. 'I was disgusted to see …' letter from Winston Churchill to Clementine Churchill in August 1934, quoted in *The Great Outsiders*, p. 290.

329. 'Success was due to your …' letter from Lord Londonderry to Winston Churchill, 4 May 1936, quoted in *The Great Outsiders*, p. 308.

330. 'He combined awareness …' *Sunday Times* of 26 March 1939, quoted in *The British Press and Germany, 1936–39*, p. 33.

331. 'The enemies who so persistently…' *Daily Mail*, 30 January 1936.

332. 'That three years of contact …' *The Times*, 31 January 1936.

333. 'I only wish I could …' *Ambassador Dodd's Diary, 1933–1938*, p. 319.

334. 'They made rich reading …' *Berlin Diary: The Journal of a Foreign Correspondent, 1934–1941*, p. 44.

335. 'The Nazis at Garmisch …' *Berlin Diary: The Journal of a Foreign Correspondent, 1934–1941*, p. 45.

336. 'You are the channel through which …' letter from William Crozier

to Frederick Voigt, 12 January 1936, quoted in *The British Press and Germany, 1936–39*, p. 82.

337. 'Their existence is one of extreme…' *Manchester Guardian*, 5 February 1936.

338. 'A man of great charm…' *Manchester Guardian*, 17 February 1936.

339. 'I think we can do…' letter from William Crozier to Frederick Voigt, 3 August 1934, *The British Press and Germany, 1936–1939*, p. 77.

340. 'If we were not…' letter from Frederick Voigt to William Crozier, 5 Feb 1936, *The British Press and Germany, 1936–1939*, p. 8.

341. 'What the country is not…' *The British Press and Germany, 1936–1939*, p. 9.

342. 'Money prize contest,' *The British Press and Germany, 1936–1939*, p. 9.

343. 'Hitler won't see…' *Extra-special Correspondent*, p. 223.

344. 'Germany's latest stroke…' *Daily Mail*, 9 March 1936, quoted in *The British Press and Germany, 1936–1939*, p. 94

345. 'Have bitten off our…' *Daily Herald* line quoted in *The British Press and Germany, 1936–1939*, p. 95.

346. 'I rushed hopefully…' *Editorial: The Memoirs of Colin R. Coote*, p. 170.

347. 'It is the moment…' *The Times*, 9 March 1936.

348. 'The people at the head of this show…' letter from Ebbutt to Dawson, quoted in *History of the Times Volume IV*, p. 900.

349. 'For Germans to insist on…' *Manchester Guardian*, 10 March 1936.

350. 'Great Britain would herself…' *Telegraph* leader of 9 March 1936.

351. 'Cleverly attuned to the weakness' *Manchester Guardian*, 9 March 1936.

352. 'The biggest organiser…' *Morning Post*, 12 March 1936, quoted in *The British Press and Germany, 1936–1939*, p. 101.

353. 'The number of Germans who…' *The Times*, 28 March 1936.

354. 'What other answer…' *Manchester Guardian*, 31 March 1936.

355. 'It grows more and more…' *Manchester Guardian*, 1 Apr 1936.

356. 'No one but yourself…' letter from William Crozier to Frederick Voigt

on 31 March 1936, quoted in *The British Press and Germany, 1936–1939*, p. 82.

357. 'At least thirteen times' statistic from *The British Press and Germany, 1936–1939*, p. 84.

358. 'I don't think you would…' letter from William Crozier to Frederick Voigt on 18 March 1936, quoted in *The British Press and Germany, 1936–1939*, p. 84.

359. 'It is madness…' *Daily Mail*, 7 July 1936.

360. 'Everyone is agreed…' *The Times*, 6 July 1936.

361. 'To live in Germany…' *When Freedom Shrieked*, p. 12.

362. Pegler fears mentioned in *Berlin Diary: The Journal of a Foreign Correspondent 1934–1941*, p. 47.

363. 'Although Boshevism has made…' *Daily Mail*, 2 September 1936.

364. 'The idea of a Germany…' *Daily Express*, 17 September 1936, quoted in *The British Press and Germany, 1936–1939*, p. 104.

365. 'An ambassador who is only…' *Manchester Guardian*, 26 November 1936.

366. 'He had been…' *The Parting of Ways*, p. 79.

367. 'The *Manchester Guardian* was…' *Unreliable Sources*, p. 221.

368. 'Robson, who spent three years…' *Chicago Tribune*, 3 December 1936.

369. 'In general be of a soothing…' *The Times*, 28 January 1937.

370. 'Says he is for cooperation…' *Manchester Guardian*, 1 February 1937.

371. 'Second thoughts only…' *Manchester Guardian*, 2 February 1937.

372. 'There is a virtual…' *News Chronicle*, 3 February 1937, quoted in *The British Press and Germany, 1936–1939*, p. 110.

373. 'Suggests that the path…' *The Times*, 4 May 1937.

374. 'What is the destiny…' *The Times*, 5 May 1937.

375. 'Normally Norman Ebbutt presides…' *Berlin Diary: The Journal of a Foreign Correspondent*, p. 41.

376. 'The British Empire is...' *The Times*, 24 May 1934.

377. 'Dawson eats out of his hand...' *Diplomatic Diaries of Oliver Harvey*, p. 140.

378. 'It would interest me to know...' letter on 23 May 1937 from Geoffrey Dawson to H. G. Daniels, quoted in *The British Press and Germany, 1936–1939*, p. 114.

379. 'Not only is the tone...' *Editorial: The Memoirs of Colin R. Coote*, p. 169.

380. 'Geoffrey Dawson spent much time...' *Editorial: The Memoirs of Colin R. Coote*, p. 167.

381. 'Feelings and friendships...' *Editorial: The Memoirs of Colin R. Coote*, p. 168.

382. 'Dawson's insurance against...' *Editorial: The Memoirs of Colin R. Coote*, p. 169.

383. 'Downing Street on a...' *Failure of a Mission*, p. 52.

384. 'The British colony in Berlin...' *Failure of a Mission*, p. 55.

385. 'A remarkable production...' *Failure of a Mission*, p. 14.

386. 'His speech contained...' *Failure of a Mission*, p. 38.

387. 'He had restored to Germany...' *Failure of a Mission*, p. 39.

388. 'In England, far too...' *The Times*, 2 June 1937.

389. 'Careful writer, against whom...' *When Freedom Shrieked*, p. 196.

390. 'The faith is in danger!' *When Freedom Shrieked*, p. 293.

391. 'Norman Ebbutt of the London *Times*...' *Berlin Diary: The Journal of a Foreign Correspondent*, p. 78.

392. 'Terribly highly-strung...' *Berlin Diary: The Journal of a Foreign Correspondent*, p. 78.

393. 'He was a man in the prime...' *When Freedom Shrieked*, p. 196.

394. 'The most important decision...' *History of The Times Volume IV*, p. 815.

395. 'Objective testimony gives little support...' *History of The Times Volume V*, p. 465.

396. Robson's reports after his expulsion mentioned in *The British Press and Germany, 1936–1939*, p. 50.

397. Chamberlain views on *Morning Post* closure mentioned in *The British Press and Germany, 1936–1939*, p. 49.

398. 'Anyone who lived in Berlin...' *A Man of The Times*, p. 18.

399. 'Traditional eve-of-Waterloo...' *A Man of The Times*, p. 19.

400. 'The sheer magnitude...' *A Man of The Times*, p. 19.

401. 'He more than once...' *A Man of The Times*, p. 20.

402. 'Cease this hypocrisy...' *Insanity Fair*, p. 359.

403. Chamberlain's attitude to press, *Twilight of Truth*, p. 8.

404. Sir Joseph Ball's phone tapping, *Twilight of Truth*, p. 9.

405. *Truth* ownership, *Twilight of Truth*, p. 10.

406. Diplomatic correspondents network, *Twilight of Truth*, p. 18.

407. Leak by Leeper in 1935, *Vansittart in Office*, pp. 44–6.

408. Dell criticism, *Twilight of Truth*, p. 19.

409. 'Were not both of these...' *The Appeasers*, p. 57.

410. Voigt's opinion on leak, *Twilight of Truth*, p. 37.

411. 'We cannot expect...' *Daily Mail*, 21 March 1934.

412. Halifax's conclusion, *Twilight of Truth*, p. 40.

413. 'Need for the press...' *Twilight of Truth*, p. 40.

414. 'The spiteful taint...' *Twilight of Truth*, p. 41.

415. 'The most troublesome' *Twilight of Truth*, p. 43.

416. 'Unjustly cruel cartoon...' *Twilight of Truth*, p. 43.

417. BBC censorship, *The Appeasers*, p. 57.

418. 'I have the greatest...' *Failure of a Mission*, p. 65.

419. 'I wish he would not...' *The Fateful Years: Memoirs 1931–1945*, p. 109.

420. 'The incident is over...' letter on 17 November 1937 from Frederick Voigt to William Crozier, quoted in *The British Press and Germany, 1936–1939*, p. 135.

421. 'There is a great...' *The Fateful Years: Memoirs 1931–1945*, p. 109.

422. 'He ought to have...' *Editorial: The Memoirs of Colin R. Coote*, p. 167.

423. 'Has not abated for one…' *Manchester Guardian*, 29 January 1938.

424. 'I do not believe…' *The Appeasers*, p. 76.

425. Gordon-Lennox tears, *Twilight of Truth*, p. 51.

426. Halifax meeting Harmsworth, *Twilight of Truth*, p. 46.

427. 'Been some reflection…' *Twilight of Truth*, p. 44.

428. 'As political extremists…' *Change and Fortune*, p. 71.

429. 'Almost the entire press…' *Change and Fortune*, p. 70.

430. 'From the very start…' *News Chronicle* report on 16 February 1938, quoted in *The British Press and Germany, 1936–39*, p. 144.

431. 'The Führer went so far…' *Telegraph* report on 16 February 1938, quoted in *The British Press and Germany, 1936–39*, p. 144.

432. 'The twittering of sparrows…' *Telegraph* piece on 17 February 1938, quoted in *The British Press and Germany, 1936–39*, p. 145.

433. 'Nothing, [Hitler] said, could…' *Failure of a Mission*, p. 115.

434. 'When I got there…' *Failure of a Mission*, p. 90.

435. 'Ein Reich! Ein Volk!…' *Extra-special Correspondent*, p. 228.

436. 'Never indeed, has the mailed' *Daily Telegraph* line on 12 March 1938, quoted in *The British Press and Germany, 1936–1939*, p. 153.

437. 'Remember that what has happened…' *News Chronicle* line on 14 March 1938, quoted in *The British Press and Germany, 1936–1939*, p. 159.

438. 'Arm, arm, arm…' *Daily Mail* on 12 March 1938, quoted in *The British Press and Germany, 1936–1939*, p. 164.

439. 'Is that a rape?' *Extra-special correspondent*, p. 229.

440. 'In my wildest nightmares…' letter from *Times* Vienna Correspondent to Geoffrey Dawson, 16 March 1938, quoted in *History of The Times Volume IV*, p. XX.

441. 'Over the frontiers…' *The British Press and Germany, 1936–1939*, p. 154.

442. 'There, you damned Jew…' *The Last Chronicle of Bouverie Street*, p. 73.

443. 'Had done more for…' *The Appeasers*, p. 106.

444. 'Felt that things…' *The Appeasers*, p. 113.

445. 'We have no alliance…' *Sunday Times* line on 20 March 1938, quoted in *The British Press and Germany, 1936–1939*, p. 18.

446. 'Nazi heart and soul' lines taken from *Times* archive, quoted in *Twilight of Truth*, p. 56.

447. 'Has spent the last…' *Daily Express* on 12 May 1938, quoted in *The British Press and Germany, 1936–1939*, p. 33.

448. 'Czechoslovakia is not of the remotest…' line from *Daily Mail* on 6 May 1938, and Cranfield reference taken from *The Appeasers*, p. 118.

449. 'A lot of the journalists…' *The Reluctant Press Lord: Esmond Rothermere and the Daily Mail*, p. 2.

450. 'No man in the service…' *When Freedom Shrieked*, p. 266.

451. 'Probably you know this…' *Trail Sinister*, p. 213.

452. 'Only very foolish newspaper…' *Trail Sinister*, p. 213.

453. Voigt's espionage involvement mentioned in *Colonel Z: The Life and Times of a Master of Spies*, p. 184.

454. 'Hundreds of victims…' letter in *Daily Telegraph*, 23 August 1940.

455. 'By refusing to be…' *Daily Mail*, May 1938.

456. 'Skilful precautionary measures…' *Manchester Guardian*, 23 May 1938.

457. 'I am afraid you will think…' Crozier to Voigt letter on 22 May 1938, quoted in *The British Press and Germany, 1936–1939*, p. 168.

458. 'Without the championship…' *Daily Telegraph*, 28 June 1938, quoted in *The British Press and Germany, 1936–1939*, p. 17.

459. 'A joint note to Berlin…' *The Appeasers*, pp. x–xi.

460. 'See Germany for yourself…' *The British Press and Germany, 1936–1939*, p. 173.

461. 'I don't myself object…' Crozier letter to Voigt on 26 July 1938, quoted in *The British Press and Germany, 1936–1939*, p. 17.

462. 'You do not seem to know…' Rothermere letter printed in *News*

Chronicle on 16 August 1938, quoted in *The British Press and Germany, 1936–1939*, p. 18.

463. 'I listened to the barrage...' *When Freedom Shrieked*, p. 316.

464. 'The parliamentary reports...' *A Man of The Times*, p. 19.

465. Captain Wiedemann meeting and Chamberlain response, *Twilight of Truth*, p. 66.

466. 'A more homogenous state...' *The Times*, 7 September 1938.

467. 'Well, that's not my reading...' *The British Press and Germany, 1936–1939*, p. 54.

468. Beaverbrook backing for Chamberlain, *Twilight of Truth*, p. 56.

469. 'Mr Chamberlain stepped...' *Failure of a Mission*, p. 149.

470. 'A stiff wing-collar...' *Extra-special Correspondent*, p. 231.

471. 'Question of her excellent...' *Failure of a Mission*, p. 83.

472. 'If England means...' *Failure of a Mission*, p. 152.

473. 'We have chosen...' Voigt diary entries from *The British Press and Germany, 1936–1939*, p. 8.

474. 'An absolute determination...' *Daily Telegraph*, 15 September 1938, quoted in *Twilight of Truth*, p. 78.

475. 'From every part...' *Extra-special Correspondent*, p. 233.

476. 'Grave, like masks...' *When Freedom Shrieked*, p. 317.

477. 'Some went one way...' *When Freedom Shrieked*, p. 317.

478. 'There was to be...' *When Freedom Shrieked*, p. 317.

479. 'The whole place...' *History of The Times, Volume IV*, p. 943.

480. 'If at first you don't...' *Daily Mail*, 30 September 1938.

481. 'If you hear any reference...' *Extra-special Correspondent*, p. 233.

482. 'The nation cannot prudently...' *Daily Telegraph* article on 26 September 1938, quoted in *The British Press and Germany, 1936–1939*, p. 196.

483. 'If that's the news...' *The British Press and Germany, 1936–1939*, p. 39.

484. 'Most dreadful man' *Editorial: The Memoirs of Colin R. Coote*, p. 172.

485. 'Millions of mothers…' *Failure of a Mission*, p. 168.

486. 'Journals were all but…' *The British Press and Germany, 1936–1939*, p. 7.

487. 'An almost complete…' *Twilight of Truth*, pp. 79–80.

488. Harrison report blocked, *The British Press and Germany, 1936–1939*, p. 39.

489. 'I fear that so blunt…' *Twilight of Truth*, p. 101.

490. Junior staff resignations, *History of The Times, Volume IV*, p. 945.

491. 'Your speech was one…' *Old Men Forget: The Autobiography of Duff Cooper*, p. 249.

492. 'Silent, mournful, abandoned…' *Man of The Times*, p. 39.

493. 'Damp squib' *Old Men Forget: The Autobiography of Duff Cooper*, p. 250.

494. 'Most of the office…' *Man of the Times*, p. 48.

495. 'With their cartoons and comments…' *Twilight of Truth*, p. 94.

496. 'Obtained, through the machinery…' *Daily Telegraph* article on 13 October 1938, quoted in *The British Press and Germany, 1936–1939*, p. 197.

497. Arthur Mann's objection to appeasement, *Twilight of Truth*, p. 62.

498. 'I believe that most editors…' *Twilight of Truth*, p. 100.

499. 'German troops are tonight…' *Daily Mail*, 3 October 1938.

500. 'Today they march in…' Voigt diary quoted in *The British Press and Germany, 1936–1939*, p. 9.

501. 'Never again shall…' *Daily Mail*, 4 October 1938.

502. 'We don't normally…' author's interview with Herbert Kaden, 21 February 2015.

503. 'The landlord said…' author's interview with Herbert Kaden, 21 February 2015.

504. Emigration statistic, *Germany: The Third Reich*, p. 92.

505. 'News of such crimes…' *When Freedom Shrieked*, p. 262.

506. 'They threw over…' *When Freedom Shrieked*, p. 259.

507. 'Ardent Nazis and Storm Troopers…' *When Freedom Shrieked*, p. 262.

508. 'The murder (in Paris) ...' *When Freedom Shrieked*, p. 246.

509. 'Primed with tales ...' *When Freedom Shrieked*, p. 258.

510. 'Jewry fired on the ...' *Daily Mail*, 11 November 1938.

511. 'Thus, thousands were doomed ...' *When Freedom Shrieked*, p. 261.

512. 'The German people has not ...' *When Freedom Shrieked*, p. 269.

513. 'To look on, helpless ...' *When Freedom Shrieked*, p. 270.

514. 'The World Protests' *Daily Mail*, 14 November 1938.

515. ''The world is appalled ...' *Daily Mail*, 14 November 1938.

516. 'I felt an ever-increasing ...' *When Freedom Shrieked*, p. 12.

517. 'Bread was grey...' *Halifax Courier*, 16 December 1939.

518. 'Who is contented ...' *When Freedom Shrieked*, p. 234.

519. The assertion comes in *The Reluctant Press Lord: Esmond Rothermere and the Daily Mail*. Reynolds is referred to fleetingly and the basis for the assertion is not given, though it may have come from his assistant Izzard, who was interviewed for that book.

520. 'Emigrants are not infrequently...' *When Freedom Shrieked*, p. 267.

521. 'So many people are ...' *When Freedom Shrieked*, p. 267.

522. 'It is pleasant to be ...' *When Freedom Shrieked*, p. 13.

523. Oxford undergraduates speech, *The Times* obituary, 2 September 1940.

524. 'This house is like ...' letter from Rothay Reynolds to Cuthbert Reynolds, 22 December 1939.

525. 'The things seen and heard ...' *When Freedom Shrieked*, p. 13.

526. 'Seriously deficient ...' *The Appeasers*, p. xii.

527. 'Certifiable lunatic' Wells articles on 2 and 3 January 1939, mentioned in *The British Press and Germany, 1936–1939*, p. 41.

528. 'The uncensored truth' *The British Press and Germany, 1936–1939*, p. 47.

529. 'That is correct' taken from Gedye's entry in *Oxford Dictionary of National Biography*, Oxford University Press, 2004.

530. Chamberlain playing golf, *Twilight of Truth*, p. 106.

531. 'The only real consolation...' *News Chronicle* article on 16 March, quoted in *The British Press and Germany, 1936–1939*, p. 252.

532. 'War was avoided last...' *Daily Mail*, 13 March 1939.

533. 'The hushed and shaking...' *Daily Mail*, 16 March 1939.

534. 'Hitler has killed Munich' *Daily Mail*, 17 March 1939.

535. 'The whole crisis had...' *Failure of a Mission*, p. 209.

536. 'With regard to the Jews...' *Extra-special Correspondent*, p. 219.

537. 'Had I anticipated...' *Failure of a Mission*, p. 227.

538. 'The whole general atmosphere...' *Failure of a Mission*, p. 288.

539. 'It was a complete...' *Failure of a Mission*, p. 241.

540. Legal threat, *The British Press and Germany, 1936–1939*, p. 65.

541. 'Nearly every day...' *News Chronicle* article on 10 July 1939, quoted in *The British Press and Germany, 1936–1939*, p. 10.

542. 'If dictators would have...' Chamberlain letter to his sister on 15 July 1939, quoted in *The Appeasers*, p. xiii.

543. 'Hitler has concluded...' Chamberlain letter to his sister on 22 July 1939, quoted in *The Appeasers*, p. xiv.

544. 'I have been tied...' letter from Rothay Reynolds to Muriel Reynolds, 15 November 1939.

545. 'The title of this book...' *When Freedom Shrieked*, p. 5.

546. 'It was built around...' *The Reluctant Press Lord*, p. 2.

547. 'All the young people...' *Some Memories of my Life*, p. 24.

548. 'London is frightening...' letter from Rothay Reynolds to Muriel Reynolds, 15 November 1939.

549. 'The best contribution...' letter from Rothay Reynolds to Cuthbert Reynolds, 22 December 1939.

550. 'Extensive experience joined with...' *Daily Mail*, 13 November 1939.

551. 'Now that the war...' *Melbourne Argus*, 30 December 1939.

552. 'A heart-breaking book' *The Observer*, 19 November 1939.

553. 'Its first-hand impressions…' *Manchester Guardian*, 12 December 1939.

554. 'Bring home to the Englishman…' *The Spectator*, 1 December 1939.

555. 'Wire-pulling politicians…' *Twilight of Truth*, p. 129.

556. 'It is a struggle…' *Halifax Courier*, 16 December 1939.

557. 'Turned out to be…' *Daily Telegraph*, 2 March 1940.

558. 'Italy's Heart is Not…' *Daily Telegraph*, 2 March 1940.

559. 'Amongst journalists Reynolds was…' *The Tablet*, 31 August 1940.

560. 'Divergent Reports on Brenner Talks' *Daily Telegraph*, 19 March 1940.

561. 'I saw a lot of him…' *The Tablet*, 24 August 1940.

562. 'A Vatican concert…' *The Tablet*, 31 August 1940.

563. 'Mussolini declared war…' *Daily Telegraph*, 15 June 1940.

564. 'I find Belgrade…' *Daily Telegraph*, 21 June 1940.

565. 'The Russian ultimatum…' *Daily Telegraph*, 2 July 1940.

566. 'You will stay at…' *Daily Telegraph*, 15 July 1940.

567. 'The attitude of French…' *Daily Telegraph*, 16 July 1940.

568. 'The beautiful city of…' *Daily Telegraph*, 15 July 1940.

569. 'Apart from the critical…' *Extra-special Correspondent*, p. 238.

570. 'The British are betraying…' *Trail Sinister*, p. 367.

571. 'Alt! What d'yes think…' *Trail Sinister*, p. 368.

572. 'The French debacle…' *Daily Telegraph*, 15 July 1940.

573. 'The whole family…' author's interview with Herbert Kaden, 21 February 2015.

574. 'He knew all the…' *Catholic Herald*, 23 August 1940.

575. 'Accounts of contemporary Germany…' *The Thirties*.

576. 'When I went out…' *The British Press and Germany, 1936–39*, p. 41.

577. 'I must send my story…' *The Last Chronicle of Bouverie Street*, p. 73.

578. 'Alerted the world …' Jewish Telegraphic Agency, 20 August 1981: http://bit.ly/2cw6AcB

579. 'Blesses and encourages...' *News Chronicle* piece on 31 August 1937, quoted in *The British Press and Germany, 1936–39*, p. 33.

580. 'Together the Harmsworth...' *The Life and Death of the Press Barons*, p. 114.

581. 'All the papers...' *Twilight of Truth*, p. 183.

582. 'I shall put in...' *When Freedom Shrieked*, p. 99.

583. 'Never have I been...' *When Freedom Shrieked*, p. 317.

584. 'The poor old *News Chronicle*...' *Towards the End of the Morning*, p. vii.

INDEX

Aitken, William Maxwell (Baron
  Beaverbrook) 43, 78, 81, 113,
  131, 285
  interference in newspaper content 85, 121–2, 276
  support for *Express* reporters
  141, 194
Albert, Frederick William Victor
  35, 51
Astor, Lady Nancy (Viscountess
  Astor) 228
  and 'Cliveden Set' 142, 194
Attlee, Clement 121

Baker, Aelred 13, 282
Baldwin, Stanley 122, 144, 155, 177,
  190–92, 230
  criticism of press 120–21
  and East-Fulham by-election 125–6
Ball, Sir Joseph 190–91, 244
Barrington-Ward, Robin 185, 223
  on staff opposition 228
Bartlett, Vernon 97, 103, 109,
  113–14, 117, 124, 145, 175, 191,
  244, 249, 275
  and Jewish boycott 102
  and Munich Agreement 224, 226,
  229
  on Göring's press threats 115–16

Beaverbrook, Lord (see Aitken, Wil-
  liam Maxwell)
Beckett, Rupert 230
Beneš, Edvard 217, 220
Bennett, John Wheeler 105
Berry, James, (Viscount Kemsley)
  123, 220, 287
  negotiates with Nazis 247
Berry, William (Viscount Camrose)
  123, 186
  distance from British government
  229
Binchy, Daniel 57–8
Bretherton, Paul 208
Brooke, Rupert 270
  death 44
  studies in Berlin 30
Brown, Harrison 119
Brüning, Heinrich 71, 79–80, 85–6,
  104

Camrose, Lord (see Berry, William)
Cardozo, Harold 138–9
Carlyle, Aelred 12–14
Catholic Herald 280
  Ronald Reynolds interview
  271–2
Chamberlain, Neville 98, 177, 212,
  217, 247, 275–8, 287

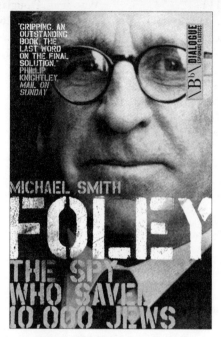